ALCOHOL, REFORM AND SOCIETY: the liquor issue in social context,
ed. by Jack S. Blocker Jr. Greenwood, 1979. 299p ill (Contributions in American history, 83) bibl index 78-73800. 23.95 ISBN
0-313-20889-1. C.I.P.

An expansion of the basic theme set forth by Joseph Gusfield's *Symbolic
crusade* (1968) that reform movements involving beverage alcohol are best
understood as symbolic manifestations of social conflict. The contributors
to the present collection tend to be more functionalist in their approaches.
The general focus is historical assessment of use and effects of beverage
alcohol upon the social structure and vice versa. Interpretive histories of the
19th and 20th centuries as well as some sociological analyses are provided.
The chapters are well organized and present a coherent picture. Adequate
index; full bibliography. The book is of value at all levels, though advanced
undergraduates and graduates will gain most.

Alcohol, Reform and Society

Alcohol, Reform and Society

THE LIQUOR ISSUE IN SOCIAL CONTEXT

Edited by

Jack S. Blocker Jr.

Contributions in American History, Number 83

GREENWOOD PRESS
WESTPORT, CONNECTICUT ● LONDON, ENGLAND

Library of Congress Cataloging in Publication Data
Main entry under title:

Alcohol, reform, and society.

(Contributions in American history; no. 83
ISSN 0084-9219)
    Bibliography: p.
    Includes index.
    1.   Temperance societies—United States—History—
Addresses, essays, lectures.   2.   Prohibition—United
States—Addresses, essays, lectures.   3.   Liquor
problem—United States—History—Addresses, essays,
lectures.   I.   Blocker, Jack S.
HV5292.A384   322.4'4'0973   78-73800
ISBN 0-313-20889-1

Library of Congress Catalog Card Number: 78-73800
ISBN: 0-313-20889-1
ISSN: 0084-9219

First published in 1979

Greenwood Press, Inc.
51 Riverside Avenue, Westport, Connecticut 06880

Printed in the United States of America

10   9   8   7   6   5   4   3   2   1

To My Grandmothers,
Irene Guertler Reifenstahl
and
Katherine Snead Blocker

Contents

Tables

Figures

Alcohol, Reform and Society

1.

JACK S. BLOCKER JR.

Introduction

The temperance movement in the United States has traditionally attracted scholars less for its intrinsic interest than for the insight it may provide into larger social processes. This volume seeks to extend and enrich that tradition by posing new questions and finding new ways to answer old ones.

The ideal inquiry would illuminate not only particular events but also the underlying structures—demographic, social, economic, political, and cultural—shaping those events. In keeping with this ideal, this volume seeks to achieve two basic goals:

1. To explain the use of beverage alcohol and its response in terms of social structure, and
2. To identify and explain the effects of alcohol use and its response upon social structure.

One shortfall from the ideal must be confessed at the outset—the lack of a cross-cultural analysis in all but the first two of our studies. This is particularly unfortunate in a field which has produced one of the first rigorous attempts at comparative explanation of reform movements.[1] Ross Paulson's example has thus far simply failed to enlarge the parochial focus of temperance studies—or any other type of American studies, for that matter.

The principal structure which has thus far gone unexamined in

American temperance studies is the structure of drinking. Even when data on aggregate consumption levels have been available, temperance scholars have preferred to emphasize other factors in explaining the temperance movement's varying fortunes. A case in point is that starting point for modern reform studies, Richard Hofstadter's *The Age of Reform*. Hofstadter explained the coming of national prohibition by the mysterious spread of a metaphorical "rural-evangelical virus."[2] Had Hofstadter extended his pioneering foray into social science literature, however, he would have discovered in a classic article by E.M. Jellinek that apparent per capita consumption of absolute alcohol during the decade immediately preceding national prohibition had reached its highest level since 1860.[3] Had he looked even further, he would have found a well-established correlation between alcohol consumption and deaths from both alcoholism and liver diseases.[4] More recent studies have demonstrated similar myopia with less excuse.[5] Estimates of aggregate consumption levels are now available at five-year intervals back to 1790, although the post-1850 figures are calculated on a more solid data base than those before.[6]

In describing and explaining drinking patterns, it would seem obvious that the work of historians and that of other social and medical researchers should proceed hand in hand, with medical, sociological, and anthropological theory enriching historical studies and vice versa. To advance this process B. Gail Frankel and Paul C. Whitehead have contributed to this volume a critical review of social science research on drinking and alcohol-related damage. As they show, other social scientists have attempted to explain cross-cultural and individual variations in alcohol use; it is now for historians to explain variation over time.

In conducting our investigation, we have the advantage of beginning with a series of testable propositions generated by proponents of the two competing sociological explanations of consumption and alcoholism, the "sociocultural" and the "distribution of consumption," as well as by attempts, such as that of Frankel and Whitehead, to reconcile the two. Our analysis could lead from known variations in alcohol use to the structural changes linked with these variations.

As the rate of per capita consumption climbed from a low in 1875 (1.8 gallons of absolute alcohol per capita of the drinking age population, fifteen years and over) to a peak in 1910 (2.6 gallons), was it accompanied by increasing integration of drinking practices into general social customs and by an increase in prescriptions for moderate drinking, as the Frankel-Whitehead formulation would predict?[7] And were those prescriptions, assuming they appeared, accompanied by a decline in proscriptions against excessive drinking? To put the problem in terms more familiar to historians, did American Victorianism reach its peak in the 1870s? The work of cultural and intellectual historians suggests rather the opposite, that the Victorian value structure lasted into the early twentieth century.[8] From this apparent disjunction between values and behavior springs a new set of questions about elite vs. mass values, cultural lag, the effect of renewed immigration after the Civil War, and the work of the temperance movement.

Such questions can be answered only when we move beyond aggregate drinking patterns to an examination of their internal structure and to an analysis of the meaning of drinking and of drunken behavior. Again, other social scientists' research can be useful. As Frankel and Whitehead note, application of the lognormal curve to any society (or any date in U.S. history) for which the gross consumption level is known can produce estimates of the proportion of the drinking population consuming at any given level. In addition, any inquiry into consumption patterns must investigate changes in the type of alcohol consumed. The major change to be explained in American history is the great shift from distilled liquors, the drinkers' favorite before the Civil War, to beer, the principal drink of Americans since then.

Probably the key to the shift from liquor to beer—and by far the major unanswered question in historical temperance studies—is: Who drank? We need to know the size of the drinking population throughout American history. We need to describe that population by sex, age, location, ethnicity, class, and religion, and we need to know how each of these variables changed over time. So far as I know, only one study has begun this task, and it has been neglected by historians.

A decade ago, the sociologist Robin Room used vital statistics reports from the 1890 U.S. Census to analyze alcohol-related urban death rates by sex, marital status, neighborhood status, and ethnicity.[9] His findings confirm some commonsense notions, bring others into question, and pose fascinating new questions. He found that the Irish ranked highest of all groups in deaths from both alcoholism and liver diseases—but they showed the lowest excess of male over female deaths, with Irish females exceeding males in deaths from liver diseases. Among native-born whites of native-born mothers, Irish and Germans, the share of wives in alcohol-related deaths of married persons was far higher than that of unmarried women in alcohol-related deaths of unmarried persons. This finding parallels Durkheim's on suicide, raising the intriguing possibility that, in the nineteenth century as in the twentieth, the home may have been a source of oppression rather than the center of tranquility the protection of which, according to some historians, lay at the heart of the temperance movement.[10]

As Room writes, his work "represents a small-scale strip mine on the rich lode of 'social statistics' on alcoholism collected around the turn of the century, but since almost totally neglected."[11] Hospital records can provide material for further comparative analysis of alcohol-related death rates. Local court records often identify drinkers in the course of prosecuting them or the saloonkeepers who sold to them. Jail registers can identify drinkers considered deviant by local police authorities. With the sources at hand and the drinking surveys of the past thirty years to provide both a basis for comparison and a methodological guide, there is no reason for further neglect of the crucial question of who drank.

Once we know who drank, we can proceed to ask why they drank. Historians often act as if they know the answer to this question, assuming that people generally drink in order to reduce tension and positing connections between high consumption levels and widespread social stress. This is the procedure used in the most sophisticated recent interpretation of the temperance movement, Norman H. Clark's *Deliver Us from Evil*.[12] Unfortunately even this cherished commonplace is in doubt. As a review of the abundant experimental literature makes clear, the evidence for tension reduction as a consequence of drinking is negative, equivocal, and often contradictory.[13] Other theories have been proposed, but at the moment no formulation appears to command widespread assent.[14]

When we know why people drink, we will still have to explain why they behave as they do when drunk. This is another of those questions whose answer has long been assumed but for which our assumptions have recently been severely shaken. In this case the agent of demolition was Craig MacAndrew and Robert D. Edgerton's classic, *Drunken Comportment: A Social Explanation* (London, 1969). Their demonstration that drunken behavior is determined culturally and not physiologically and that it varies from society to society as well as temporally and situationally within a given society, gave the field of alcohol studies a shock from which it has yet to recover. Their findings open vast and exciting new possibilities for historians in the description and explanation of historical variations in drunken comportment.[15] As learned behavior, drunken comportment offers another key to shifts in cultural structures.

Thus our first strategy for integrating historical liquor studies into social studies must be a thoroughgoing examination of past drinking patterns with an aim to discovering who drank how much of what, when, where, and why. Other social scientists have provided us with potentially valuable clues and starting points. It is up to historians to return the favor with some solid answers and theoretical contributions based upon their special access to behavioral change over time.

The history of those who produce and sell liquor is necessarily a part of any examination of the social use of and response to beverage alcohol. As a consumer goods industry, the liquor trade offers a window onto shifts in economic and cultural structures. As a business continuously under legal restriction or the threat of it, the liquor industry provides insight into business-government relations at various levels over several centuries. For the nineteenth and twentieth centuries, statistical sources are abundant, company records are sometimes available, oral history is possible,[16] and retailers are traceable through directories, censuses, tax and court records. Yet despite the pioneering studies listed in the Bibliography, among which Thomas C. Cochran's study of the Pabst Brewing Company still stands out after thirty years, and some recent work on the urban saloon,[17] little has been done. In this area our volume again reflects rather than advances the state of the art.

That studies of temperance reformers are far more abundant than studies of the makers, distributors, and consumers of liquor is testimony to American historians' general fascination with movements for social change. It is not, however, a guarantee to understanding social change. It is true that from the beginning temperance historians have sought to understand their subjects in relation to widespread social change. The crucial question has always been which type of change provides the most appropriate context for understanding temperance reformers.

Temperance historians have generally agreed that the movement was produced by nineteenth-century industrialization and urbanization, but there has been considerable disagreement over the specific issue of which of the many changes attendant upon these meta-changes was responsible. Status shifts, [18] class conflict, [19] and the development of bourgeois values [20] have recently been put forward as candidates. A corollary question is whether there has been a single temperance-prohibition movement produced by a single long-term change [21] or a series of different movements with different constituencies, goals, and strategies, each the product of a different social context. [22]

Since social change can only be expressed through social structure, the proper strategy for study of temperance reformers is to examine them within their respective social structures. Only by so doing can we fully identify temperance reformers by systematically comparing their backgrounds and behavior with those of their contemporaries. And only then can we assess the differential effects of various kinds of social change.

This effort to place temperance reformers in social context is the main thrust of the essays in this volume focusing upon the temperance movement. By studying no-license men and their opponents in an industrializing community, Ian R. Tyrrell shows that early nineteenth-century temperance supporters, like abolitionists, stood in the vanguard of social change. His discussion of the motives for support of no-license by farmers, industrial entrepreneurs, and industrial workers takes us a long step forward in understanding the connections between economic change, cultural change, and temperance reform. In a less theoretical piece, Charles A. Isetts examines the social standing of women temperance reformers within the context of their community social system. Comparison of Tyrrell's and Isetts' findings suggests a contraction in the sources of temperance support from the early to late nineteenth century. [23] One way to resolve this issue would be to meet the most urgent need in temperance movement studies today, a systematic, long-term, community-based study of the Independent Order of Good Templars. [24] Such an inquiry would enrich not only temperance studies but women studies as well, since the Good Templars were one of the few nineteenth-century national organizations to admit women on an equal basis with men.

The view, suggested by Tyrrell's study, that temperance in the early nineteenth century acted as a social cement, drawing together otherwise antagonistic groups, finds confirmation in David R. Huehner's exhaustive inquiry into temperance on antebellum New England college campuses. Although students and faculty fought over other issues, they united in a commitment to temperance. Nevertheless, students and faculty retained different reasons for adopting this position. This intellectual elite's temperance commitment probably helps to explain the churches' increasing support for the temperance cause during the course of the century.

My own essay places another elite, the leadership of the Prohibition Party and of the Anti-Saloon League, on the community-society continuum which some scholars have seen as a key to understanding social change. Use of this tool reveals that the institutional modernization of the prohibition movement was not, as might have been expected, carried out by a relatively more modern leadership group. Indeed, the opposite was true, and no direct link can therefore be shown between the processes of modernization within and outside the movement. Modernization within the prohibition movement represented not adaptation to social change but insulation against it.

George G. Wittet has made the most ambitious attempt to place the mass voting support for prohibition within its proper context and thus to explain its motivations. Using a theoretically structured multivariate analysis developed at the University of Western Ontario by Richard S. Alcorn, [25] Wittet evaluates the relative impact of situational, structural, and socialization variables upon voters in Ohio's 1883 prohibition constitutional referendum. This highly sophisticated approach marks a major step forward in both temperance studies and historical voting analysis. When such studies are extended over time we shall at last have a firm basis upon which to generalize about the social sources of alignments on the liquor issue.

Although less sophisticated methodologically, the essays by Larry Engelmann, David E. Kyvig, and Jay L. Rubin share Wittet's working principle that the temperance movement can only be understood in contrast to its opposition. Engelmann and Kyvig examine the background and process of repeal of the Eighteenth Amendment; Kyvig's national focus is complemented by Engelmann's detailed case study of Michigan. Both document the increasing political isolation of the prohibition movement in the late 1920s and early 1930s, as, ironically, a narrowly based, elite-dominated repeal movement imitated its methods and proclaimed allegiance to its goals. Kyvig goes on to elucidate the effect of repeal on early New Deal alignments and policies. [26] Rubin's study of the liquor issue during World War II confirms the prohibitionists' isolation and weakness after repeal and sheds new light on the role of war in bringing on national prohibition in the first place.

Clearly we have not exhausted all the themes or topics suggested by the history of the temperance movement in the United States. We have focused upon the national scene or the Northeast, where the organized movement was strongest, and upon the years when the liquor issue was most resonant in American society and politics. The arguments developed here must be tested in other regions, and social responses to beverage alcohol before 1820 and since 1945 should be explored. Nevertheless, we believe we have proposed significant revisions of older interpretations, tested new methodology, and raised important new questions.

Completing the volume, Jacquie Jessup's bibliography seeks to provide both a guide to work already done and a starting point for the work we and others have yet to do. It is in the achievements of the future that this volume will find its best measure of failure or success.

Notes

1. Ross E. Paulson, *Women's Suffrage and Prohibition: A Comparative Study of Equality and Social Control* (Glenview, Ill., 1973).

2. *The Age of Reform: From Bryan to F.D.R.* (New York, 1955), p. 290.

3. E.M. Jellinek, "Recent Trends in Alcoholism and in Alcohol Consumption," *Quarterly Journal of Studies on Alcohol* 8 (June 1947): 8.

4. Clark Warburton, *The Economic Results of Prohibition* (New York, 1932), pp. 73-98.

5. Paulson, *Women's Suffrage and Prohibition*, pp. 144-68; Jack S. Blocker Jr., *Retreat from Reform: The Prohibition Movement in the United States, 1890-1913* (Westport, Conn., 1976), pp. 235-42. James H. Timberlake,

Prohibition and the Progressive Movement, 1900-1920 (Cambridge, Mass., 1963), pp. 102-03, notes increased consumption only as a sign of liquor industry strength. Norman H. Clark, *Deliver Us from Evil: An Interpretation of American Prohibition* (New York, 1976), cites consumption rates to explain the rise of the early nineteenth-century temperance movement, but as an explanation for national prohibition he resorts to generalized social disorder caused by industrialization and urbanization. Joseph R. Gusfield, *Symbolic Crusade: Status Politics and the American Temperance Movement* (Urbana, Ill., 1963), p. 101, notes rising consumption only to show erosion of temperance norms; he does not mention alcoholic damage.

6. W.J. Rorabaugh, "Estimated U.S. Alcoholic Beverage Consumption, 1790-1860," *Journal of Studies on Alcohol* 37 (March 1976): 357-64.

7. Ibid., p. 361.

8. Henry F. May, *The End of American Innocence: A Study of the First Years of Our Own Time, 1912-1917* (New York, 1959); Daniel Walker Howe, "American Victorianism as a Culture," *American Quarterly* 27 (December 1975): 507-32; Stanley Coben, "The Assault on Victorianism in the Twentieth Century," *American Quarterly* 27 (December 1975): 604-28.

9. Robin Room, "Cultural Contingencies of Alcoholism: Variations between and within Nineteenth-Century Urban Ethnic Groups in Alcohol-Related Death Rates," *Journal of Health and Social Behavior* 9 (June 1968): 99-113.

10. Clark, *Deliver Us from Evil*. This would depend on establishing a connection between oppression and pathological drinking behavior.

11. Room, "Cultural Contingencies of Alcoholism," p. 110.

12. Clark, *Deliver Us from Evil*, p. 52.

13. Howard Cappell and C. Peter Herman, "Alcohol and Tension Reduction: A Review," *Quarterly Journal of Studies on Alcohol* 33 (March 1972): 33-64.

14. A good place to begin is David C. McClelland et al., *The Drinking Man* (New York, 1972). But see also Henry S.G. Cutter et al., "Alcohol, Power, and Inhibition," *Quarterly Journal of Studies on Alcohol* 34 (June 1973): 381-89, and William J. Filstead, Jean J. Rossi, and Mark Keller, eds., *Alcohol and Alcohol Problems: New Thinking and New Directions* (Cambridge, Mass., 1976).

15. Clark, *Deliver Us from Evil*, pp. 52-67, does raise the question of drunken comportment, but his discussion then proceeds to confuse perceived and actual behavior.

16. The Bancroft Library, Regional Oral History Office, *The California Wine Industry Oral History Project*, 19 vols. (Berkeley, Calif., 1971-76).

17. Jon M. Kingsdale, "The 'Poor Man's Club': Social Functions of the Urban Working Class Saloon," *American Quarterly* 25 (1973): 472-89; Perry

R. Duis, "The Saloon and the Public City: Chicago and Boston, 1880-1920" (Ph.D. diss., University of Chicago, 1975); Larry D. Engelmann, "Old Saloon Days in Michigan," *Michigan History* 61 (1977): 99-134.

18. Gusfield, *Symbolic Crusade.*

19. Blocker, *Retreat from Reform.*

20. Clark, *Deliver Us from Evil.*

21. Ibid.

22. Gusfield, *Symbolic Crusade*; Blocker, *Retreat from Reform.*

23. For evidence to support the opposite view, see Ronald Morris Benson, "American Workers and Temperance Reform, 1866-1933" (Ph.D. diss., University of Notre Dame, 1974).

24. Abundant material to begin such a study is in the IOGT Records (1855-1970) at Michigan Historical Collections, Ann Arbor, and in the IOGT Records (1845-1962), Edward C. Sturges Papers, Cornell University Library, Ithaca, N.Y.

25. For an explication of this analytical model, see *The Landon Project Annual Report, 1976-1977* (London, Canada, 1977), pp. 26-38.

26. For a pioneering attempt to show the long-term impact of the temperance-prohibition movement, see Selden D. Bacon, "The Classic Temperance Movement of the U.S.A.; Impact Today on Attitudes, Action and Research," *British Journal of Addiction* 62 (March 1967): 5-18.

2.

B. GAIL FRANKEL AND
PAUL C. WHITEHEAD

Sociological Perspectives on Drinking and Damage

Two major sociological perspectives on the social aspects of alcohol use and alcohol-related damage have predominated during the past three to four decades. The older of the two, the sociocultural model, has particularly dominated thinking about alcohol-related damage and its prevention in the United States. The second is far more recent (circa 1960), and many of its proponents have been based in Canada, although clearly this thinking has spread to other countries as well. This second perspective has come to be called the distribution of consumption model.

These perspectives have influenced past and present thought on drinking practices and have contributed heavily to suggestions for programs and to actual programs for the prevention of alcohol-related damage. However, the two models lead to highly divergent conclusions about alcohol-related damage and how it can be prevented. Attempts to make sense of these apparently diverging perspectives have yielded two additional models which synthesize the earlier models.

This essay is adapted from a larger work in progress, B. Gail Frankel and Paul C. Whitehead, *Models of Drinking and Damage: Theoretical Advances and Prevention* (forthcoming). The authors thank William R. Avison for his helpful comments on an earlier version of these materials.

The purpose of this essay is to trace the development of these models and to assess their adequacy in predicting rates of alcohol-related damage.

The Sociocultural Approach

There has been considerable interest in the relationship between the social context of drinking behavior and rates of alcohol-related damage. The major manifestation of this interest has been in the study of the structure and quality of social norms about drinking. Three specific constructs are frequently found in discussions of drinking practices in various cultures and among various ethnic groups. The first deals with the *structure* of social norms about drinking, especially the ways in which drinking customs are learned, understood, interpreted, and integrated with other cultural traits as well as other aspects of social life. The second and third constructs involve the *quality* or *content* of the social norms governing drinking practices. Specifically, these are prescriptions for moderate drinking and proscriptions against excessive drinking.

The Structure and Quality of Social Norms

Bacon points out the importance of understanding drinking norms in his proposal for a specific sociological framework for the study of alcohol problems and drinking behavior.[1] According to this framework, an examination of the correlates of alcohol-related damage rests on the study of all aspects of drinking behavior: drinking customs; how these customs are learned; the nature and source of social controls; the functions of alcohol use; the pressures for and against drinking; and the nature and extent of drinking, among others.[2] Viewed together, the components of the framework suggest that when drinking takes place in a "settled, socially integrated manner, and when there is consistent reaction to the behavior (that is, where similar behavior is not considered acceptable at one time, pathological at another), few problems are likely to result."[3]

Bacon discusses both the structure and quality of norms about drinking, but his major focus is on the "settled, socially integrated" nature of drinking practices. In contrast, Bales emphasizes the quality of norms about drinking.[4] He examines the attitudes toward drinking held by particular cultures in order to investigate how prescriptions for and proscriptions against the use of alcoholic beverages appear to be related to the rate of alcohol-related damage in a society.

Studies of the quality or content of social norms about drinking have concluded that societies characterized by social norms that have definite prescriptive and proscriptive components governing drinking behavior are likely to have low rates of damage. Mizruchi and Perrucci contend that if a culture is characterized predominantly by proscriptive norms deviation from those norms will be associated with high rates of pathology because of the absence of prescriptive norms about how to behave if one does drink. Deviation in societies with predominantly prescriptive norms (with some proscriptive norms) is associated with low levels of pathology.[5]

In their Edmonton, Alberta, study of the quality of norms about drinking, Larsen and Abu-Laban found that among persons who use alcoholic beverages, those who have "received few, if any, guidelines regarding appropriate drinking behaviour are more likely to become heavy drinkers than those who are given specific directives."[6]

Much of the work in the field of alcohol studies has examined the relationship between specific constellations of norms about drinking and rates of alcohol-related damage. Four sets of normative conditions generally are reported to be associated with rates of damage. The following have been suggested:

1. Where proscriptive norms dominate and prescriptive norms are absent, the rate of alcohol-related damage appears to be high (*proscriptive environment*);
2. Where prescriptive norms dominate and proscriptive norms are absent, within the context of drinking practices that are highly integrated into the cultural structure, the rate of alcohol-related damage appears to be high (*prescriptive environment*);
3. Where the quality of social norms is ambiguous or ambivalent and drinking practices are seen as not integrated culturally, the rate of alcohol-related damage appears to be high (*ambivalent environment*); and
4. Where clear prescriptions and proscriptions exist and drinking practices are well integrated into the culture, the rate of alcohol-related damage appears to be low (*unambiguous environment*).

These propositions apparently draw some support from a wide variety of studies of diverse religious, national, and ethnic groups. In order to understand the sociocultural model it is useful to review the nature of the evidence on which it is based.

Proscriptive Environment

The Mormon Church proscribes all use of alcoholic beverages by its members. In their study of drinking behavior among college students, Straus and Bacon found that among those Mormon students who drank against the prohibition of their Church, rates of intoxication were high.[7] Yet these same data reveal that male Mormon students who drink are the least likely of all four religious groups studied to score in the two highest categories of the Quantity-Frequency Index developed by Straus and Bacon. Similar results are reported for female students belonging to the Mormon Church.[8]

In his re-examination of some of the Straus and Bacon data, Skolnick concludes that "the abstinence orientation to drinking seems prone to encourage problem drinking in those who reject the norm of total abstinence."[9] It is not clear from the Skolnick data, however, whether this conclusion is warranted. Methodist students (abstinence background), those students who are current non-affiliates of any church but who come from abstinence backgrounds, and Episcopalians who do not proscribe drinking all have similar patterns with respect to the proportion in the highest levels of the Quantity-Frequency Index and the frequency of intoxication.[10]

Bales, Straus and Bacon, and Skolnick all suggest the etiological significance of *norms about drinking* in attempting to account for the apparently high rates of acute damage among those from abstinence backgrounds. They argue that the relative absence of norms about how to drink or an emphasis on the negative consequences of alcohol consumption lead to damaging drinking practices among those who choose to drink.

Different conclusions are possible. As Mäkelä points out, Straus and Bacon and Skolnick focus only on the drinkers in each religious category, thus distorting the results considerably.[11] A closer examination of the Straus and Bacon data reveals that only 54 percent of the Mormon students report ever having consumed alcoholic beverages compared with 77 percent of the Protestants, 90 percent of the Roman

Catholics, and 94 percent of the Jewish students. Mäkelä indicates that by including the non-drinkers in the Skolnick study, the rate of complications related to drinking is higher among the Episcopalians than among the more abstinence-oriented Methodists.

In summary, groups that advocate abstinence appear likely to have low rates of damage. There is little evidence that for those who do drink rates of damage would be high, despite Bacon's "guess" (based on the Straus and Bacon data) that the prevalence of alcohol-related damage among Mormon drinkers is high. [12] Bacon does agree that for all Mormons in the United States the rate of alcohol-related damage is very low. [13] Thus, the initial proposition that proscriptive environments are associated with high rates of damage appears to have little support.

Prescriptive Environment

There is general agreement that for the French rates of physical pathology related to the consumption of alcoholic beverages are among the highest in the world. [14] There are also indications in the literature that drunkenness as well as other indicators of the prevalence of acute alcohol-related damage are relatively high among the French. [15]

The use of wine is widespread in French culture. Children learn to drink wine with meals at an early age. Unlike the Italians, who consume most of their daily intake of alcoholic beverages with meals, many French drinkers not only drink wine with meals but also consume alcoholic beverages between meals on a regular basis. [16]

Many of the respondents in a major study of French drinking practices believe that wine is indispensable to workers in heavy labor jobs. They report that wine is "nourishing, strengthening and necessary to complete a good lunch or dinner." [17]

The use of alcoholic beverages is highly integrated into French social life, and the use of such beverages appears to be generally prescribed. According to Blacker, there are few apparent proscriptions against excessive use. Sadoun quotes an early author who says that the French have a "tender indulgence for the joyous and glowing drunkard, a genuine admiration for the man who can handle wine well." [18] Intoxication is socially acceptable to the French who have many synonyms for intoxication in their language. [19]

Blacker has inferred the existence of a particular constellation of norms from the attitudes the French appear to have toward the use of alcoholic beverages. Thus, his conclusion about the lack of proscriptions against excessive use of alcohol is based on the apparent tolerance for drunkenness expressed by the French. The validity of the inference has neither been questioned nor examined empirically. If we accept this inference as valid, then it appears that a society that is characterized by highly integrated drinking practices and predominantly prescriptive norms is in fact likely to experience high rates of physical pathology related to the consumption of alcohol as well as high rates of more acute forms of damage, such as drunkenness.

Ambivalent Environment

The particular constellation of norms that results in ambivalent or ambiguous directives about the use of alcohol is thought to be associated with high rates of alcohol-related damage. The Irish are frequently cited as a group whose drinking practices are insufficiently integrated into the structure of the group. There is ambiguity about the age at which young people should be introduced to alcoholic beverages. Drinking for instrumental reasons is accepted, but there is concern over the damage associated with drinking. There is tolerance of intoxication among men, but abstinence is a virtue when practiced by women. Much drinking occurs in public places; so it is highly visible, and drunkenness, when it occurs, is more prominent than would be the case in a society that tended to drink in private. The Irish are regarded as having high rates of alcohol-related damage, particularly in the form of drunkenness.[20]

Bales studied the conditions in Ireland that appear to be associated with high rates of drunkenness among Irish drinkers. Traditionally, extreme poverty led to strict separation of the sexes and delayed marriages. The men were expected to spend their free time drinking together. Abstinence was proscribed; men not drinking were subject to suspicion.[21] Drinking—even to the point of intoxication—was tolerated and almost encouraged in this situation. Straus called it institutionalized intoxication.[22]

Drinking in conjunction with many ritual and ceremonial occasions was prescribed among the Irish. Drunkenness was only proscribed under certain conditions—specifically, when it began to affect the family—although frequently the drunkard was laughed at or handled with maternal care. [23] Such conflict and ambiguity in the proscriptive elements of the norms are thought to produce a high degree of ambivalence among the Irish.

Bales describes the attitude toward drinking of the Irish in nineteenth-century rural Ireland as "utilitarian." [24] The functions of drinking were to promote fun and good will, to enhance feelings of personal well-being, and to provide a release from inner tensions. Immigration to the United States created many problems for the Irish. Chafetz and Demone report that the immigrants "suffered socially, economically, and religiously . . . their status was at a new low." [25] For a group which already held utilitarian attitudes toward the use of alcohol, the solution to these feelings of despair was to resort to the pattern of frequent excessive drinking that was part of their cultural heritage.

The Irish are often cited as an example of a group with high rates of "alcoholism." It is true that the frequency of public drunkenness and social disruption among the Irish appears to be high and that the rate of alcohol-related damage as measured by specific indices relating to acute forms of damage is high. However, the rate of clinical alcoholism, the rate of death from cirrhosis of the liver, and other indicators of more chronic alcohol-related damage are all relatively low. [26] On balance, it appears that the relationship between ambiguous or inconsistent norms and rates of damage receives, at best, equivocal support. [27]

Unambiguous Environment

In groups characterized by drinking practices that are an integral part of social life, by consistent and unambiguous attitudes toward drinking, and by prescriptions for moderate drinking and proscriptions against excessive drinking, the rate of alcohol-related damage is thought to be low.

Orthodox Jews are the most commonly cited example of a group with this particular constellation of norms. This situation prevails regardless of where the Jews live. The use of alcoholic beverages is an integral part of rituals for the Sabbath and the many feast days celebrated throughout the year. [28] Glad examines the context of drinking behavior among Jews. He concludes that because these events (of which drinking is only a part) have symbolic significance, Jews have low rates of acute alcohol-related damage in the form of drunkenness. [29]

Bales also accounts for the low rates of drunkenness among Jews within the context of their drinking practices. He argues that the early socialization of Jewish children to the ritual, ceremonial, and familial use of alcoholic beverages fosters moderate use of such beverages and that the association of drinking with ritual and sacred occasions helps to protect Jews from drunkenness. [30]

The qualitative aspects of Jewish norms about drinking are explicit. Bales discusses the "discipline of all appetites," including food and drink, in order to attain the "all-inclusive state of holiness which is so much desired in the Jewish religion. Undisciplined appetites are a defilement of self." [31] Drunkenness is seen as an abomination, a perversion, or a profanity. [32] By learning those prescriptions and proscriptions relating to the use of alcoholic beverages, Jews learn to drink in moderation.

Snyder and Landman suggest that the solidarity of the Jewish group may also be important in sustaining the normative structure surrounding drinking behavior. [33] The Jew learns how to drink and, at the same time, how *not* to drink, within the structure of the group. Snyder argues that the concept of sobriety has been incorporated into the ethnocentrism of the Jewish group. [34] It is part of the "ingroup-outgroup" factor which he uses to account for Jewish sobriety. Jewish children grow up with an image of drunken Gentiles and sober Jews, an image at least partially reinforced by folk songs and ditties such as "Shikker is a Goy" ("Drunken is a Gentile"). Snyder found that several of the Jewish men in his survey remembered the song and supported its sentiments; that is, they agreed that drunkenness was associated with being Gentile, the outgroup. [35]

Regardless of the orientation taken in explaining low rates of drunkenness among Jews, it appears that there is a common theoretical conclusion. The social norms that govern drinking behavior for the Jews provide prescriptive conditions and sanctions for clearly defined ways of drinking and unequivocal proscriptions against drunkenness. Together with the highly integrated structural aspects of the social norms about drinking this particular set of drinking norms appears to be associated with low rates of acute damage or drunkenness among Jews.

Singer's report on drinking patterns in Hong Kong and Moore's earlier discussion on the social uses of wine among the Chinese indicate that the practices of the Chinese are similar to those of the Jews. [36] Drinking is sanctioned in certain situations, and alcohol is used in many rituals and ceremonies. The consumption of alcoholic beverages is an integral part of many social and cultural activities, and moderation is the expected form of behavior. "The Chinese disapprove of excessive drinking, secret drinking, drinking alone and intoxication." [37] The normative structure that surrounds Chinese drinking behavior, then, is similar to that of the Jews. Drinking practices are integrated into Chinese social life and governed by prescriptive and proscriptive norms about drinking which are unequivocal as to what constitutes appropriate drinking behavior. According to Chu, the rate of both chronic and acute alcohol-related damage among Chinese is low. [38]

Thus the cases of both the Chinese and the Jews appear to support the statement that clear and consistent proscriptive and prescriptive norms along with drinking practices that are well integrated into the cultural life of the group are associated with low rates of damage.

Less clear, however, is the support afforded by the case of the Italians. Italians are often cited as a group with low rates of "alcoholism" in spite of a very high rate of consumption of alcoholic beverages. [39] It is because of the high rate of consumption and reported low rate of damage that some authors argue that the level of consumption of alcoholic beverages cannot be taken as an indicator of the prevalence of alcohol-related damage. Instead, the focus shifts to the context in which drinking takes place. [40]

The referent for the word "alcoholism" must be specified. Italians are rarely intoxicated in public or involved in other acute and visible disruptions. The rate of acute damage is low, but the Italians have very high rates of death from cirrhosis of the liver. [41] The rate of chronic alcohol-related damage is high. Throughout the literature, however, "alcoholism" among the Italians is used in the narrow sense of drunkenness, not chronic damage, and the impression is given that Italians have model drinking practices.

Drinking for the Italians is an activity almost exclusively associated with meals and family celebrations. Children are introduced to the use of wine with meals early in their lives. "Drinking becomes a way of life earlier; it is then that liquor becomes a staple of diet for always." [42]

A major survey of the use of alcohol among Italians and Italian-Americans indicated that wine is the only beverage used by the majority of Italians. [43] Italian-Americans, on the other hand, have diversified their drinking practices to include other alcoholic beverages and different drinking habits. The results of the survey indicate that Italians drink primarily for reasons associated with health and tradition, while Italian-Americans tend to drink for reasons more associated with sociability and effect. [44] The authors also contend that drinking is associated with higher rates of alcohol-related damage for the Italian-Americans because they have lost the protection afforded by the integrated drinking behavior in Italy. [45]

Statements about the quality of social norms for Italians are considerably less explicit than for the Jews and the Chinese. Nevertheless, it appears that drinking with meals, sipping wine slowly, and drinking for reasons associated with health are prescribed forms of behavior, while consumption of alcoholic beverages between meals and intoxication are proscribed. This clarity of prescriptions and proscriptions along with the structural aspects of the norms discussed earlier appear to be associated with low rates of drunkenness among native Italians. At issue still, however, is the high rate of physical complications related to drinking that is not addressed in the sociocultural literature.

An Hypothesis Relating the Structure and Quality of Social Norms to Rates of Damage

Ullman suggests an hypothesis which relates the structural aspects of social norms about drinking to rates of alcohol-related damage in society:

in any group or society in which the drinking customs, values and sanctions—together with the attitudes of all segments of the group or society—are well established, known to and agreed upon by all, and are consistent with the rest of the culture, the rate of alcoholism will be low.

He adds:

under conditions in which the individual drinker does not know what is expected or when the expectation in one situation differs from that in another, it can be assumed that he will have ambivalent feelings about drinking. Thus, ambivalence is the psychological product of unintegrated drinking customs. [46]

Blacker notes that this hypothesis fails to explain the case of the French. [47] Drinking customs, values, and sanctions in France are well established, known to and agreed upon, and so forth, but the rate of alcohol-related damage is very high. Blacker indicates that this "shortcoming" in Ullman's theory is a result of Ullman's almost total concern with the structural aspects of norms and insufficient attention to the content or quality of these norms. [48]

Blacker amended Ullman's hypothesis in such a way as to include qualitative aspects of norms:

in any group or society in which drinking customs, values and sanctions— together with the attitudes of all segments of the group or society—are well established, known to and agreed upon by all, consistent with the rest of the culture, *and are characterized by prescriptions for moderate drinking and proscriptions against excessive drinking*, the rate of alcoholism will be low. [49]

This hypothesis constitutes the most succinct statement of what is called the sociocultural model. The interpretations on which it is based are also to be found in the works of other prominent persons in the field of studies on alcohol during this and more recent periods. [50]

Summary

There is much literature in the field of studies on alcohol which attempts to associate differences in the structure and quality of social norms across various groups with rates of alcohol-related damage among these groups. The hypothesis advanced by Blacker relates the integration of drinking practices and the clear and consistent operation of prescriptive and proscriptive norms to low rates of damage from drinking. Some support is found for the hypothesis. Among Jews and possibly the Chinese, where drinking practices are integrated and there are unequivocal norms about how to drink, rates of both chronic and acute damage appear low. Among the French, where few proscriptions appear to be associated with the use of alcoholic beverages, rates of both chronic and acute damage are reported to be high.

For the Italians, the Irish and those from abstinence backgrounds, the support for the hypothesis is less clear. According to Blacker, the Italians have low rates of damage. The situation is in fact more complex; rates of acute damage are low, but rates of chronic damage are among the highest in the world. Were the hypothesis to hold, high rates of damage would be expected among the Irish. And, indeed, the Irish do exhibit high rates of acute damage, drunkenness, and acute social disruption.[51] Their chronic damage rate, however, is low. Finally, among those from abstinence backgrounds, close inspection of the available data indicates that rates of all types of damage related to the consumption of alcoholic beverages are generally low, while the hypothesis would lead us to expect high rates because of the absence of prescriptive norms.

Thus, the evidentiary base of the Ullman-Blacker hypothesis is weak, and the hypothesis itself must be regarded as unproven. The hypothesis subsumes conclusions which have been arrived at independently by others and occupies a prominent place both in current research and in planning programs of prevention. It is because of this prominence that the hypothesis is worthy of further study and empirical testing.

Implications for Prevention

The idea that the structure and quality of social norms are associated with rates of alcohol-related damage has formed much of the focus for some approaches to the prevention of such damage. For example, the report of the Cooperative Commission on the Study of Alcoholism in the United States focuses on the idea of altering the structure and quality of social norms as the means of reducing rates of alcohol-related damage. The report contends that one way to reduce alcohol-related damage in the United States is to develop a national consensus regarding acceptable and unacceptable drinking behavior. The establishment of social norms about drinking that include clear and consistent prescriptive and proscriptive norms is seen as contributing to lower rates of damage.[52]

Changes in the structure of social norms about drinking were the focus of a book by Wilkinson, who worked for the Cooperative Commission. The changes should result in the following conditions regarding drinking behavior: drinking takes its place among other activities without special significance attached to the act of drinking itself; children are taught the customs that surround drinking behavior in a controlled and unemotional way; and the restrictions on the availability of alcoholic beverages are removed to eliminate the mystique surrounding their use. [53]

Morris Chafetz, the first director of the National Institute on Alcohol Abuse and Alcoholism in the United States, has for years advocated that American attitudes toward drinking and drinking practices be changed in such a way as to resemble more closely those of countries which he sees as having more healthful attitudes and practices. [54] Italy is an example frequently used by Chafetz. [55] "Continental drinking practices" such as those in Italy are characterized by initiation of the young into the use of alcoholic beverages, drinking with meals, and integration of drinking practices into daily activities so that they become an ordinary part of life. Thus, in spite of marginal support for the Ullman-Blacker hypothesis, variations on its theme have served as the basis for programs of prevention suggested by many influential individuals and organizations.

The Distribution of Consumption Model

The distribution of consumption perspective in accounting for alcohol-related damage also examines differences in rates of damage across social and national groups. In contrast to most of the work on the sociocultural aspects of alcohol-related damage, the distribution of consumption perspective pays special attention to rates of consumption and the overall level of consumption in a society. Rates of damage and rates of consumption are social facts, at the core of this analysis. According to Durkheim, social facts are emergent characteristics of societies. A social fact is "every way of acting, fixed or not, capable of exercising on the individual an external constraint, or again, every way of acting which is general throughout a given society, while at the same time existing in its own right independent of its individual manifestations." [56] Social facts can only be explained, said Durkheim, in terms of other social facts.

From the perspective of the distribution of consumption model, the key relationship is between rates of consumption of alcoholic beverages and rates of alcohol-related damage in particular societies. Both the rate of consumption and the rate of alcohol-related damage can be seen as social facts. Both exist in those societies in which alcoholic beverages are used. Rates of consumption and damage do not have independent meaning. For their definition, they are tied inexorably to the structural features of each society, and in that sense they exercise constraint on the individual.

Sully Ledermann and the Lognormal Curve

Sully Ledermann, a French mathematician, noted certain regularities in the distribution of the consumption of alcoholic beverages in several populations.[57] The distributions were all highly skewed and resembled the distributions that Ledermann had earlier found to obtain for contagious diseases.[58] Ledermann noted that other social and economic phenomena could be described by distributions of the same general nature and that this distribution approximated lognormality.[59]

The lognormal distribution has two parameters: the mean and a measure of dispersion. Ledermann (1956) made the assumptions that the dispersion parameter is fairly stable across societies and that the proportion of the population that consumes over 365 liters of absolute alcohol per year is a constant. These assumptions have been the subject of much controversy. However, two facts must be considered. First, any consumption of absolute alcohol in excess of 365 liters annually would be fatal, so the proportion consuming at this level is constant; in fact, it is zero. Second, work by Ledermann, by Canadian researchers, by an international group of researchers, and by Scandinavian researchers indicates that the distribution of alcohol consumption is in fact approximately lognormal and that the dispersion is quite stable among populations with the same mean level of consumption.[60] In effect, the Ledermann distribution is a one-parameter variant of the lognormal distribution which provides a good approximation of the distribution of alcohol consumption.

The Ledermann Distribution

The Ledermann distribution describes consumption of alcoholic beverages in a wide variety of societies. It is a highly skewed, unimodal, continuous distribution with most individuals having relatively low levels of consumption. As the amount of alcohol consumed increases, the proportion of the population consuming at that level decreases. Given Ledermann's assumption regarding the dispersion parameter, populations with high levels of average (or per capita) consumption will have higher proportions of drinkers who consume large amounts of alcohol than populations with low levels of per capita consumption. Knowledge of the level of per capita consumption allows the projection of estimates of the proportion of the population under any part of the curve, that is, the proportion of the population that consumes alcoholic beverages at or above any level of consumption.

For the distribution of consumption approach to be useful in explaining rates of alcohol-related damage, the relationship between rates of consumption and rates of damage must be established. Work by de Lint and Schmidt has shown that the prevalence of physical damage, social and economic disruption, and emotional problems is greater among heavy consumers of alcohol.[61] These are the types of damage often referred to in definitions of clinical alcoholism.[62] Based on the work of Lelbach,[63] de Lint and Schmidt indicate that consumption in excess of 10 centiliters of absolute alcohol per day is associated with elevated risk of physical complications, and they refer to persons who consume at such levels as "hazardous drinkers."[64]

Schmidt and de Lint have shown that estimates of the prevalence of clinical alcoholism based on data relating to consumption are similar to estimates based on more common indicators such as the death rate from cirrhosis of the liver, deaths attributed to alcoholism, and deaths due to suicide.[65] They use a level of consumption of 15 centiliters of absolute alcohol per day as an estimate of alcoholic drinking, based on investigations indicating that 15 centiliters per day is the minimum amount consumed by patients admitted to alcoholism clinics for treatment.[66]

Thus, levels of consumption have been identified in terms of presenting elevated risk of damage for the individual. Similarly, estimates can be produced that associate the average level of consumption in a society with certain rates of damage.

An Hypothesis Relating Rates of Consumption and Rates of Damage

There has been no specific formulation of the distribution of consumption hypothesis as such. The closest has been the hypothesis derived from Ledermann and de Lint and Schmidt by Whitehead and

Harvey: "in any society in which the level of per capita consumption is low, such that few persons consume in excess of 10 centiliters of absolute alcohol per day, the rate of alcoholism will be low."[67] The notion of "alcoholism" was used to be consistent with the Ullman-Blacker hypothesis. The referents for the term are the physical, social, economic, and psychological damage associated with excessive consumption.

Criticisms of the Ledermann Distribution

In the review of the literature on the sociocultural approach, it was found that the quantity of alcohol consumed was rarely considered. When quantity is mentioned in that literature, it is most often as an incidental part of the drinking pattern rather than as a determinant of the rate of damage. Bales states that "high rates of consumption do not necessarily mean high rates of alcoholism."[68] Given this point of view, it is not surprising that Ledermann's work was largely ignored by North American researchers who were busy studying the contexts of drinking practices.

In 1968, the first in a series of papers by de Lint and Schmidt on the distribution of consumption of alcoholic beverages was published.[69] These papers received little immediate attention. Discussion in the literature of the distribution of consumption approach followed the publication of an attempt by Smart and Schmidt to apply the principles of the Ledermann distribution to the prevention of alcohol-related automobile accidents.[70] Briefly, they used a two-parameter version of the lognormal distribution and fitted it to data from previous studies on the blood alcohol concentration (BAC) of drivers not involved in accidents. They concluded that the distribution of BACs of drivers not involved in accidents is approximately lognormal. Given the relationship between the mean BAC (and variance or dispersion in the case of a two-parameter curve) and the proportion of high BACs, they reasoned that a reduction in the mean BAC ought to lead to a reduction in the number of drivers with high BACs (those considered to be the most dangerous drivers). Smart and Schmidt then argue for a series of measures directed at reducing drinking and driving generally.

The responses to Smart and Schmidt took two forms. Zylman criticized the nature of the countermeasures proposed but not the statistical basis for the conclusions. [71] O'Neill and Wells took issue with the statistical basis. They used a more powerful test which revealed a significant departure from lognormality in one of the sets of data used by Smart and Schmidt. They then argued that changes in the mean BAC do not *necessarily* mean that the proportion of drivers with high BACs will change, and thus the proposed countermeasures are without empirical foundation. [72]

Eckholm takes issue with O'Neill and Wells. He uses a data reduction technique to simplify the mathematical aspects of the problem and concludes that "there are firm theoretical and empirical reasons to believe that the proportion above an arbitrary risk level will vary in the same direction as the mean BACs." [73] He goes on to qualify this statement by saying that his conclusion holds if the lognormal curve is an accurate description of the distribution of BACs before *and* after any measures are introduced to produce change. To Eckholm, the constancy of the character of the distribution is the most important factor.

The Ledermann distribution has been shown to hold true for many societies at a single point in time and for some societies over time. However, whether measures specifically designed to reduce per capita consumption will alter the shape of the distribution remains an open question.

There are many discussions of the distribution of consumption approach that do not focus specifically on its implications for the prevention of alcohol-related damage. Bruun et al. have reviewed these discussions and found general support for the central proposition of the distribution of consumption approach. They report that "an increase in the per capita consumption of a country should generally be taken to indicate an increasing prevalence of heavy users and of alcohol-related mortality." [74]

In many of the discussions of the distribution of consumption approach and the Ledermann distribution, the major point of contention is with Ledermann's attempt to attenuate variation in the dispersion parameter for any given level of per capita consumption. [75] Schmidt and Popham agree with the critics that there are serious problems with the "constants" (stable dispersion, maximum and minimum possible consumption). They also agree that the Ledermann distribution can only provide an approximation of reality.

Parker and Harman and Schmidt and Popham concur with Skog that the mean consumption of alcohol in a population cannot uniquely determine either the dispersion or the number of heavy consumers. [76] However, Schmidt and Popham also agree with Skog's conclusion that "for most practical purposes, a simple one-parametric distribution (such as the Ledermann distribution), is likely to give a fairly good approximation." [77]

As we have seen, empirical evidence now supports the assumption originally made by Ledermann in 1956, that countries with the same mean consumption have similar dispersions. Schmidt and Popham conclude that, while there may be an error caused by the variation in dispersion, this error "is not sufficiently large to seriously threaten the central proposition of the model that average and heavy consumption covary." [78] Since it is among heavy consumers that one would expect to find the highest risk of damage, the relationship between average consumption and risk of damage has implications for the prevention of alcohol-related damage.

Implications for Prevention

It has been demonstrated by de Lint that rates of per capita consumption correlate with rates of alcohol-related damage. [79] Those who favor this approach to prevention have argued for measures designed to reduce per capita consumption and thereby reduce the number of persons consuming hazardous amounts of alcohol. [80]

John Seeley published one of the first papers that attempted to use the relationship between heavy consumption of alcohol and rates of alcohol-related damage as a basis for a program of prevention. [81] He focused on manipulations of the price of alcoholic beverages as a measure designed to reduce per capita consumption and associated damage. This line of inquiry was extended by researchers at the Addiction Research Foundation of Ontario and the Finnish Foundation for Alcohol Studies. The specific issue of the efficacy of price manipulation is still a source of considerable conflict among economists and is beyond the scope of this chapter. [82]

Popham et al. point out that where alcoholic beverages are readily available and comparatively inexpensive, rates of consumption are high, as are rates of alcohol-related damage. [83] The converse is also true; that is, where alcoholic beverages are more difficult to obtain and relatively more expensive, rates of consumption and damage are low. They point to the need to control the availability and accessibility of alcoholic beverages in order to reduce per capita consumption and rates of alcohol-related damage.

The Two Approaches

Differences

The major point of departure between the sociocultural perspective and the distribution of consumption perspective is on the importance of the quantity of alcohol consumed in a population. A second difference revolves around the meaning of alcohol-related damage. Proponents of the sociocultural approach—in their discussions of the Jews, the Irish, and the Italians—usually appear to mean *drunkenness* when they talk about alcoholism. In the case of the French, alcoholism refers to physical pathology. The distribution of consumption model, on the other hand, was developed and has been defended on the basis of the relationship between consumption and rates of physical complications.

As Whitehead and Harvey have indicated, these differences in perspective have led to confusion about specific societies. A case in point is Italy. Blacker sees Italy as conforming to the Ullman-Blacker hypothesis in that drinking practices are highly integrated and the rate of alcohol-related damage ("alcoholism," in his words) is low, in spite of the high rate of consumption. In fact, Italy has high rates of chronic physical complications due to alcohol consumption, even though rates for certain acute problems such as public drunkenness appear low. A second case is Ireland, where certain acute problems such as public drunkenness are more manifest, probably because much consumption takes place in public. However, the rates of physical complications are relatively low and more in keeping with the average level of consumption in Ireland than with the stereotype of a nation of drunks.

Similarities

Eckholm has pointed out that the Ledermann distribution of alcohol consumption has yet to be either derived from sociological theory or explained in terms of that theory. The same is true for the Ullman-Blacker hypothesis. It deals with social and cultural variables but has been arrived at inductively.[84] Yet, both are sociological in the sense that they attempt to account for rates of damage in terms of certain structural variables (social facts). There are aspects of the structure and quality of social norms which are associated with the level of consumption. For instance, it is not unusual to find the following traits to covary: highly integrated drinking practices; relative inexpensiveness of alcoholic beverages; relative ease of accessibility of alcoholic beverages; and high average level of consumption. The recognition of these similarities' existence has led to at least one attempt to produce a synthesis of the two perspectives.

The Whitehead-Harvey Synthesis

Whitehead argued for a synthesis of the two perspectives on practical and programmatic grounds more than on theoretical grounds.[85] In an effort to provide such a synthesis, Whitehead and Harvey[86] tested aspects of the sociocultural and distribution of consumption models with data from Bacon et al.'s cross-cultural study of drinking.[87] Briefly, they found some—though limited—support for the sociocultural (Ullman-Blacker) hypothesis and greater support for the distribution of consumption hypothesis. Based on this analysis, they proposed a synthesis of the two models:

In any group or society in which drinking customs, values and sanctions—together with the attitudes of all segments of the group or society—are well established, known to and agreed upon by all, consistent with the rest of the culture and are characterized by prescriptive and proscriptive norms (social, legal, etc.) that keep per capita consumption low enough that few persons in that society will consume in excess of 10 centilitres of absolute alcohol per day, the rate of alcoholism will be low.[88]

According to this hypothesis, the level of integration of drinking practices is related to the extent of problems in a society in such a way that highly integrated drinking practices are associated with low levels of damage. It is also hypothesized that when prescriptions for moderate drinking and proscriptions against excessive drinking exist that function to keep the level of per capita consumption low, this low level of consumption of alcoholic beverages is associated with low rates of damage. There appear to be no hypothesized relationships between the level of integration of drinking practices and the level of consumption in a society or between the prescriptive and proscriptive norms and the extent of alcohol-related damage.

A New Synthesis

All three of the aforementioned hypotheses (Ullman-Blacker; distribution of consumption; Whitehead-Harvey) have been retested using data from Bacon et al. on sixty-eight preliterate, non-Western societies. In contrast to the previous analyses, the technique of path analysis was used, and relationships which have heretofore been neglected (e.g., the relationship between prescriptive and proscriptive norms) have been systematically examined. The details of this analysis are available elsewhere,[89] and they are further developed in other work in progress.[90] However, the principal conclusions from this work are outlined below. They involve a set of propositions which are theoretically relevant and empirically supported.

1. The rate of alcohol-related damage and the level of integration of drinking practices are inversely related.
2. The rate of alcohol-related damage and prescriptions for moderate drinking are inversely related.
3. The rate of alcohol-related damage and proscriptions against excessive drinking are inversely related.
4. The rate of alcohol-related damage and the overall level of consumption are directly related.
5. The overall level of consumption and the level of integration of drinking practices are directly related.
6. The overall level of consumption and prescriptions for moderate drinking are directly related.
7. The level of integration of drinking practices and prescriptions for moderate drinking are directly related.
8. Prescriptions for moderate drinking and proscriptions against excessive drinking are inversely related.

9. The level of integration of drinking practices and proscriptions against excessive drinking are inversely related.

These propositions can be summarized in a new hypothesis:

In any group or society in which the overall level of consumption is high and (to a lesser extent) where proscriptions against excessive drinking are few or absent, the rate of alcohol-related damage will be high. Where drinking practices are integrated into the cultural structure and where prescriptions for moderate drinking are prevalent, the overall level of consumption will be high. Societies characterized by prescriptions for moderate drinking tend to have integrated drinking practices and few proscriptions against excessive drinking.

There are several points of difference between this new hypothesis and the other formulations that we have been considering in this chapter. Regarding the Ullman-Blacker hypothesis, the most important point to be made is that the amount of alcohol consumed by a population is not an incidental or unimportant factor in determining the rate of alcohol-related damage in that population. It is, in fact, the strongest single explanatory variable and deserves far more attention than has been paid to it by sociocultural theorists.

The second major difference between our hypothesis and the Ullman-Blacker formulation lies in the importance attached to the structure and quality of social norms about drinking in explaining variation in rates of damage. Our analysis shows that the net contribution of integration of drinking practices as an explanatory variable approaches zero and that prescriptions for moderate drinking have only a small overall role to play in explaining alcohol-related damage in society. Only proscriptions against excessive drinking have a clear and important direct relationship to rates of damage. This relationship is not reduced by a relationship between proscriptions against excessive drinking and consumption because the latter relationship is zero.

The final difference between our hypothesis and the Ullman-Blacker statement is found in the relationships among the various structural and qualitative aspects of social norms about drinking. Blacker introduces the concepts of prescriptive and proscriptive norms primarily to account for the rate of damage among the French. He infers that approval of moderate drinking and disapproval of drunkenness are coexisting norms, but our analysis indicates that the two are in fact inversely related. Blacker's reformulation of Ullman's hypothesis also leads us to expect that the two qualitative aspects of social norms about drinking will be positively associated with the structural aspects of those norms. Our analysis indicates that only prescriptions for moderate drinking are positively associated with integrated drinking practices. Proscriptions against excessive drinking are negatively related to integrated drinking practices.

With respect to the hypothesis derived from the Ledermann distribution, our results affirm that the overall level of consumption in a population is the single most important factor in determining the rate of alcohol-related damage in that population. However, our results indicate that a full explanation of variation in rates of damage across population groups must take into account both those aspects of the structure and quality of social norms directly related to rates of damage and those indirectly related to rates of damage through the level of consumption.

In summary, neither of the existing theoretical orientations provides a complete explanation for variation in rates of alcohol-related damage. The synthesis proposed by Whitehead and Harvey is an attempt to combine the two, but it overlooks several important relationships. Our model provides a better portrayal of the interrelationships between the two approaches. It demonstrates that the key to explaining alcohol-related damage is the overall level of consumption of alcoholic beverages in a society. It also shows that the level of integration of drinking practices and prescriptions for moderate drinking are positively related to the level of consumption and to each other, while each is significantly, but inversely, related to the rate of damage.

Societies characterized by highly integrated drinking practices tend also to be characterized by prescriptions for moderate drinking. These two normative conditions are associated with high rates of consumption and high rates of damage. The inverse relationship between the level of integration of drinking practices and rates of damage is offset by the indirect relationship through consumption, while the negative relationship between prescriptions for moderate drinking and rates of damage is greater than the positive indirect relationship to damage through consumption. Proscriptions against excessive drinking are not related to levels of consumption but have direct negative effects on rates of damage.

Conclusions

The dominant sociological perspectives that have been used to account for rates of alcohol-related damage have been examined. We have indicated how there has been some confusion over the empirical basis for some of these hypotheses, and we have specified the nature of the evidence on which they are based. We have also summarized the results of a recent study which puts the sociocultural and distribution of consumption models to empirical test. These results lead to a set of propositions and a new hypothesis which constitutes a synthesis of the major elements of the two perspectives.

Our results are based on data from preliterate societies. One potential direction for future research is to test this model on modern societies. Another direction is to change the unit of analysis to the individual level. McClelland and his associates were able to show that drinking has some common effects on fantasy across a variety of drinking situations and across several societies.[91] Thus, the demonstration that it is feasible to examine models similar to our own in a variety of cultures, both literate and preliterate, suggests that future research along those lines is possible.

When the new hypothesis is subjected to empirical validation, further refinements will doubtlessly be required. For the time being, this analysis and the new hypothesis raise some serious questions about the suggestions for prevention that have been derived solely from one or another of the earlier models. The relationships among the variables appear more complex than the earlier models suggest.

Notes

1. Selden D. Bacon, "Sociology and the Problems of Alcohol: Foundations for a Sociologic Study of Drinking Behavior," *Quarterly Journal of Studies on Alcohol* 4 (1943): 402-45.
2. Ibid.
3. Ibid., p. 443.

4. Robert F. Bales, "Cultural Differences in Rates of Alcoholism," *Quarterly Journal of Studies on Alcohol* 6 (March 1946): 480-99; "Attitudes toward Drinking in the Irish Culture," in *Society, Culture, and Drinking Patterns*, eds. David J. Pittman and Charles R. Snyder (New York, 1962), pp. 157-87.

5. Ephraim H. Mizruchi and Robert Perrucci, "Norm Qualities and Differential Effects of Deviant Behavior: An Exploratory Analysis," *American Sociological Review* 27 (June 1962): 391-99; "Prescription, Proscription and Permissiveness: Aspects of Norms and Deviant Drinking Behavior," in *The Domesticated Drug: Drinking among Collegians*, ed. George L. Maddox (New Haven, 1970), pp. 234-53.

6. Donald E. Larsen and Baha Abu-Laban, "Norm Qualities and Deviant Behavior," *Social Problems* 15 (Spring 1968): 441-50.

7. Robert Straus and Selden D. Bacon, *Drinking in College* (New Haven, 1953).

8. Ibid., p. 111.

9. Jerome R. Skolnick, "Religious Affiliation and Drinking Behavior," *Quarterly Journal of Studies on Alcohol* 19 (September 1958): 452-70.

10. Ibid., pp. 460-62.

11. Klaus Mäkelä, "Consumption Level and Cultural Drinking Patterns as Determinants of Alcohol Problems" (Paper presented to the Thirtieth International Congress on Alcoholism and Drug Dependence, Amsterdam, September 1972).

12. Selden D. Bacon, "Social Settings Conducive to Alcoholism: A Sociological Approach to a Medical Problem," *Journal of the American Medical Association* 164 (May 1957): 177-81.

13. Ibid.

14. Edward Blacker, "Sociocultural Factors in Alcoholism," *International Psychiatry Clinics* 3 (Summer 1966): 51-80; Kettil Bruun et al. *Alcohol Control Policies in Public Health Perspective* (Helsinki, 1975); Jan de Lint, "The Prevention of Alcoholism," *Preventive Medicine* 3 (1974): 24-35.

15. Ronald Sadoun, Giorgio Lolli, and Milton Silverman, *Drinking in French Culture* (New Brunswick, N.J., 1965); Bruun et al., *Alcohol Control Policies*; de Lint, "Prevention of Alcoholism."

16. Sadoun, Lolli, and Silverman, *Drinking in French Culture*.

17. Ibid., p. 50.

18. Ibid., p. 48.

19. Ibid.

20. Bales, "Cultural Differences"; Bales, "Attitudes toward Drinking"; David D. Glad, "Attitudes and Experiences of American-Jewish and American-Irish Male Youth as Related to Differences in Adult Rates of Inebriety," *Quarterly Journal of Studies on Alcohol* 8 (December 1947): 406-72.

21. Bales, "Attitudes toward Drinking," p. 169.

22. Robert Straus, "Alcohol," in *Contemporary Social Problems*, 2nd ed., eds. Robert K. Merton and Robert A. Nisbet (New York, 1966), p. 265.

23. Bales, "Attitudes toward Drinking," p. 170; Richard Stivers, *A Hair of the Dog* (University Park, Pa., 1976).

24. Bales, "Cultural Differences."

25. Morris E. Chafetz and Harold Demone, *Alcohol and Society* (New York, 1962), p. 80.

26. See, for example, Bruun et al., *Alcohol Control Policies*, and de Lint, "Prevention of Alcoholism."

27. Discussions of the structure and quality of social norms are often only implicit in the many descriptions of drinking patterns and problems among Americans. From our reading of them, it appears that American drinking patterns are governed by social norms which are predominantly prescriptive with ambiguous and ambivalent proscriptive elements. See Bacon, "Social Settings"; Don Cahalan, Ira Cisin, and Helen M. Crossley, *American Drinking Practices* (New Brunswick, N.J., 1969); Thomas F. A. Plaut, *Alcohol Problems: A Report to the Nation* (New York, 1967); Robin Room, "Drinking Patterns in Large U.S. Cities," *Quarterly Journal of Studies on Alcohol*, supplement no. 6 (1972): 28-57; Rupert Wilkinson, *The Prevention of Drinking Problems: Alcohol Control and Cultural Influences* (New York, 1970).

28. Bales, "Cultural Differences."

29. Glad, "Attitudes and Experiences," p. 461.

30. Bales, "Cultural Differences."

31. Ibid., p. 489.

32. Ibid., p. 491.

33. Charles R. Synder and Ruth H. Landman, "Studies of Drinking in Jewish Culture: II. Perspectives for Sociological Research on Jewish Drinking Patterns," *Quarterly Journal of Studies on Alcohol* 12 (1951): 451-74.

34. Charles R. Snyder, "Culture and Jewish Sobriety: The In-group—Out-group Factor," in *Society, Culture, and Drinking Patterns*, eds. David J. Pittman and Charles R. Snyder (New York, 1962), p. 203.

35. Ibid., pp. 188-225.

36. Merrill Moore, "Chinese Wine: Some Notes on Its Social Use," *Quarterly Journal of Studies on Alcohol* 9 (1948): 270-79; K. Singer, "Drinking Patterns and Alcoholism in the Chinese," *British Journal of Addiction* 67 (1972): 3-14.

37. Singer, "Drinking Patterns," p. 6.

38. George Chu, "Drinking among San Francisco Chinese," *Quarterly Journal of Studies on Alcohol*, supplement no. 6 (1972): 58-68.

39. See, for example, Blacker, "Sociocultural Factors"; Morris Chafetz, *Liquor: The Servant of Man* (Boston, 1965); Giorgio Lolli, *Social Drinking* (Cleveland, 1960); Giorgio Lolli, "The Cocktail Hour: Physiological, Psychological and Social Aspects," *Alcohol and Civilization*, ed. Salvatore P. Lucia (New York, 1963), pp. 183-99; Giorgio Lolli et al., "The Use of Wine and Other Alcoholic Beverages by a Group of Italians and Americans of Italian Extraction," *Quarterly Journal of Studies on Alcohol* 13 (1952): 27-48; Giorgio Lolli et al., "Further Observations on the Use of Wine and Other Alcoholic Beverages by Italians and Americans of Italian Extraction," *Quarterly Journal of Studies on Alcohol* 14 (1953): 395-405; Giorgio Lolli et al., *Alcohol in Italian Culture* (New Haven, 1958); Raymond G. McCarthy, *Alcohol Education for Classroom and Community* (New York, 1964); Emidio Serianni, Mario Cannizzaro, and Aldo Mariani, "Blood Alcohol Concentration Resulting from Wine Drinking Timed According to the Dietary Habits of Italians," *Quarterly Journal of Studies on Alcohol* 14 (1953): 165-75; Phyllis H. Williams and Robert Straus, "Drinking Patterns of Italians in New Haven: Utilization of the Personal Diary as a Research Technique," *Quarterly Journal of Studies on Alcohol* 11 (1950): 51-91; 250-308; 452-83; 586-629.

40. See, for example, Bales, "Cultural Differences"; Blacker, "Sociocultural Factors"; and McCarthy, "Alcohol Education."

41. Bruun et al., *Alcohol Control Policies.*

42. Chafetz, *Liquor: The Servant of Man*, p. 212.

43. Lolli et al., *Alcohol in Italian Culture.*

44. Ibid., p. 44.

45. Ibid.

46. Albert D. Ullman, "Sociocultural Backgrounds of Alcoholism," *The Annals of the American Academy of Political and Social Science* 135 (January 1958): 50.

47. Blacker, "Sociocultural Factors."

48. Ibid., p. 67.

49. Ibid., p. 68 (emphasis as in original).

50. For example Morris E. Chafetz, "The Prevention of Alcoholism," *International Journal of Psychiatry* 9 (1970): 329-48; Morris E. Chafetz, "Prevention of Alcoholism in the United States Utilizing Cultural and Educational Forces," *Preventive Medicine* 3 (1974): 5-10; Plaut, *Alcohol Problems;* Wilkinson, *Prevention of Drinking Problems.*

51. Bruun et al., *Alcohol Control Policies.*

52. Plaut, *Alcohol Problems.*

53. Wilkinson, *Prevention of Drinking Problems.*

54. Chafetz, "Prevention of Alcoholism."

55. Chafetz, *Liquor: The Servant of Man*.

56. Emile Durkheim, *The Rules of the Sociological Method* (Toronto, 1938).

57. Sully Ledermann, *Alcool, alcoolisme, alcoolisation: données scientifiques de caractère physiologique, économique et social* (Paris, 1956).

58. Ole-Jørgen Skog, "On the Distribution of Alcohol Consumption" (Paper presented to the Symposium: The Epidemiological Approach to the Prevention of Alcoholism, London, June 1977).

59. A lognormal distribution is one in which the natural logarithms of the observed frequencies are normally distributed.

60. Ledermann, *Alcool, alcoolisme, alcoolisation;* Jan de Lint and Wolfgang Schmidt, "The Distribution of Alcohol Consumption in Ontario," *Quarterly Journal of Studies on Alcohol* 29 (1968): 968-73; Bruun et al., *Alcohol Control Policies*; Skog, "On the Distribution of Alcohol Consumption."

61. Jan de Lint, "Prevention of Alcoholism"; Jan de Lint, "Epidemiological Aspects of Alcoholism," *International Journal of Mental Health* 5 (1976): 29-51; Jan de Lint and Wolfgang Schmidt, "Consumption Averages and Alcoholism Prevalence: A Brief Review of Epidemiological Investigations," *British Journal of Addiction* 66 (September 1971): 97-107.

62. Mark Keller, "Alcoholism: Nature and Extent of the Problem," *Annals of the American Academy of Political and Social Science* 315 (1958): 1-11; World Health Organization, *Second Report of the Expert Committee on Mental Health, Alcoholism Subcommittee* (Geneva, 1952).

63. Werner K. Lelbach, "Organic Pathology Related to Volume and Pattern of Alcohol Use," *Research Advances in Alcohol and Drug Problems, Volume 1*, eds. Robert J. Gibbons et al. (New York, 1974), pp. 93-198.

64. De Lint and Schmidt, "Consumption Averages."

65. Wolfgang Schmidt and Jan de Lint, "Estimating the Prevalence of Alcoholism from Alcohol Consumption and Mortality Data," *Quarterly Journal of Studies on Alcohol* 31 (1970): 957-64.

66. Ibid.; Wolfgang Schmidt and Robert Popham, "Alcohol Consumption of Alcoholics" (Toronto, 1968); Patricia Wilkinson et al. "Epidemiology of Alcoholism: Social Data and Drinking Patterns of a Sample of Australian Alcoholics," *Medical Journal of Australia* 1 (1969): 1020-25.

67. Paul C. Whitehead and Cheryl Harvey, "Explaining Alcoholism: An Empirical Test and Reformulation," *Journal of Health and Social Behavior* 15 (1974): 63.

68. Bales, "Cultural Differences," p. 480.

69. De Lint and Schmidt, "The Distribution of Alcohol Consumption"; "Consumption Averages"; "The Epidemiology of Alcoholism," in *Biological*

Basis of Alcoholism, eds. Yedy Israel and Jorge Mardones (New York, 1971), pp. 423-42.

70. Reginald G. Smart and Wolfgang Schmidt, "Blood Alcohol Levels in Drivers Not Involved in Accidents," *Quarterly Journal of Studies on Alcohol* 31 (1970): 968-71.

71. Richard Zylman, "The Blood Alcohol Distribution in Drivers Not Involved in Accidents," *Quarterly Journal of Studies on Alcohol* 32 (1971): 188-90.

72. Brian O'Neill and W.T. Wells, "Blood Alcohol Levels in Drivers Not Involved in Accidents and the Lognormal Distribution," *Quarterly Journal of Studies on Alcohol* 32 (1971): 798-803.

73. Anders Eckholm, "The Lognormal Distribution of Blood Alcohol Concentration in Drivers," *Quarterly Journal of Studies on Alcohol* 33 (1972): 511.

74. Bruun et al., *Alcohol Control Policies*.

75. Jan de Lint, "Validity of the Theory that the Distribution of Alcohol Consumption in a Population Approximates a Logarithmic Normal Curve," *Drinking and Drug Practices Surveyor* 7 (January 1973): 15-17; Gary H. Miller and Neil Agnew, "The Ledermann Model of Alcohol Consumption: Description, Implications and Assessment," *Quarterly Journal of Studies on Alcohol* 35 (1974): 877-98; Douglas A. Parker and Marsha S. Harman, "The Distribution of Consumption Model of Prevention: A Critical Assessment" (Paper presented to the N.I.A.A.A. Conference on Normative Approaches to Alcoholism and Alcohol Problems, San Diego, April 1977); Robin Room, "Notes on the Implications of the Lognormal Curve," *Drinking and Drug Practices Surveyor* 7 (January 1973): 18-20; Wolfgang Schmidt and Robert E. Popham, "The Single Distribution Model of Alcohol Consumption: Rejoinder to the Critique of Parker and Harman" (Paper presented to the N.I.A.A.A. Conference on Normative Approaches to Alcoholism and Alcohol Problems, San Diego, April 1977); Ole-Jørgen Skog, "Less Alcohol—Fewer Alcoholics?" *Drinking and Drug Practices Survey* 7 (January 1973): 7-14; Skog, "On the Distribution of Alcohol Consumption"; Lancelot J. Smith, *Beer, Wine and Spirits: Beverage Differences and Public Policy in Canada, The Report of the Alcoholic Beverage Study Committee* (Ottawa, 1973).

76. Schmidt and Popham, "The Single Distribution Model," p. 6.

77. Skog, "On the Distribution of Alcohol Consumption," p. 11.

78. Schmidt and Popham, "The Single Distribution Model," p. 7.

79. De Lint, "Prevention of Alcoholism."

80. Bruun et al., *Alcohol Control Policies*; Don Faris, "The Prevention of Alcoholism and Economic Alcoholism," *Preventive Medicine* 3 (1974): 36-48;

de Lint, "Prevention of Alcoholism"; Robert E. Popham and Wolfgang Schmidt, "The Effectiveness of Legal Measures in the Prevention of Alcohol Problems," *Addictive Diseases: An International Journal* 2 (1976): 497-513; Robert E. Popham, Wolfgang Schmidt, and Jan de Lint, "The Prevention of Alcoholism: Epidemiological Studies of the Effects of Government Control Measures," *British Journal of Addiction* 70 (1975): 125-44; Robert E. Popham, Wolfgang Schmidt, and Jan de Lint, "The Effects of Legal Restraint on Drinking," in *The Biology of Alcoholism, Volume 4: Social Aspects of Alcoholism*, eds. Benjamin Kissin and Henri Begleiter (New York, 1976), pp. 597-625; John R. Seeley, "Death by Liver Cirrhosis and the Price of Beverage Alcohol," *Canadian Medical Association Journal* 83 (1960): 1361-66; Paul C. Whitehead, "The Prevention of Alcoholism: An Analysis of Two Approaches" (Paper presented to the Canadian Sociology and Anthropology Association, Montreal, May 1972); Paul C. Whitehead, "Effects of Changing Alcohol Control Measures" (Paper presented to the North American Congress on Alcohol and Drug Problems, San Francisco, December 1974); Paul C. Whitehead, "The Prevention of Alcoholism: Divergences and Convergences of Two Approaches," *Addictive Diseases: An International Journal* 1 (1975): 431-43; Whitehead and Harvey, "Explaining Alcoholism."

81. Seeley, "Death by Liver Cirrhosis."

82. For a detailed discussion of the issues involved, see Hung-Hay Lau, "Cost of Alcoholic Beverages as a Determinant of Alcohol Consumption," in *Research Advances in Alcohol and Drug Problems*, Volume 2, eds. Robert J. Gibbins et al. (New York, 1975). pp. 211-45; Hung-Hay Lau, "Consumption of Alcoholic Beverages in Canada—A Reply to Lidman" (Ottawa, 1977); Russel M. Lidman, "Economic Issues in Alcohol Control," Report No. 7, Social Research Group, School of Public Health, University of California (Berkeley, October 1976); Russel M. Lidman, "Measuring Spirits Elasticity in Canada and California: New Findings," *Drinking and Drug Practices Surveyor* 12 (1976): 9-13; Esa Österberg, "The Pricing of Alcoholic Beverages as an Instrument of Control Policy," Reports from the Social Research Institute of Alcohol Studies, no. 83 (Helsinki, March 1975).

83. Popham, Schmidt, and de Lint, "The Prevention of Alcoholism"; Popham, Schmidt, and de Lint, "The Effects of Legal Restraint on Drinking."

84. For a discussion of this point, see Whitehead and Harvey, "Explaining Alcoholism."

85. Whitehead, "An Analysis of Two Approaches"; Whitehead, "Divergences and Convergences."

86. Whitehead, "Effects of Changing Control Measures."

87. Margaret K. Bacon et al., "A Cross-Cultural Study of Drinking: V. De-

tailed Definitions and Data," *Quarterly Journal of Studies on Alcohol* (1965): 78-111.

88. Whitehead and Harvey, "Explaining Alcoholism," p. 63.

89. B. Gail Frankel, "Theories of Alcohol-Related Damage: An Examination of Some Competing Hypotheses" (M.A. thesis, University of Western Ontario, 1978).

90. B. Gail Frankel and Paul C. Whitehead, *Models of Drinking and Damage: Theoretical Advances and Prevention* (forthcoming).

91. D.C. McClelland et al. *The Drinking Man* (New York, 1972).

3.

Temperance and Economic Change in the Antebellum North

Until the last few years, American scholarship on temperance was dominated by the notion that rural and reactionary forces shaped the anti-liquor crusade of the nineteenth and early twentieth centuries. Looking back on the disastrous experiment of national prohibition in the 1920s, modern historians of the United States have depicted the temperance movement as an intolerant and futile attempt on the part of Protestant, rural, and small-town Americans to stem the flow of social change and to impose the cultural values of native-born Americans on urban and immigrant America.

American historians have been quick to seize upon the cultural, religious, and symbolic components of conflict over the drink question but slow to appreciate the relationship between temperance and economic change.[1] The reluctance to confront the economic aspects of temperance agitation may reflect either the reaction against simplistic Beardian formulations of class conflict or else perhaps the actual experience of the 1920s, when prohibition seemed to many anything but the product of rational and "progressive" economic forces. Richard Hofstadter, the doyen of that generation of historians who revolted simultaneously against both Beard and babbittry, reflected these influences in his *Age of Reform*.

To the historian who likes to trace the development of the great economic issues and to follow the main trend of class politics, the story of Prohibition will seem like a historical detour, a meaningless nuisance, an extraneous imposition upon the main course of history.[2]

Hofstadter found in prohibition not an economic but a cultural conflict; prohibition was a product of the "rural-evangelical virus" and its "drive for morality" against "the pleasures and amenities of city life."[3] A product of the city whose sympathies lay with the New Deal and its progmatic, instrumental reformism, Hofstadter could only look aghast at the varieties of intolerance which he saw as dominating American reform up to the 1920s. Yet if we are to understand the role of reform movements in shaping the American social structure, we must not read back judgments of the twenties into earlier periods of American temperance reform. Whatever the validity of Hofstadter's view of national prohibition, it does not provide a tenable or convincing explanation of the origins of temperance agitation in the early nineteenth-century United States. Temperance reform began not in the most rural sections of the country but rather in the urban, industrial areas of the Northeast; and it found support among those groups which were attempting to hasten the process of social change.

It is abundantly clear from an analysis of the origins of American temperance that the anti-liquor crusade was more than a cultural, religious, and ethnic conflict; it was, above all, a product of changes in the character and conception of work and social relationships. Temperance reform was not a hopelessly reactionary and irrational movement. Rather, it was part of a widespread movement to discipline society and to create a society of predictable individuals devoted to self-improvement. By no means opposed to industrialization, temperance reform was rather the product of that crucial transition to an urban-industrial, commercial society.

Any explanation of the origins of temperance agitation in the United States and its relationship with economic change must begin with the character of temperance support and then proceed to analyze the goals and functions of temperance for its supporters. There are clear indications that not all Americans regarded drinking as a social problem, and only a minority demanded such solutions as total abstinence and prohibition. Within ten years after the formation of the American Temperance Society in Boston in 1826, there were over eight thousand temperance societies in the United States claiming over 1.5 million members, or about one in every ten Americans. These figures were only approximations and may have greatly exaggerated the solid support for total abstinence. Yet the temperance movement, even by its own sanguine calculations, catered to a selective group of Americans. Nine-tenths of the population did not join a temperance society. Not only was the range of recruits restricted; so, too, was the geographic distribution. In 1831, over one-third of all the temperance pledges came from New England, a region which held only 18 percent of the nation's free population. In contrast, the Southern states supplied 8.5 percent of temperance pledges but comprised about 22.5 percent of the free population.[4] These patterns of temperance activity broadly correlate with the growth of urbanization and the beginnings of industrialization in the Northeast. Yet there remains the important question of the exact relationship between the anti-liquor crusade and the character of those social changes. More precise information on the membership, tactics, and social outlook of temperance reformers must be sought if we are to elucidate those relationships.

The search for the character of temperance support leads directly to community studies, since it is only at the local level that we can find representative groups of supporters; only there can we hope to relate social structure and social processes to temperance commitment. A large part of the evidence presented here concerns such a case study of the town of Worcester, Massachusetts, in the 1830s. Once the character of support for temperance in that town has been established, the remainder of the essay will explore the wider implications of the findings.

Worcester presents us with an almost ideal case study of the origins of temperance reform. The town lay within that northeastern belt which was experiencing the dislocating effects of urbanization and the first signs of industrialization at precisely the same time that the temperance movement began to command attention in the region. Worcester presents a microcosm of those social changes. An expanding iron industry, wire manufacturing, textiles, and, in the mid-1830s, introduction of the railroad brought rapid population growth and industrial prominence.[5] This economic activity meant increased prosperity but not without the multiplication of intractable social problems. By 1834, a vigorous temperance society had emerged to combat the increase in crime, drunkenness, and poverty which seemed to many of the town's residents to accompany the process of social change. The attempts to solve these perceived social problems reached a climax between 1835 and 1838 in the temperance society's efforts to abolish all liquor licenses in the town.

This so-called no-license campaign was an early form of local prohibition, but it was also made a test of loyalty to the town's temperance society. The evidence offered here stems primarily from the study of sixty supporters of no-license in Worcester. Comparisons with membership files and other impressionistic evidence suggested that this vote was the best available test of temperance sentiment in the town and in similar Massachusetts communities in the 1830s.[6] A control group of seventy-eight was formed by combining the small published list of opponents of no-license in 1835 with a comparable and larger list of anti-prohibitionists published during the campaign against the "fifteen gallon law" in the town in 1838. This law outlawed the sale of spirits in Massachusetts in smaller quantities than fifteen gallons and, like the no-license agitation, was aimed at suppressing the taverns and retail outlets. Though three years apart, the two incidents were part of the larger controversy over drink in the town, and the alignment on the two issues proved to be identical.[7] Unfortunately, the lists used in compiling the data which follow do not amount to a random sample of temperance support in the town, since such evidence was unobtainable. The group surveyed represented all those reported in newspapers as committed to the no-license campaign; naturally this group represented an *elite* of supporters. For the moment, the focus will be on this elite, the vanguard of temperance supporters who shaped temperance ideology and tactics in the 1830s.

The no-license campaign in Worcester won strong support among groups working to promote an industrial society. Manufacturers and skilled tradesmen constituted the most important categories. The dividing line between the two was slight in the Worcester of the 1830s, and some of the names on the list could not be put with complete certainty into one category or the other. Manufacturers in the town often began as skilled tradesmen and retained close links with the shop floor as their businesses expanded, as they became employers of larger numbers of workers, and as they introduced machines and steam power into their industries. The workers who supported temperance in Worcester were also prosperous. They were not downwardly-mobile workers threatened by incipient industrial development but came rather from highly paid and highly skilled trades in expanding industries, such as textile machinery manufacture, wire manufacture, and the building and printing industries. They were from the elite of Worcester's skilled workers.[8]

Altogether, manufacturing industry accounted for more than 40 percent of the total sample. Since 47 percent of the town's labor force was engaged in manufacturing industry, according to the 1840 census, it seems at first glance that manufacturing was somewhat underrepresented in the no-license sample. But the census figure included the *unskilled* as well as skilled tradesmen and entrepreneurs; the latter two groups were actually present in the no-license camp out of proportion to their numerical importance in the town. Moreover, the manufacturing group was *underrepresented* in the no-license sample through the predominance of a small group of articulate professional people among the speakers at temperance meetings. The ward committees of the no-license supporters, formed to get out the vote for prohibition, more accurately represented the rank and file. These included 50 percent manufacturers and skilled tradesmen. The remainder of the no-license sample consisted of farmers and professionals, together with some people in commerce who through financial investments had links with the town's manufacturing sector.

The prominence of industrial entrepreneurs and skilled tradesmen in the temperance camp was in striking contrast to their absence among opponents of prohibition. Of seventy-eight opponents, only 6 percent were from manufacturing industries. Most came from the commercial classes (merchants, small shopkeepers, tavernkeepers) or were lawyers who based their opposition on the belief that prohibition would bring all law into disrepute. Much of the shopkeepers' opposition stemmed from the fact that grocers' shops carried liquor along with general merchandise. Nevertheless, commercial people of all types opposed the temperance society's drive for no-license. Altogether, over half of the sample of opponents of no-license came from commercial occupations. Again, the figure was out of proportion to the importance of commerce in the town's employment and much larger than in the no-license sample.[9]

The campaign of 1835-38 was not an isolated event in Worcester's social history; the social forces revealed therein continued to shape attitudes toward the use of alcohol as Worcester's industrial revolution proceeded. In 1848, an attempt to elect a "temperance mayor" dedicated to a more stringent enforcement of Worcester's liquor laws produced a pattern of support very similar to that in the campaign of 1835-38. A group of thirty-nine committeemen appointed to get out the vote for the temperance (read prohibitionist) forces in 1848 included nineteen manufacturers, or 49 percent of the total.[10] These men ranged from large-scale manufacturers with more than 150 employees to small-scale employers with four to ten workers. Six of the group employed more than a hundred workers. In all, twenty-eight (72 percent) of the temperance campaigners had links with the town's manufacturing sector, and the group included small-scale, self-employed tradesmen and factory employees as well as the town's most prominent industrial entrepreneurs. These figures for 1848 show an even stronger association between manufacturing interests and campaigns for prohibition than do the results for the 1835-38 no-license group. As the temperance movement in Worcester shifted attention from the relatively mild "no-license" form of prohibition to demands for tough prohibitory laws and more stringent enforcement of existing restrictions on the liquor trade, the influence of the manufacturing sector in general and industrial entrepreneurs in particular seems to have grown steadily stronger.

It is not intended to offer a narrow occupational analysis here. What is stressed is not the occupation but the experiences in that occupation and the values surrounding that working life. In Worcester the temperance conflict was not just manufacturers versus merchants. It seems to have pitted those who looked to the emergence of an industrial society against the merchant, the small country storekeeper, the tavernkeeper, and the drinking culture which sustained these economic interests.

This "entrepreneurial" interpretation can be further illustrated by looking at the responses of farmers to temperance. Of the no-license sample, 32 percent were farmers, as opposed to 19 percent of the pro-license group. There was no significant difference between the median landholding of farmers supporting local prohibition and those opposing it in Worcester. What distinguished temperance farmers in Worcester was the attitude they took toward commercial farming and scientific agricultural practices. Darius Rice, for example, was described in contemporary biographical references as "an active, enterprising, prosperous farmer" who "possessed an inventive genius and constructed some of the earliest implements for the saving of both time and labor in cultivating the farm."[11] Temperance farmers like Rice were quick to respond to the market opportunities presented by the expanding population of the factory town of Worcester by moving into dairy, produce, and market gardening.

The connection between entrepreneurial activity, scientific farming, and temperance support would be tenuous indeed if it rested on such examples alone. Yet there is much evidence to support the link between temperance and entrepreneurial farmers in the proceedings and publications of agricultural improvement societies. In a speech delivered in 1826 before the Anniversary Cattle Show and Exhibition of Manufactures of the Worcester Agricultural Society, Emory Washburn (a lawyer and town booster) advised farmers to exploit the markets which the factories were creating in New England. In addition to scientific farming, the men on the land who wished to benefit from "the cheerful hum of industry" which was "rising around us" must "shrink from the cup" of intemperance, for "health and industry" were the farmer's "greatest wealth."[12]

As opportunities to produce marketable surpluses in the urban and industrial areas of the Northeast increased, farmers seem to have heeded the advice of Washburn and others who exhorted them to work hard and abstain from strong drink. The columns of agricultural papers such as the *New England Farmer* were filled with broadsides against the "demon rum." The special focus of the attack was "the old custom of supplying a barrel of whiskey for farm workers during the harvest season."[13] It was widely believed among rural workers that a ration of liquor would "strengthen them for labor" and "preserve their health" especially "when extreme heat, or extreme cold, endangers them in their labours."[14] These pressures for prohibition intensified among commercial farmers during the 1840s and 1850s as Irish immigrants began to enter the farm labor force and as machines for threshing and harvesting began to be introduced. Drunken and inattentive farm hands could then cause grisly and costly accidents. For farmers concerned with both human welfare and the making of profits, temperance made sense.[15]

The growing support for temperance among commercial farmers in

New England was, then, a logical outgrowth of changing market conditions and commercial opportunities. The temperance movement's appeal to farmers lay not in some collective paranoia at the growth of urban society—as the traditional interpretation of the temperance movement discussed in the introduction would suggest—but was the result of changes in work and social relations which farmers themselves were helping to promote.

If entrepreneurial values seem important, it is still possible that other variables were more important. Yet a study of ethnicity, party allegiance, religious preference, and family connection has failed to dislodge the central conclusion: nothing rivalled the importance of the mercantile-industrial split in the town over the temperance issue in the 1830s. Family connection tended to reinforce the findings of the study since none of the sixty prohibitionists was related to any other, while twelve of their seventy-eight opponents were. What the no-license people had in common was not kinship but business connections and participation in voluntary organizations and moral reform societies. Ethnicity was clearly not a factor in the vote, since the Irish population at the time was tiny and since the conflict over the no-license question split respectable, native-born residents. Nor was the issue a strictly partisan one, for the town committee of the Whig party, the dominant party in the town, split down the middle over local prohibition. On the other hand, religion clearly was important. Of the sixty no-license men studied, religious preference could be established for thirty-four, and of these over half (nineteen) were evangelicals. Thus the traditional interpretation linking temperance reform to the evangelical churches clearly has some validity, yet the churches did not take a prominent part in the 1835-38 campaign, and temperance support was by no means limited to such groups in any case. Unitarians and men who expressed no public religious convictions were also well represented in the campaigns for no-license in Worcester.

The conclusions of the Worcester study parallel in some respects Leonard Richards' comparison of abolitionists and anti-abolitionists in three Northern communities. More recently, further support for this thesis has come from Bruce Laurie in his study of Philadelphia and from Paul Faler and Alan Dawley in studies of Lynn, Massachusetts. Laurie and Faler, in particular, point to the dominance of manufacturers and artisans in the various temperance societies they studied.[16] My own research in progress on two Southern counties (Rowan in North Carolina, and Allegheny in Virginia) indicates that temperance support in the South also came from artisans and entrepreneurs but that these groups were relatively insignificant in the South. Thus in part the failure of antebellum temperance in the South can be explained in the same terms that can be used to explain its success in the North.

We need many more local case studies linking temperance ideology with social structure before we can make confident statements about the social composition of the temperance movement over long periods of time; yet we can, nevertheless, explore the appeal of temperance for manufacturers and artisans in the antebellum North and analyze the contribution temperance made toward the creation of mentalities appropriate to an industrializing society.

The temperance movement's growing appeal for manufacturers and artisans was directly connected with problems of work and efficiency posed by mechanization and mass production. The development of industry enhanced the concern among employers for the regularity and predictability of their labor supply, yet the work force which industrial entrepreneurs had to utilize consisted largely of rural people and pre-industrial artisans unused to the discipline of factory conditions. Inefficient or irregular labor could spell financial loss for employers through under-utilization of capital stocks, failure to fill orders in competitive periods, wastage of fuels where steam engines were used, and damage to machinery.

Industry could not prosper with an inefficient work force, and in antebellum America, drink was a major source of inefficiency. Pre-industrial artisans had the same traditional attitudes toward the use of liquor that distinguished rural laborers. Artisan groups had long been accustomed to the heavy use of alcohol both on and off the job. The many examples of concern expressed by factory owners make this abundantly clear. To quote just a few: Factory owners in New York complained to the city temperance society of "blue Mondays which run pretty well into the week," caused by "the intemperance of workmen." In East Dudley, Massachusetts, three separate factory owners refused to sell liquor in factory stores because "the profit derived from the sale of liquor was nothing, when compared with the losses they occasioned, in time spent by their workmen in drinking, in bad debts, etc., to say nothing of the poverty and misery, the scenes of riot and wickedness thus produced." The concern of Pennsylvania employers with workers' intemperance was such that the state legislature passed numerous acts forbidding the use of liquor within three miles of specified mines and iron foundries.[17]

These concerns for the efficiency of labor were reflected in the Worcester temperance movement, not only in the dominance of employers in the early temperance societies and no-license agitation but also in efforts at the work place to get employees to abstain from alcohol use. Worcester's pro-temperance newspaper, the *Massachusetts Spy*, confirmed that "the agents and proprietors of the manufacturing establishments" in the Worcester region "have taken an active interest in the promotion of the cause,"[18] by sponsoring temperance societies among the mill workers and by discouraging the use of alcohol during working hours.

The relationship between the beginnings of mechanization and temperance activity was also apparent in Worcester. Of the nineteen employers in the Worcester sample of 1835 engaged in the manufacturing sector, more than half used machinery, and some had more than twenty-five employees as early as 1831. Moreover, some of these Worcester entrepreneurs won reputations as innovators in the use of mechanization for industrial production. William A. Wheeler "probably had the first steam engine operating in Worcester"; Ichabod Washburn and Benjamin Goddard "made the first condenser and long-roll spinning jack ever made in Worcester County"; while Thomas H. Rice "put into operation the first planing machine that went by power" in the county.[19]

None of these temperance supporters directly mentioned the mechanization of their shops, the specialization of production, and the need for more precise workmanship when they discussed prohibition, though one would not expect such a frank admission from men attempting to persuade a reluctant public to forgo its drinking pleasures. Yet Thomas Kinnicut, the secretary of the Worcester Temperance Society and a prominent banker in the town, did note in general terms that the "manufacturers, who have tested the [temperance] experiment, uniformly assert, that their workmen are not only more constant in their attention to their business, but that they can actually perform more labor of any kind, than when under the influence of any artificial stimulus."[20]

The evidence is overwhelming that employers were restricting the opportunities for employees to drink by various means: paternalistic supervision of workers in mill towns, strict rules about drinking on the job, rigid hiring and firing policies, and attempts to support a wider temperance movement. Temperance was not merely, to use Joseph Gusfield's famous phrase, a symbolic crusade for status. Temperance had instrumental functions in an industrializing society. [21]

Bruce Laurie has suggested that this process may have been confined to the larger manufacturing establishments; traditional artisan drinking habits may have been preserved in the smaller shops where masters needed the skills of the artisans and were in no position to force their temperance morality on their employees. Yet the Worcester case provides evidence of the wider ramifications of the drive toward an abstinent labor force. As early as 1831, there was a clear trend in the small "mechanics shops" to prohibit the use of liquor. In that year Thomas Kinnicut reported that the use of "spirituous liquors" had been prohibited in "twenty-six mechanics shops," and in six "manufactories" embracing over "two hundred hands." [22] In addition, the use of liquor was rapidly passing out of fashion on building construction sites and on the farm. In Worcester, the small master craftsmen seem to have embraced abstinence as readily as larger manufacturers in an effort to improve labor efficiency and thus compete with the larger and more efficient producers.

For the proprietor of a manufacturing establishment, temperance was a way to achieve a disciplined labor force. But it was much more than this. Dealing with problems of factory and labor discipline gave these men a coercive mentality. Seeing discipline, sobriety, and industry as the answer to their own labor problems, they projected this view on society and perceived temperance as the solution to wider social problems of poverty, crime, and insanity. As David Rothman has shown, reformers were obsessed with the presence of temptation in society. A highly individualistic, competitive society sustained and encouraged the obsession with problems of personal restraint and morality. [23] But we must go further than Rothman and ask again which Americans harbored such obsessions. Those who were especially concerned with the temptation of liquor were deeply influenced by personal experience. The manufacturers studied in Worcester were successful men; whether they came from humble backgrounds or not, they attributed personal success to sobriety.

An excellent example was Ichabod Washburn. Washburn lost his father, a sea captain, at an early age, then began his own working life as an apprentice blacksmith. He had to borrow two hundred dollars from one of the richest men in Worcester to get his start in business in the early 1820s. By the 1830s, Washburn was running a flourishing iron foundry in the town. At about the same time, he began to specialize in wire manufacturing, which became the basis for his fortune. In 1860, Washburn was producing 58 percent of all the wire manufactured in the United States. By the time he died in 1868, Washburn left $424,000 in his will. The Washburn and Moen Manufacturing Company which he founded was eventually absorbed into the United States Steel empire at the turn of the century. [24]

The title of Washburn's posthumously published autobiography gives some insight into his social philosophy: *Autobiography and Memorials of Ichabod Washburn, Showing How a Great Business Was Developed and Large Wealth Acquired for the Uses of Benevolence.* [25] To quote the editor of his autobiography, Washburn

thought that the mechanics and artisans of our American cities in successive ranks, beginning at the bench and the forge with nothing but their labor, as he had done, and making it a rule like himself not to spend except to produce, should be all along lifting themselves by industry, economy, and temperance, out of the condition of labor alone into the position of capital also. [26]

Washburn was an exceptionally successful man, but there were other successful men in Worcester's temperance ranks and more with similar aspirations and a similar social outlook. [27]

Since sobriety seemed to work for these upwardly mobile temperance men, it was natural that they should analyze the failures of others in similar terms. When they saw poverty and destitution around them, they blamed drink. For example, Neal Dow, the most famous prohibitionist of them all, was the owner of a tannery in Portland, Maine, and a promoter of railroads and real estate. Dow used to ferry visitors around the town, and whenever he came across a particularly galling case of poverty, he would exclaim, "Rum did that!" [28] Temperance reformers like Dow assumed that the distribution of wealth and power in American society corresponded to the distribution of talent, initiative, and moral worth. Although these temperance reformers preached self-help, their coercive mentality and their concern for discipline in the labor force and in society at large all led them inexorably toward prohibition. They were not content to practice temperance themselves; they wished to use law to impose total abstinence on society.

So far the temperance movement has been discussed as the ideology of an elite of entrepreneurs. Yet if the crusade had remained the province of a narrow and self-serving employing class, it is unlikely that temperance would have won the widespread support that it did. Several recent studies suggest that temperance sentiment was not confined to the employing classes either in England or in the United States. [29] These studies differ in their assessments of working class temperance; however, all agree that temperance was not imposed upon workers but adopted by working class groups to suit working class ends. Paul Faler showed that temperance sentiments were compatible with a critical analysis of capitalist exploitation of workers. Early labor radicals who came close to a Marxist analysis of exploitative economic conditions nevertheless urged workers to practice self-restraint in order to survive and maintain self-respect. The same quest for self-respect distinguished the artisans who joined the Washingtonian movement in the early 1840s. The Washingtonians, who took their name from the nation's first President, began in Baltimore among groups of reformed alcoholics who related their experiences on the temperance platform in earthy and sometimes crude language. By the end of 1841, there were reputedly over 200,000 adherents throughout the United States, most of them in the Northeast, including an active group in Worcester. [30]

The new organizations brought important departures in both tactics and support to the temperance movement. As the "experience speeches" suggest, the Washingtonian societies differed in style and purpose from previous temperance organizations and took their converts from lower social strata, with skilled and even unskilled workers represented in their ranks. [31] Although individual Washingtonians sometimes favored prohibition, the reformed men did nothing to promote legal action through their organization and thus occasioned a good deal of hostile commentary from those reformers who were committed to prohibition. Moreover, the new societies often displayed considerable mistrust of the established temperance leaders, whom some Washingtonians went so far as to denounce as censorious and self-serving moralizers. [32]

Clearly, the new organizations did not represent simply an imposition of temperance on sections of the working classes. Rather, sections of the working classes and lower middle classes appropriated temperance to their own purposes. The temperance movement had several uses for these people. For the alcoholics who joined, the benefits were obviously psychological therapy. John B. Gough, an intemperate Worcester bookbinder before he became the most famous temperance speaker of his era, explained the special appeal of Washingtonian assistance for him: "I was not alone in the world; there was a hope of my being rescued from the 'slough of despond' where I had been so long floundering." [33] Mutual protection for embattled artisans at a time of economic depression was another purpose. Drink was a pervasive and pressing problem in the artisans' world, and if artisans were to survive in the hostile economic climate of the depression of 1837-43, they had to practice frugality and exert self-discipline. As with manufacturers, support for temperance among artisans had more than symbolic uses. [34]

Yet it would be misleading to exaggerate the autonomy of the self-help temperance organizations with predominantly lower-class support. These organizations had an ambiguous and reciprocal relationship with the wealthy and powerful patrons of the older and more respectable temperance societies. The Washingtonians were at the same time an outgrowth of the mainstream temperance organizations and yet in important ways distinct from those larger and more powerful structures. The problem is well illustrated in the case of New York, which produced the nation's largest and most active Washingtonian society of the 1840s. The city's most respected and respectable temperance leader was probably John Marsh, the secretary of the American Temperance Union, the nationwide teetotal society with its headquarters in the Empire City. Although Marsh represented the temperance establishment, he often presided over Washingtonian meetings and contributed to the Washingtonian coffers. Yet he denounced the "excesses" of the Washingtonians in their "experience" meetings and feared they would forget the work of the older temperance reformers who had prepared the way for the Washingtonians. [35] The responses of Washingtonian leaders were similarly ambivalent. James H. Aikman, the president of the Young Men's Washingtonian Society, defended the reformed men against Marsh's criticisms yet accepted Marsh as an officer of the society of which Aikman was president. Moreover, Aikman urged Washingtonians and temperance regulars of the American Temperance Union not to fight each other but to work together. He pointed out that the Washingtonians needed the financial resources and organizational expertise which the more respectable and middle class groups could command. [36] The reciprocal relationship between Washingtonians and temperance regulars could also be seen in the Worcester case. There the Washingtonians pursued different tactics from the older societies. Nevertheless, the reformed men received extensive patronage from wealthy and upwardly mobile manufacturers who wished to encourage among the working people of Worcester the values of self-help espoused by the Washingtonians. [37]

Both the Worcester study and Faler's study of Lynn emphasized the independent nature of temperance support among workers. But, as Faler himself points out, the workers who formed their own temperance organizations in Lynn nevertheless shared some common values with their employers. Both groups stressed self-discipline and self-improvement; both could cooperate in the 1850s and 1860s in support of the free labor system against the alleged threats from the South.[38] Temperance organizations did reflect subtle class distinctions, but at the same time, temperance cut across class lines. A common commitment to temperance did give employers and some sections of the working classes common cultural values.

This commitment to sobriety and self-discipline set pro-temperance workers and industrial entrepreneurs apart from the great majority of immigrants entering the country in the late 1840s and 1850s, and so set the stage for a bitter cultural conflict. German and Irish immigrants brought with them their customs and traditions. Most of these immigrants came from pre-industrial environments where the use of liquor was not under attack as it was in early- and mid-nineteenth-century America from acquisitive industrial entrepreneurs. Immigrant attitudes toward drink were much more akin to American attitudes of the eighteenth century than to native American attitudes shaped by the conditions of a modernizing, industrializing society. German immigrants did not regard drinking as a sin or as an economic liability. Partly this reflected their preference for the lighter, fermented liquors, partly the fact that the liquor industry presented opportunities for advancement for enterprising German brewers and beer hall proprietors. The 1850s saw a rapid increase in the production of fermented liquor through the introduction of lager beer brewed by and largely for Germans. [39]

The Irish were scarcely more sympathetic to prohibitionist aims. In Worcester, the large influx of Irish in the 1840s, which gave the city an Irish population of 25 percent by 1855, made the Irish the most important target of prohibitionists by the 1850s. Though the Father Mathew movement of Irish Catholic abstainers appeared in the town in 1849, Irish Catholics were also prominent in the statistics of arrests for drunkenness in Worcester and in similar industrial towns in Massachusetts, and riots often accompanied attempts to enforce the liquor laws in the Irish section of town. [40]

The temperance movement, then, prospered among those whose values were shaped by an incipient industrial capitalism (and this applies to workers as well as employers), but temperance had little appeal for immigrants who came from traditional, rural societies such as Ireland and pre-industrial Germany. As Herbert Gutman observes, it was the clash of America's modernizing, capitalistic culture with wave after wave of peasant cultures between the 1850s and the 1920s which in large part explains the extraordinary longevity of the prohibition movement in America. [41]

Given this analysis of the character of temperance support, it may now be possible to say something about the relationship between the temperance movement and antebellum social change. Here it will be necessary to generalize about the values and character of temperance reform, to ignore factional disputes over prohibition and moral suasion, and to stress the things which temperance reformers held in common.

The evidence above casts doubt on the popular stereotype of the temperance movement as provincial, rural, and backward-looking. [42] The temperance movement won support from at least some groups which stood to benefit and hoped to benefit from the material changes taking place in American society. And the temperance movement embraced the values which were becoming dominant in that society. Individualistic, competitive, capitalistic, these are some of the adjectives which come to mind when one thinks of the kind of society then evolving in the United States. The temperance reformers accepted and promoted the ascendant values of this society.

This can be seen most clearly in the way that temperance entrepreneurs sought a more sober work force, but the temperance movement also worked in other ways to promote the development of a more recognizably "modern" society.[43] Temperance reformers displayed some of the attributes and worked for some of the changes which contemporary sociologists choose to call modernization. Temperance reformers stood for universalistic values against particularistic ones; they had no respect for diversity of cultures, as the attempts to suppress deviant ethnic subcultures through prohibition in the 1850s suggest. Temperance reformers sought to root out localistic, traditional customs and create a uniform moral standard throughout the country. They wished to create a predictable universe of sober, industrious individuals—a homogeneous America. This they would do by exerting influence over public opinion through pressure group activity. Temperance reformers readily abandoned the deferential politics of the colonial period in favor of interest group politics. Like Jacksonian Democracy itself, temperance reformers bypassed old elites of high status, well-connected individuals. [44]

The temperance reformers were among the earliest groups to exploit the potential of voluntary organizations in the cause of moral reform. They quickly realized the importance of the new mass techniques for mobilizing public opinion which Jacksonian politics vividly demonstrated. "All that is wanting," reformers argued, "is for the friends of temperance to manifest the same energy in the cause, which they enlist when other interests are at stake. If an obnoxious president were to be removed, all the means which would enlist the omnipotent power of public opinion would be zealously employed."[45] Reformers recognized that numbers, noise, and money counted most in a society which had abandoned any semblance of deferential politics.

If the temperance reformers accepted and exploited organizational change in Jacksonian America, they also embraced technological change. Temperance reformers praised American technological development, especially the advances in transportation—the canals, railroads, and turnpikes.[46] Edward C. Delavan, a prominent New York state temperance reformer, praised "the construction of rail roads canals etc" as means "to advance the good of mankind." Reformers like Delavan were quick to realize that these technological advances could be exploited to further the temperance crusade. Improvements in transportation allowed the temperance message to be spread all over the country quickly and efficiently. Steam power, above all, earned the praise of reformers. It made sense to sing the praises of the "mighty steam engine," not only because of its impact on transportation, but also for its effects on the printing industry. The introduction of the steam printing press greatly reduced printing costs and so facilitated the cheap and abundant temperance propaganda on which temperance reformers relied to spread their message. Through such means "the moral world" would "be changed and elevated." [47] One might go further and say that temperance reform could only prosper in a society which already possessed many of the characteristics of modernity: not only a mechanized transportation network but also adequate channels of communication, such as newspapers, high rates of literacy, [48] and the beginnings of urbanization. [49]

At the same time, a word of caution is in order when considering the concept of modernization and its application to the history of the temperance movement. "Modernization" threatens to become an overarching rubric which can obscure rather than illuminate social history. There is nothing inherently "modern" about an attack on alcohol. Only from the perspective of the early industrial revolution does the temperance crusade seem "modern" in its implications. It would be well to remember that the temperance crusade occurred at a specific point in the early history of that transition to an industrial-urban order and in response to specific conditions which those social changes created. Those conditions included the widespread availability of alcohol, a high initial consumption of alcohol, especially among the lower classes, a work force which proved difficult to discipline to the forms and demands of industrial production, and the belief among entrepreneurs like Ichabod Washburn that energies had to be focused on production rather than consumption in the early stages of industrialization so as to generate profits for capital accumulation. By the end of the nineteenth century these conditions had begun to change, and by the middle of the twentieth century the emergence of a consumer society devoted to spending rather than saving had rendered the Ichabod Washburns of this world as archaic and irrelevant as they thought the consumers of liquor were in the early nineteenth century.

Yet it would be wrong to read back the subsequent fate of the temperance movement into its early nineteenth-century origins. In retrospect, total abstinence and prohibition seem eccentric panaceas for complicated social problems; from the perspective of reformers, it was possible to see the temperance movement in the vanguard of social progress. Because of their role in and commitment to industrial development and economic growth, temperance reformers looked forward to the creation of a society of predictable, self-disciplined individuals. Drink seemed to be a major obstacle to the development of those qualities which reformers believed explained the success of wealthy and influential men among them, and these were also the qualities which they believed appropriate for the rest of society. If the experience of the antebellum period gives any guide, the prohibition movement was not an "historical detour" away from the "development of the great economic issues," as Professor Hofstadter would have us believe, but a critical episode in the emergence of an industrial society.

Notes

1. The key interpretations of the temperance movement referred to here are: the work of the ethnocultural historians, Richard J. Jensen, *The Winning of the Midwest: Social and Political Conflict, 1888-1896* (Chicago, 1971); Ronald P. Formisano, *The Birth of Mass Political Parties: Michigan, 1827-1861* (Princeton, N.J., 1971); Paul Kleppner, *The Cross of Culture: A Social Analysis of Midwestern Politics, 1850-1900,* 2nd ed. (New York, 1970); the interpretation of temperance as symbolic status conflict in Joseph R. Gusfield, *Symbolic Crusade: Status Politics and the American Temperance Movement* (Urbana, Ill., 1963); and Andrew Sinclair's entertaining *Prohibition: The Era of Excess* (Boston, 1962).

2. Richard Hofstadter, *The Age of Reform: From Bryan to F.D.R.* (New York, 1955), pp. 289-93.

3. Ibid., pp. 289-90.

4. John A. Krout, *The Origins of Prohibition* (New York, 1925), p. 129.

5. Worcester's economic development is briefly charted in Charles G. Washburn, *Industrial Worcester* (Worcester, 1917). For a comparative anal-

ysis of economic development and social structure in Worcester and four other Massachusetts towns, see Robert Doherty, *Society and Power: Five New England Towns, 1800-1860* (Amherst, Mass., 1977).

6. When I refer to "temperance reformers" in the context of this study of Worcester, I therefore mean those who supported local prohibition in the town. It must also be noted that in the America of the 1830s, "temperance" meant total abstinence, though there were important divisions between those who supported only abstinence from hard liquor and those who included fermented liquor in their pledges of abstinence. In the discussion of Worcester temperance which follows I am not attempting to measure the sources and character of this latter division.

7. The no-license group was taken from the *Worcester Palladium*, April 8, 1835; and the *Massachusetts Spy*, April 8, 1835. The list of their opponents was created by combining the lists in the *Spy* of April 8, 1835; and the *Worcester National Aegis*, October 3, 1838. For further detail and explanation of methodology, see my "Drink and the Process of Social Reform: From Temperance to Prohibition in Ante-Bellum America, 1813-1860" (Ph.D. diss., Duke University, 1974), ch. 3.

8. For a similar view of temperance supporters in Lynn, Massachusetts, see Alan Dawley and Paul Faler, "Working-Class Culture and Politics in the Industrial Revolution: Sources of Loyalism and Rebellion," *Journal of Social History* 9 (Summer 1976): 469.

9. Respectively, 10 percent and 9 percent; see Tyrrell, "Drink and the Process of Social Reform," p. 80.

10. The lists of temperance supporters were printed in the *Massachusetts Cataract*, April 6, 13, 1848.

11. "Flagg Family in Worcester," *Proceedings of the Worcester Society of Antiquity* 19 (1903): 207.

12. Emory Washburn, *Address, delivered before the Worcester Agricultural Society, October 11, 1826; being their Eighth Anniversary Cattle Show and Exhibition of Manufactures* (Worcester, 1827), pp. 13-14.

13. Albert L. Demaree, *The American Agricultural Press, 1819-1860* (New York, 1941), p. 77.

14. Quotations are from *Journal of Humanity*, January 17, 1831; and Cotton Mather, *Sober Considerations on a Growing Flood of Iniquity* (Boston, 1708), p. 5. See also *New England Farmer*, January 27, 1826.

15. See David E. Schob, *Hired Hands and Plowboys: Farm Labor in the Midwest, 1815-60* (Urbana, Ill., 1975), pp. 247-48, 254. This work has larger implications than its title would indicate, and it contains a useful summary of labor conditions and mechanization in New England.

16. Leonard L. Richards, *"Gentlemen of Property and Standing": Anti-*

Abolition Mobs in Jacksonian America (New York, 1969); Bruce Laurie, "'Nothing on Compulsion': Life Styles of Philadelphia Artisans, 1820-1850," *Labor History* 15 (Summer 1974): 337-66; Paul Faler, "Cultural Aspects of the Industrial Revolution: Lynn, Massachusetts, Shoemakers and Industrial Morality, 1826-1860," *Labor History* 15 (Summer 1974): 367-94; Dawley and Faler, "Working-Class Culture and Politics in the Industrial Revolution." See also Robert Doherty, "Social Bases for the Presbyterian Schism of 1837-1838: The Philadelphia Case," *Journal of Social History* 2 (Fall 1968): 69-79; David Montgomery, "The Shuttle and the Cross," *Journal of Social History* 5 (Summer 1972): 416-46.

17. *Eighth Annual Report of the New-York City Temperance Society* (New York, 1837), p. 51; *Journal of Humanity*, February 3, 1831; Asa E. Martin, "The Temperance Movement in Pennsylvania Prior to the Civil War," *Pennsylvania Magazine of History and Biography* 49 (July 1925): 213-14. There are many more examples in Herbert G. Gutman, "Work, Culture, and Society in Industrializing America, 1815-1919," *American Historical Review* 78 (June 1973): 531-88.

18. *Massachusetts Spy*, September 24, 1834.

19. Washburn, *Industrial Worcester*, pp. 143, 189; *Collections, Worcester Society of Antiquity* 16 (1899): 365.

20. *Massachusetts Spy*, October 26, 1831.

21. Gusfield, *Symbolic Crusade.*

22. *Massachusetts Spy*, October 26, 1831; cf. Laurie, "'Nothing on Compulsion,'" p. 345.

23. David Rothman, *The Discovery of the Asylum: Social Order and Disorder in the New Republic* (Boston, 1971).

24. Victor S. Clark, *History of Manufactures in the United States*, 2 vols. (Washington, D.C., 1929), 1:518.

25. Henry T. Cheever, ed. (Boston, 1878).

26. Ibid., p. 117.

27. For further examples, see Tyrrell, "Drink and the Process of Social Reform," ch.3.

28. John Kobler, *Ardent Spirits: The Rise and Fall of Prohibition* (New York, 1973), p. 80.

29. Brian Harrison, *Drink and the Victorians: The Temperance Question in England, 1815-1872* (London, 1971), pp. 24-25; Faler, "Cultural Aspects"; Laurie, "'Nothing on Compulsion'".

30. *The New Impulse, or Hawkins and Reform* (Boston, 1841), p. 18.

31. Of the Worcester Washingtonians' thirty-six office bearers in 1843, one-third (the largest single group) comprised skilled, semi-skilled, and un-skilled workers. An additional fifth comprised men so obscure that they either

could not be identified or no occupation could be ascertained. Drawn from the files of the *Worcester County Cataract* for 1843.

32. See John Zug, *The Foundation, Progress, and Principles of the Washington Temperance Society of Baltimore, and the Influence It Has Had on the Temperance Movement in the United States* (Baltimore, 1842), pp. 14, 53, 60-64; *The New Impulse*, pp. 19-21.

33. Gough, *Autobiography and Personal Recollections of John B. Gough, with Twenty-Six Years' Experience as a Public Speaker* (Springfield, Mass., 1870), p. 135.

34. These points are dealt with in detail in Tyrrell, "Drink and the Process of Reform," ch. 6; Faler, "Cultural Aspects," passim; and Laurie, "'Nothing on Compulsion,'" passim.

35. *Journal of the American Temperance Union* 7 (August 1843): 118, and 7 (September 1843): 137.

36. Editorials, *Crystal Fount* (New York), October 12, December 14, 1842.

37. Jesse W. Goodrich to William K. Mitchell, June 5, 1841, in *Massachusetts Spy*, July 21, 1841; *Worcester County Cataract*, August 23, 1843, for a list of office bearers in the Worcester Washingtonians and a committee to nominate new officials.

38. Dawley and Faler, "Working-Class Culture and Politics," p. 477.

39. For surveys of German involvement in the liquor industry, see William L. Downard, *The Cincinnati Brewing Industry: A Social and Economic History* (Athens, O., 1973), pp. 15-20; Thomas C. Cochran, *The Pabst Brewing Company: The History of an American Business* (New York, 1948), p. 39; Stanley Baron, *Brewed in America: A History of Beer and Ale in the United States* (Boston, 1962), p. 211.

40. On Irish drinking in Worcester, see *Worcester Daily Spy*, June 18, 1850; "Report of the City Marshall," *Massachusetts Cataract*, October 23, 1852, September 23, 1852.

41. Gutman, "Work, Culture, and Society," p. 583.

42. See, for example, Sinclair, *Prohibition: The Era of Excess*, pp. 18-22, and Richard Hofstadter, foreword to Sinclair, *Prohibition: The Era of Excess*, p. vii; Harrison, *Drink and the Victorians*, p. 149; Kobler, *Ardent Spirits*, passim.

43. A useful starting point for a consideration of modernization theory is P. Berger, B. Berger, and H. Kellner, *The Homeless Mind: Modernization and Consciousness* (Harmondsworth, Middlesex, 1974), while a critical assessment of the limitations and imprecision of concepts of modernization can be found in E.A. Wrigley, "The Process of Modernization and the Industrial Revolution in England," *Journal of Interdisciplinary History* 3 (Autumn 1972): 225-59.

44. Cf. Lynn Marshall, "The Strange Stillbirth of the Whig Party," *American Historical Review* 72 (January 1967): 445-68.

45. *Journal of Humanity*, November 18, 1831.

46. E.C. Delavan to Gerrit Smith, April 25, 1851, box 10, Gerrit Smith Miller Collection, Syracuse University; editorial, *New York Organ*, September 8, 1849.

47. Ibid., and July 9, 1849. On the printing revolution, see James L. Crouthamel, "The Newspaper Revolution in New York, 1830-1860," *New York History* 45 (April 1964): 91-113.

48. It is interesting to note that the temperance movement flourished where literacy was high, in New England, and languished where it was low, in the South. Whitney Cross makes this point about literacy and reform in *The Burned-over District: The Social and Intellectual History of Enthusiastic Religion in Western New York, 1800-1850* (New York, 1950), pp. 93-100.

49. Reform leaders tended to come from cities, and temperance organizations tended to develop first where population density was highest, e.g., eastern Massachusetts.

4.

"Water Is Indeed Best": Temperance and the Pre-Civil War New England College

Despite recent historical interest in pre-Civil War reform behavior, temperance remains a little studied phenomenon. Widely publicized, relatively popular, and a significant precursor of the prohibition movement, temperance occupied an important position in the galaxy of antebellum reforms. What limited attention historians and sociologists have paid to temperance and its advocates is colored by some unfortunate biases which hinder our understanding not only of this movement but also of other pre-Civil War reform crusades. Most often, temperance is studied from the perspective of the later prohibition movement or as a strange manifestation of the misguided desires of particularly anti-libertarian fanatics. Moreover, most studies are content to map the broad history of the movement or chart only the careers of those in leadership positions.[1] This limited focus neglects those numerous individuals or groups who provided the temperance crusade with its basic support. Such studies, restricted to leadership groups, limit our understanding of basic reform motives, group dynamics, and the general transmission of social values. Given this situation there is a need to study not only leaders but also those they led in order to clarify these problems, test motivational theories, and

Research for this essay was partially funded by the National Endowment for the Humanities and the University of Wisconsin Center System. Special thanks to Richard S. Alcorn for his friendship, encouragement, and criticism.

broaden our basic understanding of temperance and other pre-Civil War reform efforts.

One neglected but significant group of reformers existed within the pre-Civil War New England college community. Although many academics played leading roles in founding and sustaining the national temperance movement, few historians have studied their influence on the academic community itself.[2] This neglect is surprising given New England's prominence in reform, the religious and moral quality of antebellum higher education, the close ties between many of these colleges and pietistic religious groups that supported temperance, and the role these institutions played in shaping and transmitting specific social values.

Several advantages can be gained by concentrating on this institutionally isolated group. It is an ideal situation in which to study internal group relations and to measure any changes in the general reform impulse. Closely studying temperance within the confines of New England's colleges also provides a fuller understanding of the nature of antebellum reform, the content of informal pre-Civil War higher education, and the interaction between reform and the academic community. Given these ends, emphasis is placed on revealing behavioral relationships among these important supporters of the temperance movement. On one level, exploring the process of conversion to temperance allows evaluation of leadership motives, roles, and techniques. On another, inquiry into this process provides an opportunity to highlight the involvement of youthful supporters, their acceptance of specific values, and their response to this acculturation process.[3]

Intensive historical interest in early nineteenth-century reform associations has generated numerous explanations for this reform impulse. Early students of the subject emphasized the importance of humanitarian goals fostered by the Enlightenment. Others, noting the prevalence of New England leadership, have argued that antebellum reform represents cultural imperialism. This emphasis on the spreading of Yankee cultural values in order to shape the nation in their section's image has in turn spawned several more sophisticated explanations. Some authors have pictured these early reformers as psychological misfits or conservative leaders obsessed with the notion that they were divinely chosen as the special stewards of the young republic's destiny. Relying on sociological models, still others have argued that pre-Civil War reform represents an effort by displaced New England social elites to regain their lost status and influence. This theme is fully pursued by Joseph R. Gusfield who sees the temperance crusade as a symbolic manifestation of this fundamental social conflict.

More generally, antebellum reform, and temperance in particular, have been viewed as a great national exercise in social soul searching for a national identity. Most of these studies emphasize the crucial importance of the revival spirit, which resulted from the religious enthusiasm of the Second Great Awakening, as the vehicle or initial impulse for these reform activities. But few historians have attempted to measure this relationship. While noting the centrality of the revival spirit to reform efforts, recent scholarship also tends to emphasize America's search for community stability and the use of reform as a means for social control. Although this wide variety of interpretations offers some intriguing and revealing insights, the focus on reform leadership excludes a valuable dimension for evaluating reform motives.[4] In exploring such groups, we must explain not only why people led but why large numbers chose to follow. When viewing the New England college community's responses to the temperance movement, it appears that simplistic causal models can be misleading. On the old-time campus there was a complex interplay of factors involving a number of these motives which accounted for many students and faculty together concluding that "Water Is Indeed Best."[5]

Although most earlier reform scholarship concentrated on leaders, student activism of the 1960s generated an interest in the historical dimensions of undergraduate reform activity. Lewis Feuer, intrigued by an apparent similarity among world student movements, employs a sociological model of intergenerational conflict to explain international student activism during the past century and a half. Assuming conflict to be the natural state of student-faculty relationships, Professor Feuer uncovers a unique Anglo-American condition in antebellum U.S. colleges which he labels a "generational equilibrium." According to Feuer, this stable situation was broken only by a handful of abolitionist students and by specific social tensions which resulted in student riots.

Feuer's work, however, suffers from numerous deficiencies. To begin with, he underestimates the extent of abolitionist sympathy on pre-Civil War campuses. More importantly, he neglects to investigate the wide variety of antebellum student reform activities and thus to gauge the differing impact of specific movements on pre-Civil War higher education. At the same time, Feuer employs a cloudy distinction between student movements and movements which involve students. He maintains that students seek "carrier" crusades to further their own goals but fails to consider movements that seek to employ students as "carriers" or are built on reciprocal relationships. With regard to the specific reform issue of temperance, there was a "generational equilibrium" or, more accurately, a unity of interest on the old-time college campus. But the mechanisms involved remain only partially studied and are not universally applicable to all antebellum student-faculty relations.[6]

A more recent study by Lois Banner also seeks to illuminate antebellum student involvement in social reform. Supporting, with reservations, Feuer's notion of "generational equilibrium," Professor Banner believes greater insights are afforded by Kenneth Keniston's model of contemporary alienated youth. Comparing Andover and Lane theological seminary students, she discovers two differing patterns. At Andover, Feuer's "generational equilibrium" seems to explain student reform activities. In explaining Lane activism, however, Professor Banner favors Kenniston's notions of committed alienated youth and generational conflict. Although Professor Banner glosses over the importance of "role models," this clash between older religious meliorists and younger social crusaders reveals an important source of internal tension among some reformers.[7] As a general model, though, this explanation for student reform motivation is severely restricted. Her comparison overemphasizes differences and conceals similarities. Overlooking the initial positive reception of abolitionism by Andover students distorts their overall response and inflates the uniqueness of the Lane experience.[8] A more troubling problem involves using two theological seminaries and the antislavery crusade to explain pre-Civil War student reform motives. Looking only at Lane and Andover student reformers builds a sociological model on a dangerously narrow and biased sample. Both seminaries were specialized institutions containing an extremely small and select portion of the nation's student population. Abolitionism itself, because of its radical social implications, evoked extreme responses and found limited, although intense, student support.[9] Thus, abolition-ism is a risky foundation at best for structuring generalizations about student reform impulses. In emphasizing student antislavery activi-ties, Banner neglects, as did Feuer, other examples of antebellum undergraduate reform activities. In particular, they ignore the more popular temperance crusade. Also, emphasizing intergenerational conflict greatly distorts our picture of antebellum student life and diminishes the general utility of these motivational explanations.

Faculty members were the most conspicuous temperance advocates in antebellum New England colleges. Analysis of their motives reveals many long-range and immediate considerations which are in accord with some conventional explanations. Pietistic religion was an un-deniably important influence. Adherence to evangelical Protestant beliefs gave many old-time college faculty members both formal and informal ties to pre-Civil War America's benevolent empire. Some New England colleges, such as Amherst, were direct products of the Second Great Awakening and fostered a continuing desire to help forge a "Christian Commonwealth." Older schools, such as Yale and Dartmouth, exhibited the same spiritual vitality that produced new colleges.[10] In many New England colleges this religious spirit was fostered and maintained through several institutional forms designed to direct student behavior into accepted channels. Senior moral phi-losophy courses capped the curriculum with Christian ethics.[11] For-malized and regular reinforcement was provided by daily compulsory chapel. But the evangelical side of American Protestantism was often served through extracurricular methods familiar to antebellum Americans. Should formalized religious experience fail in stirring undergraduate spiritual behavior there was always the revival. In fact, revivals were so prevalent that they formed a permanent extension of the curriculum. Any antebellum student who, during his four-year stay on campus, failed to experience at least one spiritual outpouring might justifiably have felt denied a full college education. During President Heman Humphrey's tenure, Amherst experienced at least one revival every three years. Unsurpassed, Yale, between 1800 and 1840, underwent no less than fifteen periods of spiritual renaissance, averaging a college revival almost every two and a half years.[12] But, as we will discover, it would be a mistake to overemphasize the influence of religious revivals on student interest in temperance.

Antebellum college faculties also faced some very critical conditions requiring new methods to control. Reflecting pre-Civil War America's intense social instability, the old-time college was faced with a bewildering array of problems. Demographic shifts in the student population base undermined older forms of "paternal" governance and helped punctuate campus life with town-gown riots, bombings, stabbings, and rebellions.[13] Not the least of these problems was student drinking. It was a popular belief that "Demon Intemperance" had a particular fondness for undergraduates as it was often discovered that the "poor, filthy drunkard, lounging about a barroom and tavern stable" was once a college student.[14] Some believed that undergraduate wine consumption was responsible for most "riots and insubordination and habits of drunkenness."[15] The actual extent of student intemperance cannot be accurately gauged, but if it reflected the general public consumption of alcoholic beverages then colleges faced serious problems. Most important was the belief of many academics that the problem was real and extensive. For example, Edward Hitchcock of Amherst College believed college students were particularly prone to use alcoholic beverages because of their delicate constitutions.[16] Under these circumstances student temperance societies offered an attractive solution for restraining student intoxication.

Faculty desires to guide real or imagined student deviant behavior encompassed more than calculated attempts at social control. Existence of what appear to be social control mechanisms may not in fact arise from those kinds of desires but may be part of broader and more complex motives. Espousal of an accumulated set of social values prescribing acceptable behavior, such as religion, is a subtle and pervasive—but not necessarily overt—form of normative control. Campus revivals might ultimately promise some control over undisciplined students, but the immediate goal was to develop acceptable evangelical Christian behavior. Social control in this sense is implied by the behavior model and not sought as a conscious goal. Failure to look beyond the apparent manifestations of social control may prevent a full understanding of the complex interplay between ideas and events.[17] Thus, college faculties had a specific need to control many student activities, such as drinking, which might upset educational routines. But they also were motivated by a broader and more significant vision.

Two basic conditions both shaped and accounted for faculty espousal of temperance doctrines. Generally, the men responsible for antebellum higher education shared a commitment to evangelical Protestantism. The vast majority of pre-Civil War college presidents were Protestant ministers affiliated with the Presbyterian, Methodist, or Baptist churches. [18] As such, these men, along with others of similar religious persuasion, were vitally interested in moral reform movements. These same men shaped New England educational institutions to further their goal of educating ministers to prepare the nation for the millennium. Heman Humphrey, president of Amherst College, was unequivocal when he stated that his purpose was to prepare students as "soldiers for this holy war, who will cheerfully march to the frontiers, and pitch their tents in the dark interminable forest of the west and south." [19] Given this general goal, Humphrey and his colleagues understandably viewed temperance as an important prerequisite for attainment of a perfect society.

More specifically, along with other leaders of the temperance crusade, antebellum academics shared a common aversion toward intemperance. Optimistically viewing the United States as achieving general material and moral progress, they saw temperance as a solution to its remaining social disorders. Drinking, a longstanding problem, was viewed as particularly responsible for dulling individual moral sense and thus interfering with man's ultimate earthly mission to achieve salvation. In this way temperance became an important part of faculty millennial hopes. Beyond these considerations a number of additional reasons drew New England's colleges closer to the temperance crusade. In order to assure the nation's future sobriety, temperance leaders consciously sought to enlist young people in the movement and to educate ministers dedicated to the temperance cause. Moreover, the major thrust of the temperance movement, particularly in the 1830s, was not to convert the drunkard but to convince all temperate persons to continue that behavior. [20] Clearly, for faculty members committed to the temperance crusade, these goals might readily be achieved through student temperance activities. Thus, even in the absence of excessive student drunkenness, temperance would have emerged as an important facet of antebellum New England higher education.

This commitment is clearly revealed by faculty involvement in the temperance reformation and as either models for student behavior or immediate leaders for their activities. By providing important temperance arguments, faculty commitment to the cause generally reached beyond the old-time college campus. In 1826, reflecting temperance's close ties to religion, Andover Theological Seminary provided three charter members for the American Society for the Promotion of Temperance. The Reverends Ebenezer Porter, Moses Stuart, and Leonard Woods signed the society's first charter, and their colleague Justin Edwards became the group's first agent. Both Woods and Stuart served the crusade as leading formulators of biblically based temperance arguments. Stuart, in particular, believed that biblical texts only supported consumption of the mildest fermented grapes and called for excluding tipplers and liquor dealers from God's holy congregation.[21] In the same year Andover's faculty worked to establish a national organization, Andover students followed their lead and subscribed to a temperance pledge. This oath bound signatories to "abstain from the use of distilled spirits, except as medicine in the case of bodily infirmity." Again in 1835, at the height of faculty attempts to suppress a student antislavery society, 228 students in the seminary and academy signed a total abstinence pledge.[22] In this manner, Andover faculty symbolically emphasized the primacy of the traditional evangelical belief in individual regeneration over the general social redemption implicit in abolitionism.

Brown University's reforming president, Francis Wayland, was another charter member of the American Temperance Society. While president of Brown he maintained an active interest in many benevolent associations and was reportedly the "greatest single factor in support of the temperance reform in Providence."[23] Not content to confine his views on the immorality of intemperance to his moral philosophy course, Wayland actively promoted temperance beyond the confines of the college. In 1831, before the Providence Association for the Promotion of Temperance, President Wayland clearly indicated his sympathies. Rhetorically he queried, "Can it be right for me to derive my living from that which is debasing the minds, and ruining the souls of my neighbors" or "from that which is known to be the cause of nine-tenths of all the crimes which are perpetrated against society?" For Wayland, individuals who knowingly sold alcoholic beverages were as morally guilty as a person who abetted a murderer by furnishing the weapon.[24] The direct impact of Wayland's activities on his students remains undocumented, but it is known that during the early 1840s forty or fifty of the University's students signed the pledge of a temperance group in the City of Providence. At least one observer was overjoyed at seeing these young men "rescued from the dark abyss of the drunkard's woes."[25]

Yale's faculty also supported the temperance crusade. Prior to the founding of a national temperance society, President Timothy Dwight hosted on the Yale campus the organizational meeting of the Connecticut Society for the Reformation of Morals. This group, which was one of the earliest state temperance societies, sought to battle the twin evils of intemperance and Sabbath breaking. Personally, Dwight was noted for his attempts to curb undergraduate drinking and was widely credited with inaugurating a new phase in the temperance cause with his attacks on both intemperate and temperate drinking. His successor as college president, Jeremiah Day, was a charter member of the American Society for the Promotion of Temperance.[26] Among Yale's faculty, Professors Chauncey A. Goodrich and Benjamin Silliman stand out as noted temperance advocates. Goodrich was a staunch believer in total abstinence and the moral obligation of every man to combat this great destroyer of communities. Professor Silliman, however, was more concerned about the medical benefits that accrued upon renouncing all alcoholic "stimulants."[27] Although undoubtedly serving as a model for student behavior, Yale faculty support only indirectly influenced the founding of the first of several Yale student temperance groups in 1826.

Conversely, Harvard faculty response to temperance provided a direct inspiration to students. Drawing on different traditions and religious sources, Harvard moral philosophers nevertheless developed an ethical system which was remarkably similar to those imparted to undergraduates of other New England institutions. Thus, it is not surprising to find the college's Professor of Pulpit Eloquence, the Reverend Henry Ware, Jr., among the leading temperance advocates. Ware, author of several works on the subject, was convinced that debate over temperance was impossible. He believed that "No proposition seems to me susceptible of more satisfactory demonstration than, . . . in the present state of information on this subject, no man can think to act on Christian principles . . . and at the same time sell the instrument of intoxication."[28] Only limited evidence remains showing direct influence by Ware on student temperance activities. But circumstantial evidence suggests that his interest sparked and provided continuity for student activities. During the course of Ware's academic tenure, Harvard had a very active temperance society. Although continually beset with problems arising from misunderstandings about its pledge and lax withdrawal rules, the Harvard Anti-Wine Society lasted from 1836 to 1840. In 1841, the last year of Ware's life, the group was briefly resurrected as the Harvard Total Abstinence Society only to fail two years later. Hinting as to Ware's importance, its demise left Harvard without a student temperance group until the eve of the Civil War. [29]

With temperance finding a congenial reception among faculty members on New England's oldest college campuses, it is understandable that enthusiastic support penetrated some of the area's newer institutions. Williams's President Edward Dorr Griffin was an early member of the American Temperance Society. His successor, Mark Hopkins, along with at least one other faculty member, also were active members in the Massachusetts state society. [30] Certainly, both these men provided a model for student behavior, yet there is no evidence linking them directly to the formation of student temperance groups. Faculty members, however, were worried about student drinking habits. The president's brother, Albert Hopkins, was so concerned about student intemperance that he listed it among examples of the college's earlier "dark days" along with "abuse of the Sabbath and Bible, lying to college officers, stealing, [and] card playing." Apparently, the college corrected this condition, for he reported, "drunkenness, in the daylight, and open profanation of God's name, do not show themselves boldly as they once did." [31] By the time Mark Hopkins became president of Williams, students evidenced an active interest in temperance. In the year following the formation of the national society, a group of Williams students, following a temperance lecture, formed a total abstinence society. The pledge, however, proved too stringent for some undergraduates, and in the fall of 1828, a dissident group withdrew to form the New Temperance Society of Williams College. Believing that they should limit their activities to the Williamstown area, this new group decided to concentrate on reforming local public opinion. Initially some fifty-five students signed the pledge of the "new" temperance society. [32] How long the group lasted is unknown, but beginning in 1845 the college assumed the society's primary function by requiring all students to sign a temperance pledge. [33]

Bowdoin's President Jesse Appleton, who was very active in the peace crusade, also was one of Maine's leading temperance advocates. [34] Unfortunately, his influence on Bowdoin's undergraduates remains undocumented. In 1829, however, when the first student temperance society was formed within the Maine Medical School of Bowdoin College, his successor President William Allen and Professor Parker Cleaveland were among the society's first honorary members. These men along with other members of the faculty remained active in the organization throughout the society's existence down to 1840 and usually served as the main speaker at the society's annual meetings. [35] With most activities centered on these annual lectures, the faculty provided both a means for organizational continuity and an important voice for temperance. Some speakers came from outside the college community, but the vast majority were drawn from among Bowdoin's faculty. One outside speaker, Dr. Ruben Mussey of Dartmouth, had an immediate impact on his audience. Three days after the doctor's address, an attempt was made to bring the society's pledge into conformity with Mussey's belief in total abstinence. This sudden move fell two short of the required twenty-two votes. [36] Unaccountably, by 1840, interest in the cause was at a low ebb, and on April 17, after listening to a temperance lecture by the college's president, Leonard Woods, the society's student president and four remaining members resigned. [37] Temperance activity at Bowdoin was again manifested in the 1850s, but faculty members do not appear to have played a major role in this renaissance.

On other New England campuses enthusiastic faculty direction and guidance was even more conspicuous, crucial, and direct. Dartmouth's President Bennet Tyler was another New England academic who was a charter member of the American Society for the Promotion of Temperance. Tyler's interest in the formation of a national temperance society was quickly reflected in the founding of a Dartmouth student society in 1827. Nathan Lord, Tyler's successor, who eventually opposed abolitionism and openly defended slavery, was at the same time a vigorous supporter of the temperance crusade. [38] Following the demise of this initial group, Dartmouth temperance activities, under the direction of Dr. Ruben Mussey, centered in the medical school. Reflecting the medical profession's interest in temperance, Mussey won national awards for his writings on the subject. [39] This medical school society was formed late in 1832. During the first year, seventy of the school's seventy-one medical students subscribed to the society's pledge to reject all spirits unless "prescribed as a medicine by a physician." Besides hearing guest lecturers, the society sent representatives to state temperance society meetings and engaged in a vigorous correspondence with students on other New England campuses. An important change in the constitution was made in 1835, when the society voted to become a total abstinence society. Unfortunately, the results of this important modification are unknown because no further records of the society are available. [40] It is very likely that interest in the group declined as it became more radical and that the final blow was Dr. Mussey's departure from the school in 1838. [41]

By far the strongest and most protracted faculty support given temperance on New England campuses occurred at Amherst. Here support was completely institutionalized. Both President Heman Humphrey and his successor as president, Edward Hitchcock, were vitally interested in temperance. Humphrey, like many of his academic colleagues in New England, was a charter member of the American Society for the Promotion of Temperance. His interest, however, predated the formation of this national group. Prior to assuming Amherst's presidency, Humphrey had assisted Lyman Beecher in launching the Connecticut Society for the Promotion of Morals. Concurrently, Professor Hitchcock, in a famous lecture addressed to his students, crusaded against even the moderate use of alcoholic beverages. Alcohol, he believed, released energy stored in the body. Finally, its victim "is seized with fever, or dropsy, or apoplexy: but never suspects that his prudent use of spirit or wine is the cause." [42]

Protracted temperance activity at Amherst was sparked, in part, by Mr. John Tappan, a merchant from Boston and one of the founders of the American Temperance Society. In 1830, he offered a prize of five hundred dollars for the best temperance essay delivered at the following four commencements. [43] Fearing it would appear they were bribed, the students rejected Mr. Tappan's proposal. They did, however, form an undergraduate temperance society—the Antivenenean Society. So successful was this group that it existed until at least

1873.[44] This rather remarkable persistence was the direct result of faculty involvement. With Dr. Heman Humphrey as the society's first president and Professor Edward Hitchcock as secretary, the society enjoyed abundant faculty approval and became an integral part of the campus community. The society's main purpose involved inducing students to sign a temperance pledge which, "relying on Divine Aid," charged signatories to abstain from the use of ardent spirits, wine, opium, and tobacco. Exempted, as was generally the case, were spirits prescribed as medicine and "the use of Wine at the Lord's Supper."[45]

Continuing student adherence at Amherst was gained by direct, simple, and effective means. President Hitchcock confronted every entering class and asked them to add their signatures to a twenty-six-foot long roll containing the names of former students who had subscribed to the pledge. As Hitchcock himself pointed out, "To unroll this before a class generally produces a strong impression, as it ought to do, and such an array of the names of their predecessors in college calls loudly upon them to follow the example."[46]

On one side of the picture, the enthusiastic participation of faculty members in temperance activities reflects Protestant concerns about that issue. Generally, this faculty concern for temperance served as a model for student behavior. In part, their immediate involvement reflects a desire to shape student behavior in the interest of campus stability. Temperance activism also reflects their broader commitment to the perfection of American society through adherence to Christian behavior norms. But faculty involvement is only part of the picture. Even if the aim of these men was to dictate undergraduate behavior, it remains necessary to explain student acquiescence. Students who at times violently disrupted campus routines seem unlikely audiences for lengthy discourses on the evils of ardent spirits. Faculty desires do not fully explain the continual effect of President Hitchcock's appeal on Amherst's freshmen. Nor do these efforts account for students debating, within their own literary societies, a seemingly endless number of temperance issues when the choice of topics was open to their decision.[47]

A variety of reasons might account for this student response to temperance. All student organizations serve basic social functions. Unfamiliar campus surroundings cause students to seek companionship within organized activities. Student organizations, particularly in the nineteenth century, often self-consciously replicated adult activities. With pre-Civil War American society cluttered with voluntary societies, students could be expected to mirror this phenomenon. Poorer students entering college in great numbers for the first time may have embraced activities such as temperance as a symbol of their acceptance of college community values. Moreover, given religion's importance in nineteenth-century American society, endorsement of temperance by minister-presidents and faculty provided a positive reference for student behavior. Thus, undergraduates seeking acceptance in an unfamiliar setting might reasonably be expected to follow their mentors' lead. [48] Undoubtedly, all of these reasons help explain student temperance involvement. None, however, offers more than a general explanation for actions which ultimately required an individual decision by each student.

Recent scholarship which explores the historical dimensions of child rearing, adolescence, and youth offers a deeper insight into the problem of student temperance activism. Although faculty members, in part, supported temperance societies and revivals as campus stabilizing agents, students more likely found, within these socially and religiously accepted activities, a psychological means for easing the transition from youth to adulthood. As Joseph Kett points out, growing up in a world of "jarring discontinuities," nineteenth-century male children faced early acceptance of adult responsibilities and early confrontation with religious anxiety. [49] A young person's teenage years offered no respite from a cycle alternating between adult role playing and childlike submission. Among college students, further tensions were introduced by colleges demanding semi-dependence at a time when young people were better able to obtain economic independence. For most, however, the Second Great Awakening offered a release from these adolescent anxieties. This great national religious movement offered teenagers, through the positive vehicle of religious conversion, "at least temporary therapy for doubt and uncertainty." [50]

The importance of conversion marking the advent of adulthood is a basic component in explaining undergraduate temperance activities. On the old-time college campus, conversion experience was institutionalized and encouraged in two important ways. The most obvious method involved periodic campus revivals and the formation of student religious societies. Less obvious, but equally important, was the formation of campus temperance societies. Within these temperance societies both institutional and personal needs merged in a most fortuitous manner. Signing a temperance pledge was a symbolic conversion experience. For young people pressured to make positive and absolute religious choices, the same social and psychological ends could be served or reinforced by declaring for temperance as announcing for Christ. Given the religious atmosphere within the old-time college, the need for new institutionalized stabilizing forms, and the culturally induced predilection of young persons for affirmative religious responses, it is easy to understand wholesale undergraduate conversion to the temperance cause.

Collegiate religiosity was a prominent force in shaping student acceptance of temperance doctrines. Within antebellum colleges, which in most cases were associated with evangelical Protestant sects, governed by a Protestant minister, nurtured by revivalism, and dedicated to the forging of a "Christian Commonwealth," there was a strong inclination toward meliorist activities. Because of this condition most recent scholarship has stressed and analyzed the close ties between revivalism and benevolent activities.[51] But, as will be shown, revivalism can be overemphasized as the primary mechanism for student involvement. On campuses where temperance enjoyed enthusiastic faculty support their advocacy was paramount. In these cases revivalism provided little more than positive reinforcement. On the other hand, in the limited number of cases where faculty espousal was less overt and conspicuous revivals did provide the occasion for independent student temperance activities. Less protracted or significant than faculty-directed activities, the ties between revivals and temperance within some New England colleges reveals religious enthusiasm as a limited, but important inspiration for student activism.

At Yale, members of the faculty, among the earliest supporters of the temperance cause, continued to display a lively interest. Although their attitudes undoubtedly provided a model for student activities, no direct link can be established between their interests and student organizations. A more likely source for the displaying of undergraduate temperance enthusiasm is found in Yale's remarkable pattern of campus revivals. Between 1820 and 1860 the college underwent no less than nineteen periods of spiritual outpourings (see Table 4.1).

Table 4.1 Yale Converts, 1820–60

Year	N	Year	N
1820	45	1835	50
1821	40	1837	15
1822	18	1840	[unknown]
1823	25	1841	65
1824	25	1843	[unknown]
1825	30	1846	[unknown]
1827	30	1849	[unknown]
1828	30	1857	[unknown]
1830	"few"	1858	[unknown]
1831	104		

Note: When the range is reported in a source, the mean is used.
Sources: Chauncey A. Goodrich, "Narrative of Revivals of Religion in Yale College," *American Quarterly Register* 10 (1838): 289–314; *New York Observer*, March 31, 1827, May 30, August 1, 1835, July 15, 1837, March 27, May 1, 1841; Max Baird, "Revivals at Yale," undated ms in Yale University Archives, Yale University Library, New Haven, Ct.

Averaging almost one revival every two years, this religious spirit formed an extremely important part of Yale undergraduate life. Although only limited information remains on Yale student temperance activities, the insights afforded are revealing. Following the protracted series of revivals between the years 1820 and 1825, the first Yale temperance society emerged in 1826.[52] The next recorded temperance activity at Yale closely followed the massive revival of 1831. Between February 1830 and February 1831 the number of members in the Yale society remained at 200 students. But in February 1832 that number jumped to 267 and by November had reached 300 undergraduates. This increase in student conversion to temperance principles parallels the protracted influence of the revival of 1831 which is counted among the most profound religious experiences at Yale. So pervasive was the impact of this outpouring, it reportedly suspended any need for college government by establishing a "spirit of order, diligence and mutual affection."[53]

In the year of the next great revival, 1835, the society was reportedly advocating thoroughly cold-water principles. Student interest in temperance sporadically continued on the New Haven campus until 1870. Although specific details on this continuing support are lacking, the modulating interest of students is undoubtedly attributable to the continuing influence of the college's revival spirit. [54]

Reflecting evangelical inspiration and the impact of the great national revival of 1858, which particularly touched the nation's colleges, Harvard students displayed a renewed interest in temperance. Unlike earlier temperance activities at Harvard, this society's formation was unrelated to strong faculty interest. In early October 1859, a Temperance Society of Harvard College was founded under the energetic leadership of William Lloyd Garrison's son, Wendell Phillips Garrison. Like other student societies, this group reflected the generally friendly spirit of cooperation between faculty and students. Upon the request of the students, faculty members reviewed the society's constitution and made suggested changes which were immediately accepted by the students. This congenial relationship was especially evident when the society requested permission to include singing in their meetings. Permission was granted "provided that it is conducted with propriety." Initially, the society expressed "regret at the torpid condition of the undergraduate conscience." But, within four months their efforts met some success and the society could claim over one-fourth of Harvard's undergraduates as members. Meeting attendance, however, was generally disappointing, rarely exceeding twenty-five. By the spring of 1862, the society passed from the Harvard scene. [55]

Three other New England schools dramatically reflect both the influence of revivalism and the fact that faculty leadership, when present, transcended religious enthusiasm. At Amherst, students apparently formed their first society during a year in which a revival interrupted campus routines. In 1827, they informed fellow students at Dartmouth that their society had almost one hundred members. A majority of the undergraduates, this letter continued, was convinced that "Intemperance must be driven out. . . . Public sentiment on the subject must be reformed" so that those who manufacture, sell, and consume alcoholic beverages are made to feel that they are engaged in *"a wicked business."* [56] What happened to this early group is not known.

Once the Amherst faculty began taking an active interest in temperance they quickly changed this pattern. Between 1830 and 1861 faculty advocacy induced 1,279 out of 1,678, or 76 percent, of Amherst's students to sign the temperance pledge (see Table 4.2 and Figure 4.1). [57] During that period, however, only the revival years of 1831, 1846, and 1855 witnessed an increase in the percentage of students responding to the president's temperance appeal. In the revival years of 1835, 1842, 1850, 1853, and 1858 the percentage either remained constant or declined. Even when the intensity of a revival, reflected in the number of reported converts, is taken into consideration, only the years 1831 and 1855 show a large number of religious conversions being transformed into increased temperance pledges (see Table 4.3). Moreover, in the years 1835, 1850, and 1858, among the greatest periods of religious growth, the trend was a decline in the number of students declaring for temperance. Obviously revivalism did not guarantee conversion to the temperance cause at Amherst. Here faculty pressure provided the most significant stimulus in maintaining a high level of student pledges. [58]

Dartmouth's students displayed a pattern of temperance activity strikingly similar to that on the Amherst campus. Unassociated with any direct faculty efforts, the first recorded interest in temperance by Dartmouth undergraduates took place in the school's Theological Society. At the end of the winter term in 1825 there was a dramatic increase in student religious interest. Following the winter break, and in the wake of the annual day of prayer and fasting and the activities of the Theological Society, Dartmouth was visited by a strong religious outpouring which produced thirteen new student converts. Significantly, early in the following year, 1827, members of the Theological Society voted to form a student society "for the suppression of intemperance." Although both President Bennet Tyler and Dr. Ruben Mussey encouraged these activities, the immediate impulse came from among the students. The temperance society founded at this time was active until about 1833. During the same period the Theological Society maintained its interest, and in 1832, possibly under the influence of the mild revival of 1831, it required its members to take a temperance pledge. [59]

With Dr. Ruben Mussey directing temperance activity through the medical school society, religious revivalism remained marginally important (see Table 4.4). During the society's existence, the revival of

Table 4.2 Freshman Temperance Pledges at Amherst, 1830–61

Year	N Freshmen	Pledges	Percentage	Year	N Freshmen	Pledges	Percentage
1830	37	33	89	1846–47	35	16	46
1831–32	60	51	85	1847–48	50	37	74
1832–33	72	67	93	1848–49	52	28	54
1833–34	85	76	89	1849–50	53	36	68
1834–35	70	62	89	1850–51	40	30	75
1835–36	76	68	89	1851–52	63	47	75
1836–37	76	55	72	1852–53	57	52	91
1837–38	50	36	72	1853–54	56	50	89
1838–39	37	14	38	1854–55	66	54	82
1839–40	38	34	89	1855–56	54	41	76
1840–41	52	32	62	1856–57	64	57	89
1841–42	44	40	91	1857–58	66	37	56
1842–43	32	26	81	1858–59	74	52	70
1843–44	32	22	68	1859–60	67	41	61
1844–45	34	31	91	1860–61	52	30	58
1845–46	34	24	71				
				Totals	1678	1279	76
				Means	54	41	76

Source: Edward Hitchcock, *Reminiscences of Amherst,* p. 155; Heman Humphrey, "Revivals of Religion in Amherst," 317–28; *New York Observer,* May 2, May 30, June 27, 1835, July 16, 1842, May 30, 1846, April 27, 1850, Jan. 9, 1851, March 17, 1853, April 26, 1855, April 29, 1858.

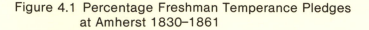

Figure 4.1 Percentage Freshman Temperance Pledges
at Amherst 1830–1861

* Revival Years.

Sources: Edward Hitchcock. *Reminiscences of Amherst*, p. 155; Heman
Humphrey, "Revivals of Religion in Amherst," 317–28; *New York Observer*,
May 2, May 30, June 27, 1835, July 16, 1842, May 30, 1846, April 27, 1850,
Jan. 9, 1851, March 17, 1853, April 26, 1855, April 29, 1858.

Table 4.3 Amherst Converts, 1820–60

Year	N	Year	N
1823	22	1846	15
1827	25	1850	30
1828	14	1853	[unknown]
1831	30	1855	25
1835	20	1858	45
1842	"considerable"		

Note: When the range is reported in a source, the mean is used.
Sources: Heman Humphrey, "Revivals of Religion in Amherst College," *American Quarterly Register* 11 (1839): 317–28; *New York Observer*, May 17, June 28, 1823, May 12, 1827, May 24, 1828, May 2, 30, June 27, 1835, July 16, 1842, May 30, 1846, April 27, 1850, January 9, 1851, March 17, 1853, April 26, 1855, April 29, 1858.

1834 failed to spark increased membership as the percentage of medical student members remained relatively constant between 1833 and 1835.[60] Following the demise of the medical school society, temperance activities briefly disappeared from the Dartmouth campus. A sudden renaissance, however, occurred in 1841 and again in 1843.

Table 4.4 Membership in the Temperance Society of the New Hampshire Medical Institution, 1832–35

Year	N All Medical Students	Temperance Members	Percentage
1832	94	70	74.5
1833	100	34	34.0
1834	106	40	37.7
1835	79	28	35.4
TOTALS	379	172	45.4

Sources: Temperance Society of the New Hampshire Medical Institution, *Constitution and Records*, ms in Dartmouth College Archives, Dartmouth College, Hanover, N.H.; Dartmouth College, *A Catalogue of the Officers and Students of Dartmouth College* (Newport, N.H., 1832–35).

The first renewal of interest resulted from a series of lectures given by a Dartmouth graduate, who was an agent for the Massachusetts Temperance Society, and activity involving the college church. The second was attributable to the death of two young brothers from excessive drinking and to the efforts of three faculty members. The result of this experience was the formation of the Dartmouth Total Abstinence Society. Although reportedly popular with most students, detailed information about its activities is lacking. Reflecting the importance of faculty support, this renewed temperance interest was unassociated with any religious revival in the college. Yet, as if to emphasize continuing ties between religion and temperance, the last recorded student temperance activity at Dartmouth involved the distribution of five hundred temperance manuals in 1850 by the Theological Society.[61]

Bowdoin provides another interesting measure of the varying influence of campus revivalism and student temperance behavior. During the period from 1820 to 1860, Bowdoin students experienced eight periods of intense religious feelings.[62] In 1827, the first recorded interest in temperance, possibly resulting from the previous year's revival, took place in the college's Praying Circle, but no immediate action to formalize this attention was taken by these students.[63] Two years later, however, Bowdoin's first society was founded in the Maine Medical School of Bowdoin College. The stimuli for its formation are obscure, but given the active participation of faculty members in the society, it is very likely that they were a major force. On April 10, 1829, members of the school assembled and were addressed by several students on the evils of intemperance. The meeting adjourned after appointing a committee to draw up a constitution for a temperance society. Six days later the students reconvened to adopt the proposed instrument which prohibited the use of ardent spirits except as an article of medicine.[64]

Reflecting a generally favorable initial response, 57 percent of the medical school students signed the constitution. But this enthusiasm was never again matched (see Table 4.5). Although an immediate downturn was checked in 1831, only to fall again in 1832, membership remained relatively constant throughout the middle of the decade. After reaching 48 percent of the school's enrollments for the second time in 1835, there was a severe downturn for the next two years. A

Table 4.5 Membership in the Temperance Society of the
Maine Medical School at Bowdoin, 1829–40

Year	Medical Students	Temp. Members	Percentage
1829	99	56	57
1830	99	33	33
1831	92	44	48
1832	90	28	31
1833	103	41	40
1834	80	32	40
1835	86	41	48
1836	100	41	41
1837	78	14	18
1838	77	33	43
1839	71	24	34
1840	70	17	24
Totals	1045	404	39
Means	87	34	39

Sources: Temperance Society of the Maine Medical School at Bowdoin,
Records, 1829–40, ms in Bowdoin College Special Collections, Bowdoin Col-
lege Library, Brunswick, Me.: Philip S. Wilder, ed., *General Catalogue of
Bowdoin College and Medical School of Maine: A Biographical Record of
Alumni and Officers 1794–1950* (Brunswick, Me., 1950), pp. 441–59.

dramatic reversal of this trend proved temporary, and the society's
membership resumed its final downward trend. It is interesting that
the revival year of 1833 saw the reversal of a membership decline but
only to slightly above the twelve-year mean of 39 percent. For the remainder of the society's existence, however, interest modulated without any obvious explanation other than student interest.[65] It appears
that, at least in the medical school, temperance interest varied independently of religious enthusiasm.

Bowdoin students founded several temperance societies independent of direct faculty influences. In 1831, the minutes of the Medical
School Temperance Society mentioned that members of the "Temperance Society . . . of Bowdoin College" were invited to attend one of
their lectures. What became of this particular group remains unknown, but most likely it was founded following the previous term's

period of "unusual spirit of prayer and desire for the salvation of souls."[66] Years later, on March 8, 1854, a group of students met to consider forming a new temperance society. "Judging from the past and present evidence of intemperance in college," the students declared, "and feeling it a duty we owe ourselves, God and Humanity to interpose a countering influence to this lamentable evil," they agreed to form a temperance society. Probably as a result of the college's recent revival, 41 percent of the students subscribed to the society's constitution (see Table 4.6). Greatest enthusiasm was found in the freshman class where over one-half joined this newest temperance group. The following year two-thirds of the incoming freshmen took the pledge. Meeting attendance, however, was never consistent. Within a year and a half of its founding declining membership forced the officers to resign and the group ceased to exist.[67] In 1859, most likely as the result of revival activity, a new temperance society was reported on the Bowdoin campus. Initially 67 percent of the undergraduates enrolled in this group. Freshmen again were most conspicuous in their enthusiasm for this latest temperance reformation. It is not known when this society ceased activities, but it was still corresponding with its Harvard counterpart in 1860.[68]

The behavior model which emerges from this study points out the difficulty of trying to explain causal relationships with too narrow a focus. In a very important way, the impact of temperance on pre-Civil War New England campuses reveals how differing means can serve the same ends. Fostered by a dynamic interaction between faculty and students, temperance thrived through a happy convergence of personal and institutional needs. The result was a harmonious cooperation between students and faculty which contrasts sharply to the image of often violent academic conflicts over abolitionism and countless other campus problems. Unquestionably, consistently active faculty espousal of temperance doctrines was the most important ingredient in tying antebellum higher education to the national crusade and in influencing student behavior. For these academics, campus stability was fostered as a concomitant of their efforts to perfect American society by inducing those who were temperate to remain so and by engaging the sympathy of young men who would serve that cause in the future.

For both students and faculty, evangelical Protestant enthusiasm

Table 4.6 Membership in the Temperance Society of
Bowdoin College, 1854–58 (by class year)

Class Year	N Students	Temperance Membership	Percentage
1854	39	6	15
1855	41	16	39
1856	38	18	47
1857	61	33	54
1858	54	36	67
Totals	233	109	47
Means	47	22	47

Sources: Temperance Society of Bowdoin College, *Records, 1854–55*, ms in Bowdoin College Special Collections, Bowdoin College Library, Brunswick, Me.; Philip S. Wilder, ed., *General Catalogue of Bowdoin College and Medical School of Maine: A Biographical Record of Alumni and Officers 1794–1950* (Brunswick, Me., 1950), pp. 100–11.

provided an important background for their temperance commitment. But revivalism on campus, most pointedly in the 1820s and 1850s, only provided the occasion for student temperance activities. When campus revivalism was at its height in the 1830s, it only marginally influenced student temperance involvement. More important for students was the promise offered by the temperance movement, faculty-sponsored or not, to release them from a pervasive early nineteenth-century psychological quandary. Raised in families which one authority describes as "nurseries of neurotic disorientation" yet infused with idealism, they found in temperance an immediate individual release from this condition.[69] Temperance, by emphasizing individual conversion, adhered to familiar forms associated with enthusiastic religion. Thus, for students temperance was a more attractive release mechanism than causes, such as the more radical abolitionism, which not only met faculty hostility but could only be successful following a general social reorganization. So important was this desire to alleviate their personal plight that in the absence of faculty temperance activity students sometimes independently enlisted in the temperance crusade. The result of this situation tied the pre-Civil War New England academic community to the temperance movement and undoubtedly had some long-term effects. Exposure to temperance ideals and conversion to the cause created a sympathetic group which later promoted and eased the acceptance of legal restrictions on the sale of alcoholic beverages. But, above all, general acceptance of temperance, by both students and faculty, signaled a strong commitment by an important segment of antebellum America's population to support the social and ethical utility of sobriety and moderation.

Notes

1. Standard monographs concerning temperance are John A. Krout, *The Origins of Prohibition* (New York, 1925); Joseph R. Gusfield, *Symbolic Crusade: Status Politics and the American Temperance Movement* (Urbana, Ill., 1963). For examples of more polemical writings and general literature, see Ernest H. Cherrington, *The Evolution of Prohibition in the United States* (Westerville, Ohio, 1920); Andrew Sinclair, *Prohibition: The Era of Excess* (Boston, 1962); Alice Felt Tyler, *Freedom's Ferment: Phases of American Social History from the Colonial Period to the Outbreak of the Civil War* (New York, 1962); J.C. Furnas, *The Life and Times of the Late Demon Rum* (New York, 1965). For more recent works reflecting new trends in the analysis of temperance and prohibition, see Jack S. Blocker Jr., *Retreat from Reform: The Prohibition Movement in the United States, 1890-1913* (Westport, Conn., 1976); Norman H. Clark, *Deliver Us from Evil: An Interpretation of American Prohibition* (New York, 1976); James H. Timberlake, *Prohibition and the Progressive Movement, 1900-1920* (Cambridge, Mass., 1963); Ian Robert Tyrrell, "Drink and the Process of Social Reform: From Temperance to Prohibition in Ante-Bellum America, 1813-1860" (Ph.D. diss., Duke University, 1974). Richard D. Brown, *Modernization: The Transformation of American Life, 1600-1865* (New York, 1976), p. 103, sees temperance as an important reflection of modernization in its espousal of nontraditional universal personality values.

2. See David B. Potts, "Students and the Social History of American Higher Education," *History of Education Quarterly*, 15 (1975): 317-27; for the fullest discussion on this neglected but emerging area of study. Academic interest is noted but not covered by Krout and Tyler.

3. Because they represent a cross section of New England higher education the following colleges were included in this study: Amherst, Bowdoin, Brown, Dartmouth, Harvard, Yale, and Williams. On the nature of antebellum higher education, see Daniel Walker Howe, *The Unitarian Conscience: Harvard Moral Philosophy, 1805-1861* (Cambridge, Mass., 1970); Donald H.

Meyer, *The Instructed Conscience: The Shaping of the American National Ethic* (Philadelphia, 1972); Frederick Rudolph, *The American College and University: A History* (New York, 1962); George P. Schmidt, *The Liberal Arts College: A Chapter in American Cultural History* (New Brunswick, N.J., 1957).

4. For extensive treatment of these themes see Clifford E. Griffin, *Their Brothers' Keepers: Moral Stewardship in the United States 1800-1865* (New Brunswick, N.J., 1960); Clifford S. Griffin, "Religious Benevolence as Social Control, 1815-1860," *Mississippi Valley Historical Review* 44 (December 1957): 423-44; David Donald, "Toward a Reconsideration of Abolitionists," in *Lincoln Reconsidered: Essays on the Civil War Era* (New York, 1956), pp. 19-36; Gusfield, *Symbolic Crusade*; Perry Miller, *The Life of the Mind in America: From the Revolution to the Civil War* (New York, 1965); Michael B. Katz, *The Irony of Early School Reform: Educational Innovation in Mid-Nineteenth Century Massachusetts* (Cambridge, Mass., 1968); David J. Rothman, *The Discovery of the Asylum: Social Order and Disorder in the New Republic* (Boston, 1971); Carroll Smith-Rosenberg, *Religion and the Rise of the American City: The New York City Mission Movement 1812-1870* (Ithaca, N.Y., 1971).

5. Motto of the Amherst student temperance society—the Antivenenean Society. Edward Hitchcock, *Reminiscences of Amherst College, Historical, Scientific, Biographical; also of Other and Wider Life Experiences* (Northampton, Mass., 1863), p. 157.

6. Lewis Feuer, *The Conflict of Generations: The Character and Significance of Student Movements* (New York, 1969), pp. 8, 319-25; for a critique of the work, see Richard Flacks, "Review Article," *Journal of Social History* 4 (Winter 1970-71): 141-53.

7. Lois Banner, "Religion and Reform in the Early Republic: The Role of Youth," *American Quarterly* 23 (December 1971): 677-95.

8. J. Earl Thompson, Jr., "Abolitionism and Theological Education at Andover," *The New England Quarterly* 47 (June 1974): 238-61.

9. Student abolitionism is currently under study by the author. For a general picture of their involvement, see David R. Huehner, "Reform and the Pre-Civil War College" (Ph.D. diss., University of Illinois-Urbana, 1972), chs. 3, 4.

10. Donald G. Tewksbury, *The Founding of American Colleges and Universities before the Civil War, with Particular Reference to the Religious Influences Bearing upon the College Movement* (New York, 1932), pp. 28, 55, 69-70; Natalie A. Naylor, "The Ante-Bellum College Movement: A Reappraisal of Tewksbury's Founding of American Colleges and Universities," *History of Education Quarterly* 13 (Fall 1973): 261-74, makes it obvious that,

although Tewksbury gives some insight into the problem, much of his research should be redone. Sydney E. Ahlstom, *A Religious History of the American People* (New Haven, 1972), pp. 640-41; Timothy L. Smith, *Revivalism and Social Reform: American Protestantism on the Eve of the Civil War* (New York, 1957), pp. 50, 60; and Robert T. Handy, *A Christian America* (New York, 1971), passim.

11. Meyer, *The Instructed Conscience*, pp. ix-xiv.

12. W.S. Tyler, *History of Amherst College during Its First Half Century* (Springfield, Mass., 1873), pp. 211, 273-79, 346-48, 350, 353, 449-58; Charles S. Cole, Jr., *The Social Ideas of the Northern Evangelists, 1826-1860* (New York, 1954), p. 75; Smith, *Revivalism and Social Reform*, p. 51.

13. David Allmendinger, Jr., *Paupers and Scholars: The Transformation of Student Life in Nineteenth Century New England* (New York, 1975), pp. 97-126.

14. *Journal of the American Temperance Union* 7 (December 1843): 185.

15. American Society for the Promotion of Temperance, *Permanent Temperance Documents*, vol. 1 (Boston, 1835), p. 567 (misnumbered 557).

16. On this problem see Clark, *Deliver Us from Evil*, pp. 14-24; Edward Hitchcock, *An Essay on Alcoholic and Narcotic Substances, as an Article of Common Use Addressed Particularly to Students* (Amherst, 1830), pp. 32-33.

17. Gregory Singleton, "Mere Middle-Class Institutions," *Journal of Social History* 6 (Summer 1973): 489-504; William A. Muraskin, "The Social-Control Theory in American History: A Critique," *Journal of Social History* 9 (Summer 1976): 559-69.

18. George P. Schmidt, *The Old Time College President* (New York, 1930), pp. 184-87.

19. Heman Humphrey, *An Address Delivered at the Collegiate Institution Amherst, Massachusetts* (Boston, 1823), p. 36.

20. Ian Robert Tyrrell, "Drink and the Process of Social Reform," pp. 3, 6, 11-12, 14, 37-64, 94-106.

21. American Society for the Promotion of Temperance, *Annual Report* 1 (1826): 27; Krout, *The Origins of Prohibition*, p. 109; David Day Williams, *The Andover Liberals* (Morningside Heights, N.Y., 1941), p. 23.

22. American Society for the Promotion of Temperance, *Annual Report* 1 (1826):58; Thompson, "Abolitionism and Theological Education at Andover," pp. 245-50.

23. American Society for the Promotion of Temperance, *Annual Report* 1 (1826):28; Krout, *The Origins of Prohibition*, p. 147 (the quotation).

24. American Society for the Promotion of Temperance, *Permanent Temperance Documents*, vol. 1, pp. 129-30.

25. *Journal of the American Temperance Union* 9 (March 1845): 39.

26. Krout, *The Origins of Prohibition*, pp. 69, 86, 147; American Society for the Promotion of Temperance, *Annual Report* 1 (1826):28; Tyler, *Freedom's Ferment*, p. 324.

27. New York Young Men's Temperance Society, *Annual Report* 2 (1836): 18-19; William Lathrop Kingsley, ed., *Yale College: A Sketch of Its History*, vol. 2 (New York, 1879), p. 50; American Society for the Promotion of Temperance, *Permanent Temperance Documents*, vol. 1, p. 560.

28. American Society for the Promotion of Temperance, *Annual Report* 5 (1832): 129; see also Henry Ware, Jr., *The Criminality of Intemperance* (Boston, 1823), and *The Combination against Intemperance Explained and Justified* (Cambridge, Mass., 1832); Howe, *The Unitarian Conscience*, fully discusses the ethical and moral systems developed at Harvard during this period.

29. Harvard Anti-Wine Society, *Records*, October 26, 1841. Ware is known to have actively taken part in meetings, see entry for June 29, 1836; Records of Harvard Total Abstinence Society are in the back of this volume. There was at least one earlier temperance society of which no records remain, see Institute of 1770, *Records*, February 5, 1834. MSS. in Harvard University Archives; Howe, *The Unitarian Conscience*, pp. 15, 314-15.

30. American Society for the Promotion of Temperance, *Annual Report* 2 (1829):27; American Temperance Union, *Annual Report* 10 (1846):28-29.

31. Albert Hopkins, "Revivals of Religion in Williams College," *American Quarterly Register* 13 (1841): 468-70.

32. Society for the Promotion of Temperance, *Annual Report* 1 (1826):58. *The American Advocate* (Williamstown, Mass.), November 5, 1828, p. 123; April 1, 1829, p. 207; Leverett Wilson Spring, *A History of Williams College* (Boston, 1917), pp. 141-43; Frederick Rudolph, *Mark Hopkins and the Log: Williams College 1836-1872* (New Haven, 1956), p. 128; Spring says this new society was founded in the spring, but evidence points to its founding in the fall.

33. Rudolph, *Mark Hopkins*, p. 128.

34. Tyler, *Freedom's Ferment*, p. 324.

35. Louis C. Hatch, *The History of Bowdoin College* (Portland, Me., 1927), pp. 57, 91, 290; Temperance Society of the Maine Medical School at Bowdoin College, *Records, 1829-1840*, Bowdoin College Library Special Collections, Bowdoin College, Brunswick, Me.

36. Temperance Society of the Maine Medical School at Bowdoin, *Records*, April 20, 23, 1835.

37. Ibid., April 17, 1840.

38. John King Lord, *A History of Dartmouth College, 1815-1901* (Concord, N.H., 1913), p. 268; Lord reports the first study society was founded in 1828, but other evidence points to 1827. Tyler, *Freedom's Ferment*, p. 324;

American Society for the Promotion of Temperance, *Annual Report* 2 (1829):55; and George P. Shedd, *Two Centuries of Student Christian Movements, Their Origins and Intercollegiate Life* (New York, 1934), p. 86.

39. As a student at the University of Pennsylvania, Mussey studied under Dr. Benjamin Rush, one of the nation's first temperance advocates, Krout, *Origins of Prohibition*, p. 146. One prize committee was composed of the following notable academics: Drs. John C. Warren, Harvard; Thomas Sewall, Columbian College, Washington, D.C.; Parker Cleaveland, Bowdoin; and Benjamin Silliman, Yale. American Society for the Promotion of Temperance, *Permanent Temperance Documents*, vol. 1, pp. 494-513. On the medical profession and temperance, see James H. Cassedy, "An Early American Hangover: The Medical Profession and Intemperance 1800-1860," *Bulletin of the History of Medicine* 50 (Fall 1976): 405-13.

40. Dartmouth College Medical School Temperance Society, *Constitution and Records*, October 19, 1832, November 20, 1833, November 4, 1834, August 19, September 9, 1835, ms in Dartmouth College Archives, Dartmouth College Library, Hanover, N.H.

41. Lord, *History of Dartmouth*, p. 262n.

42. American Society for the Promotion of Temperance, *Annual Report* 1 (1826):27; *Annual Report* 4 (1831):viii; American Society for the Promotion of Temperance, *Permanent Temperance Documents*, vol. 1, pp. 366-67, 387; Hitchcock, *An Essay on Alcoholic and Narcotic Substances*, pp. 20-21.

43. Hitchcock, *Reminiscences of Amherst*, pp. 151-58.

44. Tyler, *History of Amherst College during Its First Half Century*, p. 206.

45. Antivenenean Society of Amherst College, *Records*, brief history in front of volume, dated 1869, apparently in President Hitchcock's hand. MS in Amherst College Archives, Amherst College Library, Amherst, Mass.

46. Hitchcock, *Reminiscences of Amherst*, p. 152.

47. See, for example, Brothers in Unity, *Constitution and Records* (Brown), October 24, 1846; I.O.H. (Imps of Hell), *Constitution and Records* (Harvard), December 7, 1843; Philologian Society, *Records* (Williams), October 30, 1833; Brothers in Unity Society, *Records and Secretary's Book* (Yale), March 11, July 17, 1833; Philotechnian Society, *Minutes* (Williams), June 24, 1829. MSS in archives of college noted. Allmendinger, *Paupers and Scholars*, pp. 97-113.

48. On the nineteenth-century demographic shift in student population, see Allmendinger, *Paupers and Scholars*, pp. 8-52. On reference group theory, see Robert K. Merton, *Social Theory and Social Structure* (New York, 1967), pp. 225-386.

49. Joseph F. Kett, "Growing Up in Rural New England, 1800-1840," in *Anonymous Americans*, ed. Tamara K. Hareven (Englewood Cliffs, N.J.,

1971), p. 3; Joseph F. Kett, *Rites of Passage: Adolescence in America 1790 to the Present* (New York, 1977), especially ch. 3.

50. Joseph F. Kett, "Adolescence and Youth in Nineteenth Century America," *Journal of Interdisciplinary History* 11 (Autumn 1971): 289-90; see also John R. Gillis, *Youth and History* (New York, 1974), pp. 37-93.

51. See, for example, Lois W. Banner, "Religious Benevolence as Social Control: A Critique of an Interpretation," *Journal of American History* 60 (June 1973): 23-41; John R. Bodo, *Protestant Clergy and Social Issues* (Princeton, 1954); Griffin, *Their Brothers' Keepers*; Cole, *The Social Ideas of the Northern Evangelists, 1826-1860*; Charles I. Foster, *Errand of Mercy: The Evangelical United Front, 1790-1837* (Chapel Hill, N.C., 1960); Meyer, *The Instructed Conscience*; Smith-Rosenberg, *Religion and the Rise of the American City*; Smith, *Revivalism and Social Reform*; Wilson Smith, *Professors and Public Ethics: Studies of Northern Moral Philosophers before the Civil War* (Ithaca, N.Y., 1956).

52. James B. Reynolds et al., *Two Centuries of Christian Activity at Yale* (New York, 1901), p. 81; Shedd, *Student Christian Movements*, p. 85; Chauncey A. Goodrich, "Narrative of Revivals of Religion in Yale College," *American Quarterly Register* 10 (1838): 289-314; Max Baird, "Revivals at Yale," undated ms in Yale University Archives, Yale University Library, New Haven, Ct.

53. Goodrich, "Narrative of Revivals," p. 309.

54. Reynolds et al., *Two Centuries of Christian Activity*, p. 81.

55. Harvard Temperance Society, *Minutes*, 1859-1862, ms in Harvard University Archives, Harvard University Library, Cambridge, Mass.

56. Shedd, *Student Christian Movements*, pp. 55-86.

57. Hitchcock, *Reminiscences of Amherst*, p. 155.

58. Revival data from Heman Humphrey, "Revivals of Religion in Amherst College," *American Quarterly Register* 11 (1839): 317-28; *New York Observer*, May 17, June 28, 1823, May 12, 1827, May 24, 1828, May 2, May 30, June 27, 1835, July 16, 1842, May 30, 1846, April 27, 1850, January 9, 1851, March 17, 1853, April 26, 1855, April 29, 1858.

59. Shedd, *Student Christian Movements*, p. 86; Lord, *History of Dartmouth*, p. 268; Henry Wood, "Historical Sketch of the Revivals of Religion in Dartmouth College, Hanover, N.H.," *American Quarterly Register* 9 (1836): 181; *New York Observer*, December 3, 1836; Theological Society of Dartmouth College, *Records, 1820-30*, April 16, 1827, May 14, 1832, ms in Dartmouth College Archives, Dartmouth College Library, Hanover, N.H.; American Society for the Promotion of Temperance, *Annual Report* 2 (1829):55.

60. Temperance Society of the New Hampshire Medical Institution, *Constitution and Records*, October 19, 1832, November 20, 1833, November 3,

1834, August 19, 1835, pledges at the end of book, ms in Dartmouth College Archives, Dartmouth College Library, Hanover, N.H.; Wood, "Revivals of Religion in Dartmouth College," p. 181.

61. Lord, *History of Dartmouth*, pp. 268-69; Theological Society of Dartmouth, *Records, 1845-56*, October 14, 1850.

62. Revivals occurred in 1826, 1830, 1833, 1845, 1853, 1856, 1858, and 1859. Bowdoin College Praying Circle, *Records*, May 16, October 25, 1826, March 25, May 14, 1833, April 12, 26, May 10, 1845, July 9, 1853, annual reports for 1855-56, 1857-58, 1859-60, ms in Bowdoin College Special Collection, Bowdoin College Library, Brunswick, Me.; *New York Observer*, January 29, 1831, July 12, 1834.

63. Shedd, *Student Christian Movements*, p. 86.

64. Temperance Society of the Maine Medical School at Bowdoin, *Records, 1829-40*, April 10, 16, 1829.

65. Membership lists are in the back of Temperance Society of the Maine Medical School at Bowdoin, *Records, 1829-40*; Philip S. Wilder, ed., *General Catalogue of Bowdoin College and the Medical School of Maine: A Biographical Record of Alumni and Officers 1794-1950* (Brunswick, Me., 1950), pp. 441-59.

66. Temperance Society of the Maine Medical School at Bowdoin, *Records, 1829-40*, March 26, 1831; *New York Observer*, January 29, 1831 (the quotation).

67. Temperance Society of Bowdoin College, *Records, 1854-55*, March 15, 1854, June 19, July 17, October 9, October 30, 1855, ms in Bowdoin College Special Collection, Bowdoin College Library, Brunswick, Me.

68. *Journal of the American Temperance Union* 24 (misnumbered 23) (December 1859): 179; Harvard Temperance Society, *Minutes*, November 16, 1859, March 28, 1860.

69. Kett, *Rites of Youth*, p. 85.

A Social Profile of the Women's Temperance Crusade: Hillsboro, Ohio

The women's temperance crusade began in Hillsboro, Ohio, on December 23, 1873. Over the course of the next six months the "best" women of Hillsboro took to the streets to protest the liquor traffic. They sang, prayed, cajoled, and coerced the liquor dealers into stopping the sale of alcohol. Although the crusaders did not succeed in drying up Hillsboro, the crusade was one of the opening rounds in the struggle which led to prohibition.

In 1870, Hillsboro had a population of 2,189. It had been settled early in the nineteenth century by immigrants from Virginia and western Pennsylvania as part of the Virginia Military District, a large tract of land set aside for Virginia veterans of the Revolutionary War. Agriculture was the central source of wealth for the country for which Hillsboro was the seat. Ironically, distilleries, which consumed much of the corn grown in the county, were the most important industry in Hillsboro in the 1870s. Thus, much of the city's economic prosperity was directly dependent upon liquor. This might have been one factor which led to the crusade's failure.

The women's crusade of 1874 led directly to the formation of the Women's Christian Temperance Union. To understand the WCTU and the temperance movement it is necessary to understand the people who made up the movement. This chapter's task is to study, employing a quantitative methodology, one group of temperance activists to see where they fit socially in their own world. Since most of the crusaders left little correspondence and, with the exception of Mother Thompson's *Crusade Sketches*, there are few memoirs of the crusade in Hillsboro, counting was the only way to gather data on the entire group.[1]

There are four important questions to answer: What was the social level of the crusading women? What was their economic background? Did they have a common background? How did they relate socially and economically to the rest of the Hillsboro community?

To rank the women socially an acceptable method of vertical classification had to be chosen. The Philadelphia Social History Project developed the method finally selected. It is fully described by Theodore Hershberg and Robert Dockhorn in their article "Occupational Classification."[2] This method of vertical classification offers definite advantages because it can be easily applied to the data available on the Hillsboro women, primarily the 1870 manuscript census, and it also allows correlation of the results obtained for Hillsboro with the much larger data pool collected for the Philadelphia project.[3]

The vertical classification of occupations, as described by Hershberg and Dockhorn, divides all occupations into ten categories. It is based on the assumption that white collar occupations were highest on the social scale and that skilled occupations were higher than nonskilled. Only the first six categories give a vertical ranking; the remainder are for special cases.

1. High white collar and professional.
2. Low white collar and proprietary.
3. Skilled craftsmen.
4. Unskilled workers, who specify their occupations.
5. Unskilled workers, who do not specify their occupations.
6. Remainder of unskilled occupations.
7. Those who list their place of employment instead of their occupation.
8. Those who have no occupation.
9. Those who cannot be classified.
10. Those who left the occupation space blank.[4]

Appended to the Hershberg and Dockhorn article is an occupational index which lists the most common occupations and gives their vertical ranks.[5] Without exception, the occupations given for the people of Hillsboro are either listed directly in the occupational index or their ranking can be easily interpolated from the information given.

Several points about the index need to be mentioned because they relate directly to Hillsboro and because most readers will not have a copy of the index at hand. All those listed as "merchants" were placed in category one, while those listed as "dealers" were placed in category two. All "farmers" fall in category two. Category seven is unusual because there is uncertainty whether the person is the proprietor or a worker at the place listed. The data gathered by Hershberg and Dockhorn indicates that most people who fall in category seven are proprietors and belong in category two.[6] This indication is true for Hillsboro, where all those who gave their place of employment instead of their occupation were actually the proprietors. Thus, for this study categories two and seven have been combined. Category eight includes those who give no occupation as well as women who list themselves as "keeping house" or "at home."

The two groups of interest for this study were the Hillsboro crusaders and the whole population of Hillsboro. The crusaders were identified from a list published in the *Highland Weekly News* on January 8, 1874.[7] Using this list as a guide, 95 of the 145 listed could be accurately identified in the 1870 manuscript census. The census gives names, age, sex, race, occupation, value of real estate, value of personal estate, place of birth, number of foreign-born parents, and several other categories not used in this study.

Almost all of the crusaders listed "keeping house" under occupation, which would have put them in vertical category eight. For this reason, the husband of the crusader was used for all personal data, such as occupation, place of birth, race, and number of foreign-born parents. For wealth statistics the figure used was the combined real and personal wealth of both husband and wife, plus that of any children under twenty-one. Excluded was the wealth of other relatives or boarders in the household; in the case of two-family households, the second family was excluded altogether.

The 1870 census does not distinguish personal relationships, but in almost all cases the first person listed for a household is the head. In some cases, however, an elderly parent is listed first with the second person listed the actual head. A judgment then had to be made as to who should be considered head of household for purposes of this study. As a rule, if the first person listed was over 65 and had no occupation and there was an employed person under 65 listed second, I used the second person.

To be consistent in comparing the crusaders with the rest of Hillsboro, I used the household as the basic unit of measurement. The head of the household furnished the personal statistics, and the same standards were applied to determine total wealth. I had thus to exclude people living in boarding houses, the remainder of families living in multi-family households, live-in servants, boarders, and all others who were not members of the immediate family of the head of the household. These exclusions account for approximately 9 percent of the population. Most of these people list their occupations as either laborer or servant and would be placed in categories four and five. The effect of the exclusions is to eliminate some laborers and almost all servants from the economic picture given for Hillsboro. Had they been included the differences between the white and blue collar classes would have increased slightly.

What has been gained by these exclusions is a means to compare crusader households with the total number of households in Hillsboro. This more than offsets the slight loss in accuracy, while at the same time emphasizing a central fact of life in Hillsboro: the dominance of the family unit.

The total number of crusader households was ninety-three, with two households containing two crusaders.[8] Table 5.1 gives the rank and wealth of the crusader households by the vertical categories used for the Philadelphia Social History Project. It shows that 75 percent of the crusaders' husbands came from categories one and two, white collar occupations. Using the generally accepted distinction between white collar and manual labor as a measure of status, this table alone shows that crusading women enjoyed high social status. Also note that only the highest level of non-white collar workers, the skilled craftsmen in category three, were husbands of crusaders. Table 5.2 shows that occupational category and wealth were directly linked. Table 5.3, which shows the average household wealth in a given category, also indicates that only the wealthiest skilled craftsmen were husbands of crusaders.

Table 5.1 Rank and Wealth of Hillsboro Crusader Households, by Vertical Category

Category	Number	Percentage	Wealth	Percentage
1	36	38.7	$1,140,500	48.4
2	33	35.5	929,900	39.4
3	19	20.4	252,500	10.7
4	0	0.0	0	0.0
5	0	0.0	0	0.0
6	0	0.0	0	0.0
8	5	5.4	35,800	1.5
TOTALS	93	100.0	$2,358,700	100.0

Note: Category two includes category seven.
Source: Manuscript schedules of the 1870 census, Ohio Historical Society,
Columbus.

The vertical distribution for the entire city shows the same pattern
as the crusader table. The higher the position on the vertical scale, the
greater the wealth. Table 5.2 dramatically demonstrates that the
white collar categories, one and two, controlled 76.5 percent of the

Table 5.2 Rank and Wealth of All Hillsboro Households,
by Vertical Category

Category	Number	Percentage	Wealth	Percentage
1	58	11.0	$1,213,500	33.4
2	124	23.6	1,565,000	43.1
3	160	30.5	554,000	15.3
4	15	2.9	23,300	0.6
5	89	16.9	52,500	1.4
6	1	0.2	0	0.0
8	78	14.9	224,800	6.2
Totals	525	100.0	$3,633,100	100.0

Note: Category two includes category seven.
Source: Manuscript schedules of the 1870 census, Ohio Historical Society,
Columbus.

Table 5.3 Average Family Wealth, by Vertical Category

Category	N	All Hillsboro Households	N	Crusader Households
1	58	$20,922	36	31,681
2	124	12,621	22	28,179
3	160	3,463	19	13,289
4	15	1,553	0	0
5	89	590	0	0
6	1	0	0	0
8	78	2,882	5	7,160
Totals	525		93	

Note: Category two includes category seven.
Source: Manuscript schedules of the 1870 census, Ohio Historical Society, Columbus

wealth, while only accounting for 34.6 percent of the population. It also shows that the 105 families listed as unskilled workers (categories four, five, and six), accounting for 20 percent of the population, controlled only 2 percent of the wealth. The skilled craftsmen category, three, falls well below the wealth levels of the upper two categories, indicating that white collar workers in general were higher on the social and economic scales.

In each category the crusader households were well above the average for the whole city. The crusader who had a skilled craftsman as a husband possessed almost $10,000 more than the average for the city. This figure is probably low because the crusader families are included in the figures for the whole city.

It is particularly interesting that of the fifty-eight families ranked as category one, the thirty-six crusader families controlled 94 percent of the wealth (Table 5.4). Again, we have a clear indication that the crusaders were the social elite of Hillsboro.

The 1870 manuscript census gives the birthplace and the number of foreign-born parents for each person listed. This data can be used to determine the ethnic origins of the population.

Table 5.5 demonstrates that 92.5 percent of the heads of the crusader households were native-born whites of at least second genera-

Table 5.4 Crusader Wealth and Total Wealth, by Vertical
         Category

Category	Crusader Wealth	Total Wealth	Percentage
1	$1,140,500	$1,213,500	94.0
2	929,000	1,565,000	59.4
3	252,500	554,000	45.6
8	35,800	224,800	15.9
Total	$2,358,700	$3,633,100*	64.9

*Includes figures for categories four, five, and six.
Note: Category two includes category seven.
Source: Manuscript schedules of the 1870 census, Ohio Historical Society,
Columbus.

tion standing, and most were born in Ohio of American-born parents.
The husbands of the crusaders were used in this table in order to be
consistent with the other tables and for comparison with the rest of
Hillsboro. The use of data for the crusaders themselves would only
have resulted in slight changes in the figures given. Table 5.5 strongly

Table 5.5 Ethnic Origins of the Heads of Crusader
         Households

Category	Number	Percentage
1. Ohio-born, no foreign-born parents	48	51.6
2. U.S.-born, no foreign-born parents	38	40.9
3. U.S.-born, one or more foreign-born parents	2	2.1
4. Immigrants	5	5.4
5. Blacks	0	0.0
	93	100.0

Note: Category five also includes mulattoes, who were listed separately in the
census.
Source: Manuscript schedules of the 1870 census, Ohio Historical Society,
Columbus.

suggests that the crusader households were representatives of old-line Hillsboro families.

It is also interesting to notice the results when the categories listed in Table 5.5 are applied to the general population and are then compared to the vertical ranking categories. The most important result is that for the unskilled laboring categories (four, five, and six) 80 out of 105 heads of households, or 76 percent, were either immigrants or blacks. Among the white collar categories (one and two) 140 out of 182, or 77 percent, were native-born whites of at least the second generation. In Hillsboro, then, the native-born whites without foreign-born parents tended to dominate the highest categories, while blacks and immigrants dominated the lower.

From the above data we can safely conclude that the Hillsboro crusaders formed the upper crust of their society, controlled most of the wealth, had uniformly white, native-born American, old-line family backgrounds, and were, in general, the dominant social and economic force in Hillsboro at that time.

The fact that the crusade was a failure, however, and, in a broader perspective, that it was needed at all, suggests that the crusaders were not dominant in all ways. The informal social pressures which the crusaders could normally use to get their way were of little use against the saloon owners. The hotel keepers, themselves members of the social elite, did succumb to such pressures early in the crusade, but saloon keepers such as William H.H. Dunn never did give in. Dunn even took the crusade to court and won. This episode is one indication that Hillsboro was a fragmented community and that this fragmentation was itself a possible cause of the crusade.

It is obvious that the social and economic standing of the crusaders was not accompanied by commensurate political power. Although a local ordinance against the sale of liquor was pushed through the city council in March 1874, it was not strong enough to close the saloons. When city elections were held on April 6, 1874, with temperance as the main issue, the vote was almost even between the temperance and anti-temperance factions.

It should also be noted that the interests of the husbands and the crusaders were not necessarily identical. James Henry Thomson, the husband of the leader of the Crusade, Eliza Jane Thomson, published a series of articles in the Hillsboro *Gazette* in 1873, in which he argued that law was the only practical means of solving the liquor problem, a view that was at odds with the Crusade. Thus, internal differences among the crusader households may have lessened their political power. That Hillsboro was to an extent economically dependent on the liquor traffic was another factor which inhibited the Crusade's success.

There is still much study to be done on the fragmentation within Hillsboro society before it can be fully understood why the crusade was necessary and why it failed. A study of the external fragmentation of Hillsboro society and the internal fragmentation within the crusader households would help answer these questions.

Notes

1. Eliza Jane Trimble Thompson, *Hillsboro Crusade Sketches and Family Records* (Chicago, 1896).

2. Theodore Hershberg and Robert Dockhorn, "Occupational Classification," *Historical Methods Newsletter* 9 (March-June 1976): 59-98. Other studies of occupational classification are Michael B. Katz, "Occupational Classification in History," *Journal of Interdisciplinary History* 3 (Summer 1972): 63-88; and Clyde Griffen, "Occupational Mobility in Nineteenth Century America: Problems and Possibilities," *Journal of Social History* 5 (Spring 1972): 310-30.

3. The data used in this study are drawn from the manuscript schedules of the 1870 census, which is available on microfilm at the Ohio Historical Society, Columbus, or from the National Archives. The material on Hillsboro can be found listed under Liberty Township, Highland County, Ohio.

4. Hershberg and Dockhorn, "Occupational Classification," pp. 66-68.

5. Ibid., pp. 90-98.

6. Ibid., p. 67.

7. James Henry Thompson, *The History of the County of Highland in the State of Ohio* (Hillsboro, O., 1878).

8. The occupation and vertical category ranking for the head of each crusader household can be found in the Appendix.

Table 5A.1 Occupations of Crusaders with Their Vertical Categories

Occupation	Number	Vertical Category
Baker	1	3
Banker	3	1
Brick mason	3	3
Cabinet maker	1	3
Carpenter	5	3
Carriage maker	1	3
Clerk	1	2
Clerk in store	1	2
Dentist	1	1
Deputy revenue collector	1	2
Deputy United States Marshal	1	2
Dressmaker	1	3
Dry goods merchant	3	1
Druggist	1	2
Farmer	10	2
Flour miller	1	3
Foundryman*	1	2
Grocer	2	2
Hardware dealer	2	2
Hardware merchant	2	1
Lawyer	7	1
Marble dealer	2	2
Merchant	2	1
Merchant tailor	1	1
No occupation	5	8
Physician	9	1
Preacher	1	1
Produce dealer	1	2
Probate judge	1	1
Queensware merchant	1	1
Real estate assessor	1	2
Real estate dealer	1	2
Retired farmer	1	2
Retired grocer	1	2
Retired merchant	1	1
Saddler	1	3
Seamstress	1	3
Shoe dealer	1	2
Shoemaker	2	3
Shoe merchant	1	1
Surveyor	1	3
Teacher	4	2
Watchmaker	1	3
Wolesale grocer	3	1
Woollen manufacturer	1	2

*Foundry proprietor
Source: Manuscript schedules of the 1870 census, Ohio Historical Society, Columbus.

6.

GEORGE G. WITTET

Concerned Citizens: The Prohibitionists of 1883 Ohio

As the polls closed on the evening of October 9, 1883, the prohibitionists of Ohio waited anxiously for the election returns that would confirm or deny their victory. After years of frustration caused by ineffective liquor laws and uneven law enforcement, the possibility of victory seemed near at hand.

Ironically, a large part of the frustration of the prohibitionists was caused by a no-license clause in the 1851 constitution. Article XV, section 9 of the constitution read: "No license to traffic in intoxicating liquors shall hereafter be granted in this state: but the General Assembly may, by law provide against the evils resulting therefrom."[1] This clause was placed into the constitution as a result of the pressure applied by anti-liquor forces during the constitutional convention of 1851.[2] Although the clause was intended to clear the state of the liquor traffic, practically it meant that the saloon spread virtually unhindered, providing no revenue to the state.

The 1851 Constitution neither provided for prohibition nor defined the precise status of the liquor trade. In analyzing the no-license clause, the Sons of Temperance isolated the essence of the problem: "The technical quibble is, that as the General Assembly may provide against the evils resulting from it [the liquor trade], that it is a fair inference that the traffic shall not be forbidden." If this was indeed the case, the Sons judged that the clause "means nothing at all, and leaves the Legislature just where it would be without such a declaration."[3] An attempt to define the status of the trade by submitting an amendment to the constitution repealing the no-license clause and substituting license failed in 1874. The status of the trade remained ambiguous into the 1880s.

The Republican-controlled legislature attempted to circumvent the no-license clause by "taxing" retail liquor sellers in 1882. The Pond Law imposed a tax of $100 to $300 on saloons and demanded that liquor sellers give bond to comply with the act. The Ohio Supreme Court ruled that the bond required was tantamount to license and therefore unconstitutional.[4]

In late 1882, a campaign was launched by the Ohio Woman's Christian Temperance Union (WCTU) to pressure the legislature into submitting a prohibitory constitutional amendment to the people. By February 1883, this campaign had produced petitions containing 157,000 signatures (76,000 of which were of males and possibly voters).[5] The impetus for this campaign stemmed in part from the WCTU aversion to license. At least some of the thrust, however, came from the success of prohibitory constitutional amendments in Kansas (1880) and Iowa (1882).

By late April 1883, the Republicans had passed two resolutions calling for the submission of two constitutional amendments. Whether this was the result of the petitions or because of an ongoing Republican interest in anti-liquor legislation cannot be determined.[6] The petitions did indicate that a segment of the population was concerned with the contemporary liquor situation.

The first proposed amendment concerned regulation through license and read:

The additional section in and with section eighteen of the schedule shall be repealed, and there shall be substituted for it the following: "The general assembly shall regulate the traffic in intoxicating liquors so as to provide against the evils resulting therefrom, and its power to levy taxes or assessments thereon is not limited by any provisions of this constitution."[7]

The second proposed amendment substituted the following after the preamble:

The manufacture of and the traffic in intoxicating liquors to be used as a beverage are forever prohibited, and the general assembly shall provide by law for the enforcement of this provision.[8]

The amendments were mutually exclusive; they could not be enacted simultaneously.[9]

The two amendments effectively divided the anti-liquor forces into two elements, providing an ideal opportunity to investigate the base of anti-liquor support in 1883 Ohio as well as differentiating between prohibitionists and "temperance" men. Originally no differentiation existed in the anti-liquor movement, as the movement was united in its quest for reform. Early temperance societies were indeed "temperate," concerning themselves with the salvation of the individual through moral suasion.[10] Since the early societies preferred to compromise with existing customs rather than alienate possible support, they accomplished very little in terms of lasting results.[11] But after the United States Temperance Society changed its name to the American Temperance Society in 1836, the movement adopted a more militant stance by urging total abstinence as the solution to intemperance. When moral suasion failed to diminish the intemperance surrounding them, the anti-liquor movement began to advocate legislation as a solution to the problems created by the use of alcohol as a beverage.[12] The debate between the moral suasionists and the regulationists continued through the remainder of the nineteenth century. The moral suasionists continued their traditional approach, while the regulationists gained control of the anti-liquor movement.

"Temperance" was a term embracing widely varying approaches to the liquor issue. Even after the organized movement adopted the total abstinence policy, men and women who favored moderation in drinking still called themselves "temperance people." But no matter how much and what sort of consumption they were willing to accept, temperance people divided between those who relied primarily upon moral suasion and those who put their trust in law. Among the latter, four legal remedies were advocated: taxation, license, local option, and prohibition, legislative or constitutional.

Although taxation had been used to restrict the domestic manufacture of other commodities and the federal government had taxed liquor since 1862, special state taxes were not levied against the liquor trade until Michigan legislators fixed a tax on liquor in 1869.[13] As a method of regulation, taxation is the weakest of the four remedies and has serious drawbacks from a prohibition standpoint since it rarely, if ever, prohibits. Like license, taxation guarantees a proprietor the right to carry on a business which anti-liquor forces do not wish to be allowed to function at all. Taxation merely provided revenue for the state. Taxation did have a slight meliorative effect because it did increase the cost to the consumer, but it did not include the benefits to society supplied by license.

The license remedy required liquor sellers to pay fees to state, municipal, or county treasuries in order to be allowed to sell liquor. Historically this is the oldest of the four remedies, antedating the Declaration of Independence. High License, however, came into existence around 1880, and was a contemporary of constitutional prohibition. Up to 1880 a $200 per year license fee was considered high. This was modified after Nebraska enacted the "Slocumb" Law in 1881. This law set license fees at $500 for saloons in all towns having less than 10,000 inhabitants and at $1000 for saloons in those areas with over 10,000 inhabitants. [14]

License fees rarely prohibit even when set very high. In *Deliver Us from Evil: An Interpretation of American Prohibition*, Norman H. Clark details the survival of two Pomona, California, saloons paying five thousand dollars for a licensing period of six months. [15] The strength of license, even High License, is not in the license fee itself but in the restrictions which can be placed on the saloon through license requirements. In the words of license advocate John J. Janney, "without a license a man can sell when, where and to whom he pleases; with it he agrees to sell according to the law," or his license is not renewed and he is out of business. [16]

License and taxation function more properly as a means to control than as a means to prohibit. This approach differs fundamentally from the suppression of the liquor trade sought by local option and prohibition. Local option and prohibition are frontal attacks seeking the immediate end of the liquor trade in a given area.

Local option involves special elections called when a sufficient percentage of the registered voters in a ward, city, town, township, or county petition the government for a referendum regarding the sale of intoxicating liquors within the political boundaries of that unit. If a majority of the votes are against the sale of liquor, liquor licenses are rescinded, or prohibitory legislation passed. Unlike constitutional amendments, local option does not necessarily involve the entire state. This marks an important strategic shift because the state may be gradually "dried up" by anti-liquor forces. [17]

Constitutional prohibition was advocated as early as 1856; however, it was not until 1878 that state constitutional prohibition was seriously urged. Once anti-liquor forces adopted constitutional prohibition as the means to achieve their goal, it became the most popular method of the 1880s. Campaigns for constitutional amendments took place in twenty-one states and the North and South Dakota territories by 1890. This agitation led to the holding of referenda in nineteen states and territories, six of which were successful for the prohibitionists.

Constitutional amendments to state constitutions were advocated for two principal reasons: amendments were more stable than statutes, and, when adopted by referendum, amendments directly reflected the will of the majority of voters regarding the liquor issue. Like all means to achieve the suppression of the manufacture and sale of beverage alcohol, enforcement through legislation was required before amendments could be effective.

Of the methods used to attack the liquor trade only two methods actually prohibit: constitutional prohibition and local option. Both rely heavily on legislation for their implementation. More pointedly, both methods directly involve the electorate in the decision-making process.

Unlike the regulatory temperance methods, prohibition was coercive unless adopted by an absolute consensus. This feature of prohibition divided the anti-liquor forces. The two proposed amendments divided them along the same lines. The first amendment proposed to regulate the traffic, curbing its excesses while not suffocating the trade. Since it did not attack alcohol itself it was "temperate" in nature. The second amendment clearly was prohibitive. The difference between the amendments and the methods of dealing with the liquor trade that the amendments represent are symptomatic of the shift of emphasis in the anti-liquor movement.

The 1880s and early 1890s was a transition period for the anti-liquor movement. Prior to 1880 the regulationists concentrated on statutory legislation, license, and taxation to curb the excesses of alcohol abuse. During the 1880s constitutional prohibition appeared to be the wave of the future, but by 1890 the anti-liquor movement began to shift away from prohibitory constitutional amendments to local option. This was in part because of the success of only six out of nineteen prohibition referenda. The shift to local option represented an important strategic approach to the eventual suppression of the liquor trade. Through local option, states could be gradually "dried up." This gradual increase of "dry" territory may have been an important factor leading to national prohibition.

Studies of prohibition tend to concentrate on the prohibitionist constituency during the local option and national prohibition phases of the anti-liquor movement. Although it is possible that changes in the prohibition constituency accompanied changes in method, these studies produce hypotheses which may be useful for the 1880s.

Traditionally prohibitionists have been characterized as rural white natives who belonged to the evangelical Protestant churches. They were middle class, or on the borders of the middle class, and were progressive rather than reactionary in outlook. Socially concerned and motivated by a reform impulse, they adopted prohibition as a means to improve the surrounding environment. Current scholarship attributes prohibition to rural-urban conflict, cultural conflict, or class conflict. [18]

An affirmative vote for prohibition could have been a rational response to real problems in the surrounding environment. As prohibitionists long claimed, serious social costs accompanied alcohol abuse. In contemporary rhetoric such costs included:

The yearly retail cost of liquors; the waste of grain and other crops; the loss of productive industry, to the country, of drunkards and tipplers; the support of drunken paupers and children; expenses for intemperate sick; nursing, physician bills and funeral charges for the drunkards dying annually; property damage caused by intemperate criminals; and the value of domestic suffering. [19]

Prohibitionists saw a causal link between alcohol abuse and crime, alcohol abuse and pauperism, and alcohol abuse and disease. By the late nineteenth century, anti-liquor reformers had compiled a substantial number of "scientific" studies and statistics to support their case.

The relationship of intemperance and disease received considerable support in the nineteenth century as early scientific findings were usually anti-liquor. Documented evidence and expert testimony detailed the relationship between intemperance and delirium tremens, cirrhosis, and other mental afflictions. More serious than the limited number of cases where intemperance was the cause of death was the general effect alcohol had upon health and recuperative powers.

Even the moderate use of alcohol produced inflammation of the tissues of the heart, stomach, and bowels and adversely affected the activity of these organs. The continued use of alcohol diminished the body's power to resist disease and predisposed the user to cholera, fever, gout, rheumatism, consumption, and apoplexy. [20] Since the effect of alcohol was believed to be hereditary, intemperance had a profound effect not only on the drunkard but on subsequent generations as well.

In 1886, *The Voice* sent letters to a large number of superintendents of almshouses asking the relationship between pauperism and intemperance. Among the estimates: Worcester, Mass.: among the males nine-tenths, females seven-tenths; Albany, N.Y.: about nine-tenths; Meadville, Pa.: nine-tenths; North Brookfield, Mass.: fully two-thirds; Shelley, N.C.: at least two-thirds; and, Hamilton, O.: three-fourths. [21] The Committee of Fifty softened these estimates twenty years later to 18 percent in charitable societies and 37 percent in almshouses. The indirect influence of intemperance added 7 percent and 5 percent respectively. [22] As one investigator commented, "The worst phase of the poverty occasioned by drink, is thus seen to be in the fact, not that the drinker himself suffers but that innocent persons suffer still more." [23]

The prohibitionists used similar survey and investigative techniques to establish the relationship between intemperance and crime. Long lists of statements from prison wardens, chaplains, and criminals themselves all stated that crime resulted from alcohol abuse. Some subjective estimates placed the relationship as high as 90 percent, but objective studies found intemperance as one of the causes of crime in almost 50 percent of the cases, and the sole cause in 16 percent. [24] Intemperance was cited with such factors as unfavorable environment and lack of industrial training as one of the primary causes of crime.

The prohibitionists' cure for the interrelated problems of intemperance, crime, disease, and poverty was prohibition, and as such could have been a rational response to the environment which surrounded them. Behavior, however, is not merely a response to the environment but a "response made in accordance with ideational mediation."[25] The perception of the situation and the behavior itself rests on individual interpretations of the environment; so, while prohibition could be a rational response to the environment, so could opposition to prohibition. Since the individual responds to the environment through learned forms of perception and learned behavioral options, behavior must be examined in terms of the basic behavioral model:

SITUATION (Stimulus) → ORGANISM → BEHAVIOR (Response)

Figure 6.1 presents the basic elements of the model used in this study. The model assumes that all behavior is rational in that individuals act in their own self-interest. The individual both perceives and responds through learned patterns; these patterns, however, can be restricted by structural limits on perception and behavior.[26] Behavior may be explained as a rational response to the environment. Because of this possibility analysis proceeds cumulatively through the inclusion levels listed in Figure 6.1.

Prohibitionists saw a causal link between intemperance and crime, pauperism and disease. Was the link merely perceived or was it real in 1883 Ohio? If the link was real, how much crime, pauperism, and disease was due to intemperance? Was it extensive enough to explain the behavior, or was it merely a peripheral issue? In other words, why did the prohibitionists vote for prohibition? To attempt to understand why prohibitionists voted for prohibition, we must examine the link between alcohol abuse and crime, pauperism and disease to determine the degree to which environment caused behavior. Analysis will proceed from environment, to structural limits on perception, to structural limits on behavior, and finally to socialization, as explanations for behavior.

The prohibitionists of Ohio were disappointed in their bid for state-wide prohibition. Although the prohibition amendment achieved a plurality vote of 323,129 to 226,595, it fell short of the majority of all votes cast at the election which the Constitution of Ohio required. The license amendment suffered a resounding defeat with only 99,238 affirmative votes.[27]

Neither amendment was defeated by the actual votes cast against it but by the voters who abstained from voting on the issue. Over

Figure 6.1 Basic Behavioral Model

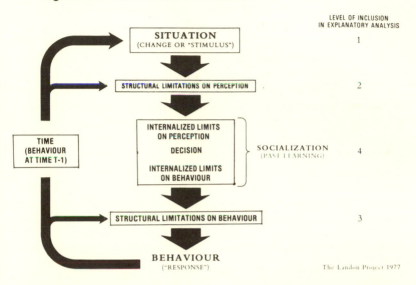

LEVEL OF INCLUSION
IN EXPLANATORY ANALYSIS

SITUATION
(CHANGE OR "STIMULUS")   1

STRUCTURAL LIMITATIONS ON PERCEPTION   2

INTERNALIZED LIMITS
ON PERCEPTION
DECISION   SOCIALIZATION   4
                       (PAST LEARNING)
INTERNALIZED LIMITS
ON BEHAVIOUR

TIME
(BEHAVIOUR
AT TIME T-1)

STRUCTURAL LIMITATIONS ON BEHAVIOUR   3

BEHAVIOUR
("RESPONSE")   The Landon Project 1977

Source: The Landon Project Annual Report, 1976–1977 (London, Canada, 1977), p. 29.

333,000 voters, or 46.4 percent of the total, failed to cast a ballot on the license issue; 24 percent (131,686 voters) failed to vote on the prohibition amendment. It is impossible to determine if the abstentions were the result of a lack of interest or merely an alternative to a negative vote (because the amendment required a majority of all votes cast, an abstention counted as a negative vote). But the importance of prohibition as an issue was verified, as 76 percent of the electorate who voted in the election voted on the second amendment, the highest percentage of any appended issue on the ballot.

Why was prohibition such an important issue? Was it entirely because of the rhetoric of the election, or was it because of what prohibition offered? The majority of the voters concerned enough to cast a ballot, whether pro or con, felt that prohibition should be enacted in Ohio. Who were these people, and what were they reacting to? Prohibitionist rhetoric spoke of causal links between alcohol abuse and crime, pauperism and disease. Did the links exist? To determine if voting behavior was a reaction to the environment we must determine if the links existed. This requires an examination of crime, pauperism, disease, and alcohol abuse in 1883 Ohio.

The Secretary of State for Ohio recorded crimes in forty-five different categories for the years 1881 to 1883. [28] The small number of prosecutions for some crime categories necessitated the aggregation of similar crimes into nine categories. Rape, gambling, and liquor offenses were preserved because of their interest to the study. "Crimes against public peace, public justice and public health" and "crimes against chastity and morality" aggregate the statutory offenses the Secretary of State originally listed under these two broad divisions. Three of the remaining nine categories aggregate similar offenses under the categories of murder, theft, and assault. The last category encompasses unclassified crimes. These crimes do not fit the other eight categories. The information lost to the study through the exclusion of eleven of the original crime categories is approximately 3 percent. [29]

The *Annual Report* also records the number of persons in the county infirmaries (a term used after 1851 for poorhouses) and the number of paupers otherwise supported on a yearly basis. Together the two variables provide an adequate measure of pauperism within the limits of the *Annual Reports*.

A wide range of diseases and accidents were and are alcohol-related. This study concentrates on the number of violent deaths superinduced by alcohol as determined by coroner's inquest. The concentration on violent deaths is due to the large range of alcohol-related diseases and to the complexity of determining the actual role intemperance played in instigating and/or spreading those diseases. In only one disease is the role of alcohol abuse clear, ebriositas, the nineteenth-century medical term for intemperance and alcoholism. [30] All other alcohol-related diseases can be induced or exacerbated by other complicating factors.

Alcohol abuse is difficult to determine for the nineteenth century. Nationwide apparent per capita consumption of alcohol (distilled spirits, wine and beer, with beer accounting for the lion's share) was calculated by the United States Department of Commerce to equal 12.21 gallons in 1883. [31] No reliable statistics are available for individual consumption. However, a surrogate for consumption, saloons per capita, may be used to measure alcohol availability and the potential for alcohol abuse. [32]

As an outlet for alcohol, saloons crudely measure potential alcohol abuse. It is a crude measure because it does not include other commercial outlets, such as grocery stores and drug stores. Using saloons per capita as a surrogate for the availability of alcohol and the potential for alcohol abuse we can attempt to determine if a link between alcohol abuse and the alleged products of intemperance existed in 1883 Ohio.

Regression analysis yields divided results (see Table 6.1). There was no statistical link between alcohol abuse and pauperism. But the relationship between the availability of alcohol and inquest alcohol deaths and ebriositas per capita reveals that prohibitionists may have been correct in attributing a causal link between alcohol abuse and disease. Ebriositas (intemperance and alcoholism) and alcohol deaths did increase with an increase in the availability of alcohol; the causal

Table 6.1 Coefficients of Determination Between Selected Dependent Variables and Potential Alcohol Abuse, Ohio Counties, 1883

Dependent Variable (per capita)	Coefficient of Determination
Murder	.00038
Assault	.01737
Rape	.00061
Theft	.08903*
Liquor	.07764*
Gambling	.01251
Public peace, public justice, public health	.06697
Chastity and morality	.00996
Paupers	.02817
Inquest alcohol deaths	.14170*
Ebriositas	.16267*

*Statistically significant at the .05 level.
Source: Study data (see Notes 28 and 29).

relationship between crime and intemperance, however, rests on shakier ground. [33]

The relationship between alcohol availability and two of the eight crime categories is statistically significant at the .05 level. [34] Theft per capita did increase with an increase in the availability of alcohol, but liquor offenses per capita decreased with an increase in the availability of alcohol.

At first glance the relationship between liquor offenses per capita and the availability of alcohol appears to be the opposite of the relationship hypothesized by the prohibitionists. If the hypothesis is true we would expect liquor offenses to increase with an increase in the availability of alcohol, but this is not the case. Liquor offenses per capita decreased with an increase in the availability of alcohol. Were the prohibitionists incorrect in their hypothesis? Perhaps. But an examination of the nature of liquor offenses is in order before we can reject the hypothesis.

Eric Monkkonen found that liquor offenses were sporadically prosecuted, with prosecution most likely dependent upon public pressure. [35] Areas with a low social acceptance of public drinking were more likely to prosecute liquor offenses than areas with a high social acceptance of public drinking. Conversely, areas with a high social acceptance of public drinking were more likely to accept a larger number of saloons than areas with a low social acceptance of public drinking. As a commercial outlet for alcohol and, more importantly, as a commercial outlet where alcohol was consumed on the premises, saloons would be the most visible outlets of alcohol abuse. Saloons per capita therefore may measure the social acceptance of drinking in public. If we reinterpret saloons per capita as the social acceptance of public drinking, the relationship with liquor offenses become positive. Areas with a low social acceptance of public drinking prosecuted liquor offenses, and areas with a high social acceptance of public drinking did not prosecute liquor offenses. [36]

To this point in the analysis, it is evident that a link between intemperance, alcohol deaths, and the potential for alcohol abuse did exist. The relationships between the potential for alcohol abuse and pauperism and crime, however, are less revealing. In the latter case the crudeness of the measurement may have played a significant role. The use of police blotters and infirmary admission records might provide much better data, but the use of these records is beyond this limited study. It is entirely possible that even the use of such records would not provide an answer to the relationship of alcohol abuse and crime, pauperism, and alcohol deaths. But statistics that are more readily available suggest otherwise.

Eric H. Monkkonen's data base for his study of pauperism in Franklin County, Ohio, employed manuscript infirmary admittance records. These records included the individual's name, age, residence, birthplace, "disease," admittance and discharge dates, and additional remarks. Although intemperance was a recognized "disease" in the nineteenth century, there is no mention of intemperance as a reason for admittance to county infirmaries in Monkkonen's study. This does not mean that intemperance did not play a role in causing pauperism. More likely Monkkonen, who concentrated on the relationship between industrialization, urbanization, and pauperism, felt that intemperance was extraneous to his study. The investigation of the role intemperance plays in pauperism of the nineteenth century remains unexamined. Further examination of county infirmary records may supply an answer to this question.

The role intemperance played in creating social dependents can be examined in a somewhat different light. The five major insane asylums (Athens, Central, Cleveland, Dayton, and Longview) listed intemperance as a "supposed cause of insanity" throughout the 1881 to 1883 period. Intemperance as a cause of insanity ranged from a low of 3 percent to a high of 17 percent.[37] This was a relatively low percentage; it could be easily decreased, however, through the control of alcohol.

The Secretary of State for Ohio did not list the number of paupers influenced by alcohol; however, the number of crimes probably committed under the influence of alcohol was listed for 1879 and 1880. Crimes committed under the influence of alcohol range from 2.26 to 13.14 percent of each of the three major categories of crime. The highest percentage of alcohol-related crime was in crimes against the person; the lowest occurred in statutory crimes, a catchall category. The mean percentage of crimes committed under the influence of alcohol for 1879 and 1880 was 4.95. These findings differ significantly from the findings of the Committee of Fifty.

The Committee of Fifty examined the role of intemperance in causing crime by investigating 13,402 convicts. The Committee found intemperance to be directly responsible for crime in 16.87 percent of the cases, making no distinction between crimes against the person and crimes against property. [38] In 1879 and 1880 Ohio, there was a distinct difference in the role of intemperance between crimes against the person and crimes against property (mean percentages of 12.04 and 2.71 respectively), but little or no difference between crimes against property and statutory offenses (2.71 and 2.54 respectively). The distinction between crimes against the person and the remaining two categories calls to mind the rowdy drunk and the frequency of assaults in bars. The lack of similarity between the Committee report and the Ohio statistics in the mean percentages of crimes committed under the influence of alcohol is also curious.

The lack of similarity is probably due to differences in the respective methods of investigation. The Committee conducted direct interviews with convicts. The *Annual Report* used court records. In the latter case, underenumeration was more likely possible while the methods of the Committee of Fifty lend themselves to overenumeration. Similarly, the mean percentage of crimes committed under the influence of alcohol appears to be low in Ohio given the interpretive popularity of intemperance as a cause of crime in the latter half of the nineteenth century.

Inquest records provide another readily available means to investigate the role played by intemperance. Deaths due to intemperance ranged from a low of 7.43 percent to a high of 28.82 percent. The mean for the five-year period was 16.41 deaths. This provides a fairly strong case for a single cause of violent deaths over a five-year period. This figure includes only the number of people who died violently. It does not include deaths due to ebriositas, cirrhosis of the liver, or other alcohol-related diseases.

The investigation of asylum admittances, inquests, and crimes committed under the influence of alcohol reveals support for a causal link between intemperance and crime, social dependency, and disease. Whether this link was as comprehensive as the prohibitionists claimed must be further examined. But a link did exist.

The link between alcohol abuse and crime, pauperism, and disease need not have been total. Prohibitionists were not naive enough to assume that all incidents of such deviant behavior were alcohol-related; liquor, however, was an obviously removable cause. In the words of Joseph T. Zottoli, Associate Justice of the Municipal Court of Boston, 1944:

It will serve no useful purpose to talk about non-removable causes; these will have to wait the action of a more enlightened era. Society should concentrate attention on those causes and means that are removable, for many such have been attacked and treated. But here I can deal only with what I firmly believe to be the greatest removable blot on our social fabric—intemperance due to alcohol.[39]

Society might eventually remove the other causes of crime, pauperism, and disease, but prohibitionists intended to attack the "removable cause," intemperance. By controlling liquor, first through the prosecution of liquor offenses and ultimately through prohibition, the social damage caused by intemperance would be decreased. Were prohibitionists responding to the alleged products of intemperance as if the link between them and alcohol abuse did exist?

Looking for correlates of the prohibition vote in 1883, we find that only liquor offenses, inquest alcohol deaths, and saloons per capita are statistically significant at the .05 level (see Table 6.2). The relationships between inquest deaths superinduced by intemperance and saloons per capita and the prohibition vote are inverse: the prohibition vote increased where inquest alcohol deaths and saloons per capita decreased.[40] The relationship between liquor offenses per capita and the prohibition vote is positive: the prohibition vote increased where the prosecution of liquor offenses increased.[41] Because the prosecution of liquor offenses was dependent upon public pressure, it is logical to assume that citizens in favor of prohibition would have been concerned about liquor offenses and more likely to exert pressure upon authorities for prosecution of liquor offenses than would anti-prohibitionists. Areas which prosecuted liquor offenses and had a low social acceptance of public drinking tended to vote for prohibition while areas with a high social acceptance of public drinking did not prosecute liquor offenses and tended to vote against prohibition. Similarly areas with a high public acceptance of social drinking were more likely to have more alcohol-related deaths than areas with a low public acceptance of social drinking. The prosecution of

Table 6.2 Coefficients of Determination Between the Affirmative Percentage for the Prohibition Amendment and Selected Independent Variables, Ohio Counties, 1883

Independent Variables (per capita)	Coefficient of Determination
Murder	.05322
Assault	.00094
Rape	.02613
Theft	.06357
Liquor	.21471*
Gambling	.04932
Public peace, public justice, public health	.00921
Chastity and morality	.00703
Paupers	.00220
Alcohol inquest deaths	.13926*
Ebriositas	.06479
Saloons	.41948*

*Statistically significant at the .05 level.
Source: Study data (see Notes 28 and 29).

liquor offenses and the social acceptance of public drinking rely on the attitudes of the public. Public attitudes may have been influenced by a belief in the social consequences of alcohol abuse, but until more comprehensive study is undertaken, conclusions in this direction must remain tentative.

To summarize to this point in the analysis: Both moral suasion, insofar as it lowered public tolerance of drinking, and legal prosecution seem to have worked to reduce intemperance, if not poverty and crime. But the reduction of intemperance, rather than satisfying Ohioans, increased the demand for the deployment of the ultimate legal weapon: prohibition. The fewer saloons an Ohio county had, the more its population was likely to want none. Conversely, the more saloons an Ohio county had—and the more intemperance—the less likely its voters were to accept prohibition. This all suggests that something more than the situation confronting them determined the choices of Ohio voters on October 9, 1883. What also mattered was their perception of that situation.

The behavioral model used in this study assumes that individuals act in their own self-interest. Anyone perceiving the prohibition amendment as a benefit would naturally vote for prohibition; anyone perceiving the prohibition amendment as a detriment would vote against prohibition. The perception of the situation and the behavior itself rest on individual interpretations of the environment; thus, while prohibition could be a rational response to the environment, so could opposition to prohibition.

The prohibitory amendment read in part, "the manufacture of and the traffic in intoxicating liquors to be used as a beverage are forever prohibited." [42] Saloons, distilleries, and breweries (the liquor interest) were under direct attack from the amendment, and it was in their own self-interest to discourage its passage. Regression analysis reveals that this was indeed the case: the prohibition vote decreased where the liquor interest (liquint) increased. [43] The equation is

Prohibition Vote = 50.9 — 6640.1 (Liqint)
(827.4)

The liquor interest of course was limited in its potential voting power. Individuals working in saloons, distilleries, and breweries would logically vote against anything that attacked their livelihood. But the number of people affected in this manner must have been relatively small compared to the voting population of the state. The size of the coefficient of determination, .43, suggests that some other factor may be affecting the relationship.

The complicating factor in the relationship arises from the ambiguity of the variable "saloons per capita." As noted earlier, saloons per capita is open to a variety of interpretations, including the social acceptance of public drinking which is essentially a measure of socialization. Analysis of the relationship between the prohibition vote and the social acceptance of public drinking revealed a positive relationship: areas with a low social acceptance of public drinking voted for prohibition; areas with a high social acceptance of public drinking voted against prohibition. The large number of saloons (6,451) compared to the number of breweries (159) and distilleries (60) may cause a disproportionate influence of saloons on the combined variable, the liquor interest, since the economic influence of an active brewery or distillery probably outweighed that of a single saloon.

Redefining the liquor interest as the number of breweries plus the number of distilleries per capita does produce a slight decrease in the strength of the relationship between the prohibition vote and the liquor interest. The initial coefficient of determination, .43, decreased to .36 when saloons per capita was omitted. The relationship remained inverse: the prohibition vote increased where the liquor interest decreased. The slight difference between the coefficients of determination reveals that saloons per capita does not have a disproportionate influence on the liquor interest; however, this information does not "purify" the variable of socialization influences. The liquor interest and saloons per capita are ambiguous variables and must be used with caution. If the variables are not used cumulatively (i.e., as situation and socialization variables), their use is valid. It simply must be remembered that the liquor interest is not a "pure" situation or "pure" socialization variable.

The strength of the relationship between the prohibition vote and the liquor interest is .43. The remaining unexplained variance (57 percent) must first be examined for structural limits on perception and behavior which limited people's ability to act in ways consistent with the hypothesis that variation in the prohibition vote was due to variations in the strength of the liquor interest.

Structural limits on perception are not readily discernible. If a tendency to vote for prohibition resulted from actual exposure to the detrimental effects of alcohol abuse, one might speculate that distance from centers of high alcohol consumption constituted such a perception limit, but that does not hold in this case. There were, however, a number of structural limits on behavioral options in an election. The most obvious restriction was voting qualifications. An Ohio elector had to be male, twenty-one years of age, a citizen of the United States, and resident in Ohio for one year prior to the election to vote in 1883.[44] This can be controlled for by expressing the prohibition vote as a percentage of the qualified voters.[45]

Individuals qualified to vote were allowed only those options on the ballot, regardless of the ideal choice. The options available was one factor which determined whether the individual would vote. Other reasons for a non-vote include political apathy, poor weather, distance to the polls, occupational demands on time (i.e., harvest), disease, and other personal reasons. (Because of the method used to calculate qualified voters residency requirements must be added to this list.) The nature of historical data precludes the separation or even the estimation of the importance of these factors affecting turnout. This does not cause a rejection of the variable because, whatever the reason for a non-vote, the reason did restrict behavior.

Only 81.8 percent of the estimated electorate actually voted in the 1883 gubernatorial election. Regression analysis reveals that the prohibition vote increased with an increase in turnout. [46] Adding turnout (turn) to the initial equation yields a coefficient of determination of .48. The equation becomes

$$\text{Prohibition Vote} = 4.7 + .5\,(\text{Turn}) - 4905.5\,(\text{Liqint})$$
$$(.2) \qquad\qquad (972.3)$$

Further restrictions on people's capacity to vote for prohibition resulted from the way some ballots were printed.

The ballots followed a number of forms, not all of which contained a "no" alternative for the two amendments. In the words of Attorney General Hollingsworth:

I find nothing in the law to prevent party tickets from being printed, voted and counted with either or all of the proposed amendments thereon.... It is strictly legal however, to bring party tickets with either amendment followed by the word "Yes" alone, or "No" alone or by a blank space for the elector to fill in either. [47]

The Attorney General determined that the particular form was immaterial as long as the ballot was not printed in such a manner as to deceive or influence the voter. But the use of party tickets, followed by the word "yes" alone, or "no" alone, would influence the voter to follow the party line on the amendments.

Fifteen counties did not include "no" on the ballot for either the license or the prohibition amendments (although the alternative was included for the third appended issue, the judicial amendment). The fifteen counties account for 79,486 abstentions for the license amendment and 45,142 abstentions for the prohibition amendment, leaving 253,981 and 86,444 abstentions respectively in other areas of the state.

The omission of "no" on the ballot in fifteen counties had no effect on the success of the prohibition amendment. The amendment could pass in only one way, an affirmative vote, but could be defeated in two, a negative vote or an abstention. The omission of "no" did, however, restrict the behavioral options. Confusion created by the multiplicity of issues further limited behavioral options.

As late as October 2, 1883, some voters were unaware that they could vote on both the license and the prohibition amendments. [48] That confusion existed was evident by the number of newspapers that tried to clarify the issue. The *Akron City Times* commented on this in a June 6 editorial:

> The Republican press are making "confusion worse confounded" in their attempts to make clear the effect of voting on, or not voting on, the proposed Constitutional Amendments to the Constitution in relation to the liquor traffic. "S.R.R." one of the editors of the Cincinnati "Commercial Gazette," the Ohio State "Journal" and the Akron "Beacon" have all tried their hands at it, no two of them arriving at the same conclusion. [49]

This confusion was well founded because the amendments were mutually exclusive and could not be enacted simultaneously.

Supporters of the license amendment, in and of itself, were extremely few. A fraction of the support can be explained by the following letter to the editor of the *Zanesville Signal*: "voters who prefer, like myself, the second amendment, may, as a second choice try the effect of the first. Voting for both increases the chances of carrying one or the other." [50] The absence of liquor legislation was more abhorrent to some anti-liquor voters than the evils which license was thought to represent. [51]

The importance of prohibition as an issue was verified by the fact that 76 percent of the electorate who voted in the election voted on the prohibition amendment, the highest percentage for any appended issue on the ballot (license amendment: 54 percent; judicial amendment: 75.9 percent). Despite the importance of prohibition as an issue, roughly 25 percent of those who voted in the election failed to vote on the issue. Confusion, created by the multiplicity of issues and the printing of the ballots, played an important part in these abstentions, with apathy contributing an unknown percentage.

Logically the prohibition vote would decrease with an increase in the number of abstentions, since an abstention counted as a "no" vote. Regression analysis reveals the expected trend, although the relationship is extremely weak.[52] When the fifteen counties not recording a "no" vote are excluded from the analysis the strength of the relationship increases slightly and remains inverse.[53] With the addition of abstentions (Abs) the equation becomes:

$$\text{Prohibition Vote} = 9.3 - .1(\text{Abs}) + .5(\text{Turn}) - 4972.4(\text{Liqint})$$
$$(.2) \qquad (.1) \qquad (963.4)$$

The coefficient of determination increases to .50.

The last variable to be entered into the equation is socialization. As noted earlier, prohibitionists have been characterized as rural, white, middle-class natives who belonged to the evangelical Protestant churches. All of these factors shape value systems, forms of perception, and modes of behavior. In other words, they are socialization variables.

The "rural" trait emphasized by the traditional thesis of prohibition support was common to writers of the national prohibition-repeal period of the anti-liquor movement. Clark Warburton wrote in 1934 that national prohibition "was in part an attempt by the rural and village populations of the country to retain their waning influence and to impose their ways of life upon the urban dwellers."[54] This argument saw a conflict between the traditional, rural life style and the freer, more cosmopolitan urban life style.

Scholars analyzing rurality or urbanity usually adopt one of two measures: population density or the census definition of 2,500 inhabitants constituting an urban place. The *Tenth Decennial Census* recorded a total population of 3,198,000 for Ohio, 1,031,000 of which lived in areas of over 2,500 inhabitants. Almost 50 percent of these "urban" inhabitants lived in the five principal cities of Ohio: Cincinnati, Cleveland, Toledo, Columbus, and Dayton. Despite the increase of 348,000 in the urban population between 1870 and 1880, Ohio did not cross the urban threshold until the decade between 1900 and 1910, and the state remained 67.8 percent rural in 1880.[55]

An examination of the 1880 population of municipal corporations in Ohio reveals ninety places which met the census urban definition.

These urban areas were spread among sixty-six counties, leaving twenty-two counties where the population lived in areas with less than 2,500 inhabitants. Only twelve of the latter twenty-two counties supported prohibition in 1883.[56] (See Figure 6.2 for the spatial distribution of prohibition counties, 1883.) Using the percentage of the population of a county living outside areas of over 2,500 inhabitants as an independent variable yields a positive relationship with the prohibition vote. The coefficient of determination is .28.[57]

Just as the struggle for prohibition assumed the nature of a rural-urban conflict, so did it assume the nature of a nativist-immigrant conflict. The prohibitionist caricature developed by H.L. Mencken and popularized by cartoonist Rollin Kirby of a tall grim "blue"-nosed Puritan was countered by an equally stereotypical caricature of a besotted vice-stricken immigrant.

To the poor immigrant, the saloon functioned as a "poor man's club." It was a place to escape the drudgery of daily life and converse with friends and relations. The saloon functioned as a meeting place and as a place of recreation.[58] The immigrant saw the saloon as fulfilling a social need; the nativist saw it as a place which fostered crime, vice, poverty, and suffering. The dichotomous nature of the argument was caused by the differing backgrounds in socialization of the groups involved.

The 1880 census listed 394,943 Ohioans as foreign-born, an increase of 22,450 since 1870. An overwhelming percentage of this group was German, although Ireland and England provided notable additions. Together the three countries provided over 80 percent of the foreign-born in Ohio in 1880.[59] The foreign-born were overwhelmingly urban, with over 40 percent living in the two largest urban centers, Cincinnati and Cleveland.

There were differences in the distribution of native and foreign-born between prohibitionist and anti-prohibitionist counties (a mean percentage of 92.9 and 83.9 percent native respectively) and the prohibition vote did increase where the proportion of native-born increased.[60] But a strict native-born/foreign-born split was untenable.

In Hamilton County, where the foreign-born comprised approximately 25 percent of the population, 87 percent of the electorate voted against prohibition. In Cuyahoga County, where the foreign-born comprised approximately 35 percent of the population, 68 percent of

Figure 6.2 Spatial Distribution of Prohibition Counties,
Ohio, 1883

LEGEND

░░ Anti-Prohibition

☐ Prohibition

Source: Study data (see Note 43).

the electorate voted against prohibition. Although the prohibition
vote increased with an increase in the proportion of the native-born,
not all the native-born supported prohibition.

Racial overtones to the prohibition issue were found largely in the South. During the antebellum period blacks were denied the use of liquor, an exclusion extended to free blacks as well as slaves. [61] During Reconstruction fear of drunken blacks led to increased support of prohibition; until the disenfranchisement of the blacks, however, the danger to white domination of disunity in the Democratic party stunted anti-liquor legislation. [62] Once blacks were disenfranchised and the threat to white domination politically nullified, "whites and Negroes could now join hands to protect the ignorant black man from the evils of intemperance." [63]

Anti-liquor legislation in the South and in the West functioned as a means of racial control and as a means of curbing alcoholic excesses. Restraint of the black and the Indian provided added impetus to the prohibition movement. This force appears to have been negligible in Ohio, largely because of the relatively small black population. The 1880 Census reported only 79,900, or 2.49 percent of the enumerated population, as black. Given this small percentage, it is not surprising that the relationship of the proportion of the population which was white to prohibition support was not significant in 1883 Ohio. [64]

The unifying trait for the traditional characterization of prohibition support is economic status. Status cuts across lines dividing rural from urban, nativists from immigrants, and pietists from liturgicals. It could explain urban, liturgical, and immigrant support for prohibition. As a middle-class reform, prohibition could have functioned in a number of ways: as a means of social control (operating against the black, the immigrant, and the lower class); as a means of social protection (providing a focal point to establish a middle-class consensus and legislate middle-class morality); or, as a humanitarian reform embodying the middle-class traits of thrift and abstinence.

To date, the middle-class nature of prohibition support has been tested on the aggregate level by one measure, the family-per-dwelling index used by Norman H. Clark in his Washington State study. Clark found that support for prohibition increased as the variance from the middle-class ideal of one family per residence decreased. [65] Linear regression suggests a similar inverse relationship in Ohio: the relationship, however, is a weak one. [66]

The evangelical churches were in the vanguard of the drive for national prohibition. With the advent of the Anti-Saloon League the evangelical churches moved into the field of politics and firmly fixed the religious characteristic into the prohibition stereotype. But not all Protestant churches are evangelical, and therefore Richard Jensen's and Paul Kleppner's pietist-liturgical (ritualistic) split is a more legitimate measure of cultural background than the Protestant-Catholic split. [67]

The principal criterion Jensen used for the separation of pietists and liturgicals was commitment to religious revivals. Pro-revival denominations were pietistic; anti-revival denominations were liturgical. But the separation of the two groups does not entirely rest on the dispute over revivals. Liturgical denominations stressed an adherence to the creeds, rituals, sacraments, and hierarchy of the church. These religious practices are closely associated with the lavish use of ornamentation, vestments, stylized prayers, and ritualized sacraments used in the religious worship of the Catholic Church. Comparable ritualism did, however, develop in some Protestant denominations which increasingly stressed theological scholasticism. Pietistic denominations, in contrast, rejected ritualism and stressed the idea that man could be saved by direct confrontation with Christ. [68]

The greatest difference between the pietist-liturgical and the Protestant-Catholic classifications is the separation of a large number of Lutherans, Presbyterians, and Episcopalians from the Protestant category. Numerically this amounts to a 183,028 decrease from the Protestant category. [69] This refinement of the Protestant-Catholic split does increase the validity of the variable; however, religion remains a moderate indicator of prohibition support. [70] Prohibition support did increase with an increase in the proportion of pietists in the population, but prohibitionists were not necessarily pietist.

As with all socialization surrogates, religion can sometimes measure elements of environment, but religion was not under attack by the prohibition amendment. The amendment was directed to the liquor trade and not to drinking; had it been directed toward the latter the amendment might have interfered with the sacramental use of alcohol. This was not necessarily the case with the previous socialization surrogates. The concentration of the liquor trade in urban areas meant that attacks on the liquor trade could be construed as attacks on the city. Foreign and working class groups could have construed the amendments as attacks on their culture. The latter socialization variables can be divested of their dual nature (i.e., elements of situation and elements of socialization) by careful research. This does not, however, mean that the variables can be entered individually as socialization traits because of the problem of auto-correlation.

The two socialization variables with the greatest value to the study, the proportion of the population which was pietist and the proportion of the population which was native, have a correlation coefficient of .81 (see Table 6.3). Each of the variables measures a similar underlying characteristic, the socialization milieu of most native-born Americans. Using the variables individually will improve the analysis statistically but will not improve it logically, since the same element, socialization, will be added more than once.

Religion is the most theoretically sound and practical surrogate for socialization. The most frequently used surrogate for socialization, ethnicity, has at least two major problems: (1) individuals born in the United States may be socialized in an ethnic milieu; (2) the socialization of individuals born in different countries—for example, Germany and Ireland—may be radically different.

Adding the percentage pietist (Piet) to the equation yields

$$\text{Prohibition Vote} = 2.1 + .3(\text{Piet}) - .2(\text{Abs}) + .3(\text{Turn}) - 2663.9(\text{Liqint})$$
$$(.1) \qquad (.1) \qquad (.2) \qquad (1025.5)$$

The coefficient of determination equals .59. The equation explains approximately 60 percent of the variation in the prohibition vote.

Using Beta, which normalizes the influence of each variable so they can be compared, we can determine the relative contribution of each variable to the equation. Using Beta the equation becomes:

$$\text{Prohibition Vote} = +.41(\text{Piet}) - .16(\text{Abs}) + .19(\text{Turn}) - .26(\text{Liqint})$$

Socialization (Piet) explains the greatest relative percentage of the variance in the behavior, but combined behavioral restraints (.16(Abs) + .19(Turn)) explain almost as much variance; self-interest explains approximately 25 percent of the variance.

The obvious interaction of the percentage of the population in the Pietist category and the strength of the liquor interest revealed by the marked decrease in the contribution of the liquor interest variable when pietism is introduced into the equation is troublesome. The variables correlate highly (−.64) because the liquor interest had difficulty getting a foothold in areas dominated by pietists.

Table 6.3 Correlation Matrix for Selected Variables

	Pietist	Class	Rural	Native
Pietist	1.00			
Class	−.37	1.00		
Rural	.53	−.58	1.00	
Native	.81	−.47	.66	1.00

Source: Study data (see Notes 43 and 67).

One way to get around this statistical problem is to assume simply that liturgicals would not vote for prohibition under any circumstances, and then remove them statistically from the electoral base (people willing to vote for prohibition). Conversely one might assume that all pietists voted for prohibition, remove them from the base upon which behavioral variation is measured (voting population), and independently estimate the influence of the liquor interest. Except insofar as the presence of the outward manifestations of alcohol abuse (saloons, etc.) might prompt pietists to vote for prohibition, there should be no relationship between the estimated percentage of pietists voting for the amendment and the presence of the liquor interest. This is, in fact, exactly what happened:

$$\text{Prohibition Vote} = 65.03 + 606.7(\text{Liqint})$$
$$(1506.8)$$

A coefficient of determination of .00188 reveals that an insignificant amount of the variance in the estimated pietist voting behavior was the result of variations in the strength of the liquor interest.

This analysis illustrates that the traditional thesis of prohibition support is partially correct, as socialization does explain a substantial proportion of the variance in the prohibition vote. But the complete equation also illustrates that the traditional thesis neglects important aspects of the behavioral model, such as self-interest and restraints on behavior, which together explain more of the variance in the prohibition vote than socialization.

It is logical that the prohibition vote would not increase in areas where the prohibitionists were the weakest, the areas where the liquor interest was strong. Analysis in the second section of this paper illustrated that the prohibition vote decreased in areas with a high social acceptance of public drinking and increased in areas with a low social acceptance of public drinking. Support for prohibition was dependent upon the individual's interpretation of the environment; hence, the strong relative contribution of socialization to the equation. What areas had a low social acceptance of public drinking?

The traditional view regarding prohibition support yields much better results in determining areas with a low social acceptance of public drinking than in determining areas where the prohibition vote increased. Analysis reveals that the social acceptance of public drinking (SAPD) decreased where the proportion native, pietist, rural, and middle-class increased.[71] In all cases, except the proportion pietist which decreased by .03, the coefficient of determination increased.

The traditional thesis of prohibition support does predict areas which had a low social acceptance of public drinking. Voting for prohibition was dependent upon the individual's interpretation of the environment, illustrated by the social acceptance of public drinking. Moral suasion, insofar as it lowered public tolerance of drinking, appears to be a prerequisite for prohibition; however, the difference in the coefficients of determination between the prohibition vote and the social acceptance of public drinking indicate that not everyone was prepared to make the jump from moral suasion to prohibition (see Table 6.4).

Table 6.4 Coefficients of Determination Between Selected Variables and the Affirmative Percentage for the Prohibition Amendment and the Social Acceptance of Public Drinking

Independent Variable	Prohibition Vote	Social Acceptance of Public Drinking
Rural	.30	.69
Native	.42	.63
Middle-Class	.17	.44
Pietist	.46	.43

Source: Study data (see Notes 43 and 67).

The prohibition referenda of 1883 thus revealed three groups of Ohio voters. The more urban counties held large numbers of poorly politicized voters who could not be enticed to the polls by questions of public policy or normal partisan conflict. In these counties a level of alcohol-related deaths that was high relative to other counties, although low relative to other causes of death, did not lead to a vote for prohibition. It did not because these counties contained disproportionate numbers of the statewide minority of foreign-born and liturgical voters. The socialization and behavior of these voters was reflected in the strength of the liquor interest. The result was a "no" vote on prohibition.

By themselves, however, the opponents of prohibition were insufficient to defeat it. The key to that defeat lay in the second group of voters, those who cared enough to vote in the gubernatorial election but who, out of confusion, inertia, apathy, or whatever, failed to vote on the prohibition amendment. Since they could be found in both prohibitionist and anti-prohibitionist counties, it is unlikely that this group actively opposed prohibition, although their abstentions resulted in the defeat of the amendment. Instead, these were the uncommitted and perhaps the unreached. Their existence testifies to a crucial failure of the prohibition movement, a failure to polarize the electorate in a situation in which to straddle the issue was to oppose it.

Then there were the prohibitionists, the largest single group of Ohio voters. Highly politicized, they lived in rural counties where the liquor industry was weak, its depredations effectively restricted by the legal prosecution employed against it. Sensitized by pietistic religion, they moved against a threat which was neither immediate nor, apparently, as great as their rhetoric claimed. Nevertheless, the threat was real. The prohibitionists went to the polls on October 9, 1883, to remove that threat.

Notes

1. *The Constitution of the State of Ohio*, p. 26.
2. The constitutional provision providing against license was submitted separately due to its controversial nature. The amendment passed 113,239 to 104,255. See Francis Myron Whitaker, "A History of the Ohio Woman's

Christian Temperance Union, 1874-1920" (Ph.D. diss., Ohio State University, 1971), pp. 68, 74-75.

3. S.F. Cary, H. Canfield, and Thos. H. Cummings, *Temperance Tract* (No. 1), pp. 4-5. An address delivered at Circleville, Ohio, October 20, 1852. Original held at the Ohio Historical Society, Columbus.

4. State v. Hipp, 38 Dewitt 199 (O. 1882).

5. F.M. Whitaker, "Ohio W.C.T.U. and the Prohibition Amendment Campaign of 1883," *Ohio History* 83 (1974): 94.

6. Ibid.

7. Isaac Franklin Patterson, *The Constitutions of Ohio and Allied Documents* (Cleveland, O., 1912), pp. 249-50.

8. Ibid.

9. Before the legislature adjourned, the Republicans further confused the liquor issue by amending the ill-fated Pond Law. *Dayton Daily Herald*, April 19, 1883. The law was re-enacted as the Scott Law without the bond requirement. The Scott Law was ruled constitutional prior to the 1883 gubernatorial election. State v. Frame, 39 Dewitt 399 (O. 1883).

10. For examples of these early temperance societies, see John A. Krout, *The Origins of Prohibition* (New York, 1925), which examines the anti-liquor movement from the pre-colonial period to the passage of the Maine Law in 1851. See also Joseph R. Gusfield, *Symbolic Crusade: Status Politics and the American Temperance Movement* (Urbana, Ill., 1963), chs. 1, 2.

11. Krout, *Origins of Prohibition*, p. 100.

12. Legislation regulating the liquor trade was instituted during the colonial period; however, organized anti-liquor agitation did not occur on the national level until after 1840.

13. Ernest H. Cherrington et al., eds., *Standard Encyclopedia of the Alcohol Problem*, 6 vols. (Westerville, O., 1924-30), 4:1763.

14. *Cylopaedia of Temperance and Prohibition* (New York, 1891), p. 209.

15. Norman H. Clark, *Deliver Us from Evil: An Interpretation of American Prohibition* (New York, 1976), pp. 96-97.

16. John J. Janney, "The Liquor Traffic: Constitutional Prohibition" (Address delivered in Columbus, Ohio, October 4, 1890). Original held at the Ohio Historical Society, Columbus.

17. Township local option was given to ten Ohio counties in 1846 but was repealed in 1847. Municipal local option was re-enacted by the Dow Law in 1886 after the Scott Law, which had a local option provision, was declared unconstitutional in 1884. *Standard Encyclopedia*, vol. 4, p. 2046.

18. The rural-urban split was developed in Peter H. Odegard, *Pressure Politics: The Story of the Anti-Saloon League* (New York, 1928); and Charles Merz, *The Dry Decade* (Garden City, N.Y., 1931). Recent scholarship criti-

cizing the rural-urban conflict thesis includes James H. Timberlake, *Prohibition and the Progressive Movement, 1900-1920* (Cambridge, Mass., 1963); and Norman H. Clark, *The Dry Years: Prohibition and Social Change in Washington* (Seattle, 1965). The theory for the cultural conflict thesis was developed primarily by the "ethnoculturalists." See Richard J. Jensen, *The Winning of the Midwest: Social and Political Conflict, 1888-1896* (Chicago, 1971); and Paul Kleppner, *The Cross of Culture: A Social Analysis of Midwestern Politics, 1850-1900* (New York, 1970). For an excellent review of the ethnocultural interpretation of American politics, see Richard L. McCormick, "Ethno-Cultural Interpretations of Nineteenth Century Voting Behavior," *Political Science Quarterly* 89 (1974): 351-77. The class nature of prohibition support was developed in: Gusfield, *Symbolic Crusade*; Clark, *The Dry Years*; Larry D. Engelmann, "O Whiskey: The History of Prohibition in Michigan" (Ph.D. diss., University of Michigan, 1971); and Jack S. Blocker Jr., *Retreat from Reform: The Prohibition Movement in the United States, 1890-1913* (Westport, Conn., 1976).

19. Ovid Miner, "What It All Costs," in *The Prohibitionist's Textbook, 1883* (n.p., 1883), p. 105.

20. William Reid, *The Temperance Cyclopaedia* (Glasgow, n.d.), pp. 52-142.

21. *The Voice*, November 25, December 9, December 16, 1886, January 6, 1887, as quoted in *Cyclopaedia*, pp. 466-67.

22. George E. Catlin, *Liquor Control* (New York, 1931), p. 38.

23. Ibid.

24. Ibid., p. 30.

25. Robert F. Berkhofer, Jr., *A Behavioral Approach to Historical Analysis* (New York, 1969), p. 46.

26. The Landon Project, *Annual Report, 1976-1977* (London, Ont., 1977), pp. 24-38.

27. The vote for the amendments was as follows: License Amendment: Yes—99,238; No—288,605; Prohibition Amendment: Yes—323,129; no—226,595; Total vote for Governor: 721,310. *Annual Report of the Secretary of State, 1883* (Columbus, Ohio, 1883), pp. 266-68.

28. The data for this study was taken almost entirely from the published *Annual Report* of the Secretary of State for Ohio. The dependence on this data creates some problems and requires further discussion. The number of cases of criminal prosecutions and incidents of pauperism do not represent the magnitude of either variable. Approximately 30 percent of the criminal prosecutions were reportable to the State (the State was concerned only with the number of cases which came to trial). The number of paupers does not reflect the amount of turnover in the pauper population, representing only the

number of paupers resident at the time of the yearly census. These variables represent a sample of the total number of criminal prosecutions and incidents of pauperism throughout the state. This study continues on the assumption that errors are randomly distributed and that the numerical representation of crime and pauperism is a valid sample of these variables. Eric H. Monkkonen, *The Dangerous Class: Crime and Poverty in Columbus, Ohio: 1860-1885* (Cambridge, Mass., 1975), p. 25.

29. The need for developing broader crime categories was pointed out in Monkkonen's *The Dangerous Class*. Monkkonen used eight categories with a resulting 16 percent information loss; however, some of his distinctions (i.e., the difference between theft and theft by trick) are meaningless to this study. The major distinctions between the categories used in this study and Monkkonen's categories are: all assaults, regardless of intent, were included in one category; and the original division of crimes against public peace, public justice, and public health and crimes against chastity and morality were retained. Although all of the crimes included under these two categories are statutory offenses there is an important distinction between the two categories. Crimes against public peace, public justice, and public health were essentially crimes against the legal system. Crimes against chastity and morality were moral offenses. The distribution of crime among the urban hierarchy, and the amount of variability in each hierarchal category reveals that crime did not vary significantly throughout the state. A lack of variability was also evident in the distribution of paupers and alcohol inquest deaths. See George G. Wittet, "Concerned Citizens: The Prohibitionists of 1883 Ohio" (M.A. thesis, University of Western Ontario, 1978), appendix 1. The lack of variability in crime and pauperism was confirmed in Monkkonen, *The Dangerous Class*, pp. 33-39.

30. Ebriositas was the cause of less than 1 percent of the total deaths in Ohio, 1879 to 1883.

31. *Statistical Abstract of the United States* (Washington, D.C., 1922), p. 697.

32. The distribution of saloons per capita revealed as large a variability within each category of the urban hierarchy as the previous distributions. Despite the variability it is evident that saloons were concentrated in the National and Regional Metropolises. The number of saloons was compiled from *Williams' Ohio State Directory for 1882* (Cincinnati, 1882), pp. 657-73.

33. Inquest Alcohol Deaths $= .00002 + .01$(Saloons)
$$(.004)$$

The coefficient of determination equals .14.

$$\text{Ebriositas} = .000004 + .007(\text{Saloons})$$
$$(.001)$$

The coefficient of determination equals .16.

34. Theft = .0004 + .07(Saloons)
       (.02)

The coefficient of determination equals .09.

Liquor Offenses = .001 — .3(Saloons)
                 (.1)

The coefficient of determination equals .08.

35. Monkkonen found that liquor offenses and gambling offenses responded to different stimuli from the remaining crime categories. He concluded that "the not very serious offenses of liquor and gambling violations were sporadically prosecuted probably from the influence of local pressure groups such as the temperance movement or local religious leaders like Washington Gladden." Monkkonen, *The Dangerous Class*, p. 53.

36. This in no way affects the interpretation of the relationship between the potential for alcohol abuse and the remainder of the dependent variables. The potential for alcohol abuse increased in areas with a high social acceptance of public drinking and decreased in areas with a low social acceptance of public drinking.

37. *Annual Report*, 1881 to 1883.

38. Catlin, *Liquor Control*, p. 30.

39. Joseph T. Zottoli, "A Removable Source of Crime" (Columbus, Ohio, n.d.), p. 1. Reprinted from *The Scientific Temperance Journal* (Autumn, 1944).

40. Prohibition Vote = 46.1 — 91116.7(Inquest Alcohol Deaths)
                      (24427.5)

The coefficient of determination equals .14.

Prohibition Vote = 50.8 — 6749.9(Saloons)
                  (856.3)

The coefficient of determination equals .42.

41. Prohibition Vote = 38.7 + 4463.1(Liquor Offenses)
                      (920.4)

The coefficient of determination equals .21.

42. Patterson, *The Constitutions of Ohio*, p. 250.

43. The data used in this study were made available (in part) by the Inter-University Consortium for Political and Social Research (ICPSR). ICPSR supplied: United States historical census data, 1880, 1890; United States historical election returns, 1865-90; and United States historical census of religious bodies, 1890. The data were assembled and checked by ICPSR. The

Consortium bears no responsibility for the analysis or interpretation presented here.

44. *Laws of Ohio Relating to Conduct of Elections* (Ohio), pp. 6-7.

45. The number of qualified voters was calculated from the *Decennial Census*.

46. Prohibition Vote = —43.7 + 1.0 (Turnout)
(.155)

The coefficient of determination equals .33.

47. *Steubenville Weekly Herald*, September 21, 1883.

48. *Zanesville Signal*, October 2, 1883.

49. *Akron City Times*, June 6, 1883.

50. *Zanesville Signal*, October 2, 1883.

51. Support of this kind must have been extremely limited because there is an inverse relationship between the votes on first and second amendments.

License Vote = 13.8 — .1 (Prohibition Vote)
(.03)

The coefficient of determination equals .04. The *Sandusky Daily Register* suggested in an August editorial that the Liquor Dealers Association was pro-license. *Sandusky Daily Register*, August 11, 1883. If this was the case, we would expect to find a positive relationship between the license amendment and the liquor interest. This is, in fact, exactly what happened; the relationship, however, is a weak one. The equation is:

License Amendment = 10.3 + 581.13 (Liquor Interest)
(348.1)

The coefficient of determination equals .03. It appears that in Ohio the strength of the prohibitionists influenced the liquor interest enough to begin a move in the direction of some form of regulation.

52. Prohibition Vote = 45.7 — .1 (Abstentions)
(.1)

The coefficient of determination equals .02.

53. Prohibition Vote = 45.9 — .2 (Abstentions)
(.1)

The coefficient of determination equals .03.

54. Clark Warburton, "A History of Prohibition," in *The Politics of Moral Behavior*, ed. K. Austin Kerr (Reading, Mass., 1973), p. 41.

55. *Historical Statistics of the United States: Colonial Times to 1970*, 2 vols. (Washington, D.C., 1975), vol. 1, p. 33.

56. In *Prohibition and the Progressive Movement*, Timberlake points out that in Ohio, East Liverpool, Newark, Zanesville, and Springfield voted against no-license in 1909, only to be forced dry by the rest of the county. Timberlake, *Prohibition*, p. 151. Township data, available for forty-nine Ohio counties, suggests a similar occurrence for mid-hierarchical urban areas in 1883. In Ashland, Belmont, Carrol, Gallia, Jefferson, Knox, Mahoning, and Meigs Counties the townships voted in favor of prohibition while the non-rural areas voted wet. In these counties the township vote was significant enough to produce dry majorities. In Stark County the townships voted dry, but the wet vote of Canton and Massilon was significant enough to produce a wet majority.

57. Prohibition Vote $= 16.3 + .3$(Rural)

$$(.1)$$

58. Jon M. Kingsdale, "The 'Poor Man's Club': Social Functions of the Urban Working Class Saloon," *American Quarterly* 25 (1973): 472-89.

59. Other countries included: Bohemia, British America, France, Scotland, Sweden and Norway, and Switzerland.

60. The proportion of the variance explained by place of birth equals .42. The equation is

Prohibition Vote $= -65.1 + 1.2$ (Native)

$$(.2)$$

61. Daniel Jay Whitener, *Prohibition in North Carolina, 1715-1945* (Chapel Hill, N.C., 1945), p. 39.

62. James Benson Sellers, *The Prohibition Movement in Alabama, 1702-1943* (Chapel Hill, N.C., 1943), p. 51; C.C. Pearson and J. Edwin Hendricks, *Liquor and Anti-Liquor in Virginia, 1619-1919* (Durham, N.C., 1967), pp. 227n, 230.

63. Sellers, *Prohibition*, p. 101.

64. The relationship yields the lowest coefficient of determination, .01. The linear regression equation is:

Prohibition Vote $= 86.7 - .4$(White)

$$(.5)$$

The equation was not statistically significant at the .05 level.

65. Clark, *The Dry Years*, p. 120.

66. The relationship yields a coefficient of determination of .17. The equation is

Prohibition Vote $= 113.5 - 67.7$(Families per Dwelling)

$$(16.2)$$

67. The religious variable was obtained from the 1890 Census of Religious Bodies which reported church members in forty-nine denominations for a total church membership of 1,183,756.

68. Jensen, *The Winning of the Midwest*, pp. 64-65.

69. Although neither Richard Jensen nor Paul Kleppner explicitly list a categorical enumeration of pietist or liturgical denominations, the categories can be determined from Jensen's third chapter, "Pietists and Liturgicals: The Religious Roots of Partisanship." Fourteen of the seventeen denominations which cannot be categorized by this method were classified by resorting to Jensen's major source for denominational information: H.K. Carroll's *The Religious Forces of the United States* (New York, 1893). The "pietist" category encompasses twenty-nine denominations and 664,614 church members (the denominations are listed by size, largest to smallest): Methodist Episcopal, Presbyterian, Regular Baptist (North), Disciples of Christ, United Brethren, Congregationalist, Christian Connection, Methodist Protestant, Lutheran General Synod, Evangelical Association, Friends (Orthodox), African Methodist Episcopal, Dunkard, Independent Churches of Christ, Freewill Baptist, United Brethren (Old Constitution), Universalist, Church of God, Cumberland Presbyterian, Spiritualist, Seventh Day Adventist, Friends (Hicksite), Wesleyan Methodist, Advent Christian, Unitarian, Free Methodist, Salvation Army Church, Christian Scientist, and the African Methodist Episcopal Zion Church. The "liturgical" category encompasses thirteen denominations and 431,234 church members: Roman Catholic, Joint Lutheran Synod, Protestant Episcopal, Lutheran Synodical Conference, United Presbyterian, Jewish (Reformed), Primitive Baptist, Welsh Calvinistic Church, Jewish (Orthodox), Moravian, Church of the New Jerusalem, Norwegian Lutheran, and the Two-Seed-in-the-Spirit Predestinarian Baptist church. The remaining seven denominations are either split between pietists and liturgical, or their religious style was uncertain: Reformed Church in the United States, German Evangelical, General Council (Lutheran), Amish Mennonite, Mennonite, Reorganized-Jesus Christ of Latter Day Saints, and the Reformed Church in America. This last category encompasses 87,913 church members, or 7.4 percent of the total.

70. The coefficient of determination with the proportion Protestant was .43. When the proportion pietist was used the coefficient of determination increased to .46. The equations are:

Prohibition Vote = —.1 + .5(Protestant)

(.1)

Prohibition Vote = 14.9 + .4(Pietist)

(.05)

71. $SAPD = .01 - .0001(\text{Native})$
$(.00001)$

The coefficient of determination equals .63.

$SAPD = .004 - .00004(\text{Pietist})$
$(.000004)$

The coefficient of determination equals .43.

$SAPD = .005 - .00005(\text{Rural})$
$(.000003)$

The coefficient of determination equals .69.

$SAPD = .009 + .01(\text{Middle-Class})$
$(.001)$

The coefficient of determination equals .44. All equations are statistically significant at the .05 level.

7.

JACK S. BLOCKER JR.

The Modernity of Prohibitionists: An Analysis of Leadership Structure and Background

On the issue of modernity prohibition historiography has split. For Andrew Sinclair and Richard Hofstadter, prohibition was "a pseudo-reform, a pinched, parochial substitute for reform" which represented "the final victory of the defenders of the American past. On the rock of the Eighteenth Amendment, village America made its last stand."[1] Other social historians agree. For Robert H. Wiebe, "the basic thrust to the prohibition movement" was supplied by "an enduring rural localism"; for Samuel P. Hays, the basic thrust came from rural evangelical Protestantism's "drive to protect its cultural heritage against erosion."[2] After examining the symbolic aspects of the struggle over prohibition, Joseph R. Gusfield arrives at the same conclusion as the older scholar Peter H. Odegard: the Anti-Saloon League led "the cultural struggle of the traditional rural Protestant society against the developing urban and industrial social system."[3] Although he discounts rural influence, Norman H. Clark contends that in Washington State prohibitionists sought to restore "the lost

The author wishes to acknowledge grants for computer time and typing generously provided by Huron College, as well as additional computer time made available by the University of Western Ontario. Susan M. Smith Blocker, Fred W. Burd, and the American historians' seminar at the University of Western Ontario provided a critical audience for an earlier version of this paper.

purity of the great agrarian dream."[4] These scholars emphasize evidence of prohibitionists' hostility to the urbanizing and centralizing forces of the early twentieth century. On the other side, James H. Timberlake, Paul A. Carter, and Lawrence W. Levine point to prohibitionists' commitments to efficiency and progress.[5] Ross E. Paulson recognizes the modernity of the prohibitionists' positive conception of the state, although he believes that it was accompanied by an anachronistic "religious and absolutistic style of politics."[6]

With the exception of Paulson's concern for style, the historical debate has clearly focused upon the aims and constituency of the prohibition movement. All but Clark, Carter, and Levine assume consistency between the two. Since neither the proponents of prohibitionist archaism nor the defenders of prohibitionist modernity have identified their subjects through modern methods of voting analysis, most claims rest upon inferences from dry rhetoric. For Sinclair, Hofstadter, Wiebe, Hays, and Gusfield, retrogressive aims can only emanate from a backward constituency. Explicitly or implicitly, repeal demonstrates to these scholars the retrogressive nature of prohibitionist aims. Timberlake accepts their first premise but not their second: his progressive prohibition movement emerges from a middle class which was urban and therefore located in the most dynamic part of the American landscape. Clark has a new middle class in the West seeking to restore pre-industrial ways, while Levine and Carter couple progressive goals with rural, evangelical Protestants.

I propose to explore the question of prohibitionist modernity through identification and analysis of the national and state leadership of the prohibition movement. First, I will present an empirical test of a point which is generally undisputed but whose significance has escaped both sides in the historical debate: the modern structure of the Anti-Saloon League, the leading prohibitionist organization of the Progressive era. This structure is revealed in action through the career patterns of the League leadership. Once the modernity of the League structure is placed upon a sound basis, I will examine the people who created and filled it. Were leaders of the League products of the new forces transforming American society, or were they holdovers from an earlier America? The concept of a community-society continuum will be used. If "rural localism" indeed supplied the basic thrust of the prohibition movement, the League leadership should have been composed primarily of "locals," persons oriented more toward the community than the society at large. If, on the other hand, the League represented a "modern" movement it should have been led predominantly by "cosmopolitans," men and women who were more at home on a national than a local stage. [7]

The Anti-Saloon League was not the only national dry political organization of the Progressive years. The Prohibition Party had preceded it by a generation and stubbornly refused to give way to the League until 1913. Founded in 1869, the Prohibition Party has run candidates continuously since that time, reaching its peak of influence during the 1880s and winning its largest proportion of the national vote (2.25 percent) in 1892. Although it agreed with the League upon the goal of the movement, national prohibition, the party differed with the League's choice of means. Most important, the party required for supremacy a plurality among three parties or a majority in a contest between two. The League, a pressure group, needed only a large enough bloc to swing the balance of power between the two major parties. In pursuit of its elusive plurality or majority, the Prohibition Party, with only two exceptions (1896 and 1900), put forward broad platforms including planks on questions ranging from woman suffrage to government control of railways. The League in contrast generally confined itself to the single issue of prohibition. The Prohibition Party gives us an intramovement basis for comparison with the structure and composition of the League leadership. [8]

The Anti-Saloon League leaders used for the study include 271 persons who were active during the period 1893-1913. This was the organization's formative period, and many of the early leaders continued to dominate the organization well into the 1920s. Of the 13 key men named by Odegard in 1928, for example, only one is absent from the group studied. [9] Offices held include 29 paid positions on the national level, 102 state superintendents, 118 paid positions on the state level other than superintendent, 64 volunteer positions on the national level, and 103 volunteer positions on the state level. Most of the data came from the *Standard Encyclopedia of the Alcohol Problem,* the compendium published by the League during the late 1920s; [10] the remainder from the League's periodical press before 1913.

For the Prohibition Party, we have similar data for 370 national and state leaders. Party leaders include 16 candidates for national office,

122 gubernatorial candidates, 119 national committee members, and 87 state chairmen, as well as lesser candidates and officials; all were active during the period 1890-1913. Their data came from various biographical compendia in addition to the Prohibition Party periodical press. Neither group, strictly speaking, represents a sample; nor does either comprise the universe of leaders. The material for the study does encompass, however, virtually all the data we are likely to find on the leaders of these two organizations during this period.[11]

Career Patterns

Various scholars have pointed to the League's professional staff, systematic fund raising, and centralized structure as evidence of its modernity. They have based their claims primarily upon League self-descriptions.[12] While this method may reveal the League's willingness to be seen as professional, systematic, and centralized, it does not establish the presence of those attributes. An analysis of the League's organizational structure through the career patterns of its leaders can discover them if they are present. Limited service and interchangeability of leadership roles would be congruent with a description of the League as an informal and decentralized organization. Tenure and specialization, in contrast, would indicate a more formal, centralized, and professional organization.

Let us first examine the leadership structure of the Prohibition Party (Table 7.1). Here we see the career patterns within that organization of three important types of officials: gubernatorial candidates, state party chairmen, and members of the national committee, which normally included two members from each state. Among these three positions, there was a good deal of shifting around. Nearly a third of the gubernatorial candidates served as state chairmen; over two-fifths as national committeemen. Over 40 percent of the state chairmen also ran for governor, and over 70 percent were elected to the national committee. About half of the national committeemen served in each of the other two posts.

Tenure as a gubernatorial candidate was short, as might be expected for consistently losing entries, but so was that of state chairmen, who typically served no more than four years. And although one might have expected a substantially longer term of office in the na-

Table 7.1 Prohibition Party Officeholding

	Gubernatorial Candidate	State Chairman	National Committee Member
Additional service as (percentage):			
N	122	86	119
Gubernatorial candidate	—	45.3	45.4
State chairman	32.0	—	51.3
National committee member	44.3	70.9	—
Number of positions held within same category (percentage):			
N	122	na	na
One	77.9	na	na
Two	21.3	na	na
Three or more	0.8	na	na
Years of service within same category (percentage):			
N	na	86	119
Four or less	na	68.6	42.9
4 years, one month to 8 years	na	15.1	19.3
More than 8 years	na	16.3	37.8
Date of birth (percentage):			
N	116	79	110
1810–49	48.2	35.6	49.9
1850–89	51.8	64.4	50.1
Date joined Prohibition Party (percentage):			
N	83	55	82
Before 1884	45.7	38.2	42.7
1884 and after	54.3	61.8	57.3
Age joined Prohibition Party (percentage):			
N	80	51	77
Younger than 37 years	58.9	76.5	53.3
37 years and older	41.1	23.5	46.7
Education (percentage):			
N	89	67	91
No college or professional training	37.0	41.8	41.8
College or professional training	63.0	58.2	58.2
Occupation (percentage):			
N	117	80	115
Clergy	23.1	17.5	18.3
Businessman	22.2	23.8	28.7
Lawyer	20.5	22.5	20.9
Temperance or social worker	3.4	5.0	7.8
Other	30.8	31.2	24.3

Source: Study data.

tional committee, which rarely met as often as once a year, over 40 percent of them, too, stepped down after four years or less. The state chairmen constituted a particularly important group for the party. As a group, state chairmen were younger than the other two, had joined the party younger, and had joined fairly recently, after the party had become highly visible nationally in the 1884 presidential election. Clearly the party had to retain and put to productive use the energy of these younger leaders if it was to have a future in American politics. Yet either the younger men or their colleagues found their performance as state chairmen unsatisfactory, judging from the relatively short time spent in that unremunerative position. And from there, one could only go on to a doomed gubernatorial campaign or to a place on the national committee, which after 1896 increasingly devoted itself to debilitating internal bickering. With tenure and specialization so restricted, the Party relied upon moral force and amateurism and became increasingly anachronistic in twentieth-century politics.

The League was different. Most important, it provided two distinct and parallel lines of career activity. If one wished to devote oneself to full-time League work, there were paid positions on both national and state levels carrying various burdens of responsibility. These positions did not pay very much, especially during the early years, but they usually paid enough to live on. And if one had only part of one's time to spare for prohibition, there were voluntary positions, again on both national and state levels.

Table 7.2 makes this clear. Multiple positions were usually held within one career line or the other, rarely overlapping. Over half of the paid workers below state superintendent went on to become superintendents themselves; three-fifths of the superintendents had experience in a paid state position bearing less responsibility. From among the state superintendents, the most promising or influential went on to paid positions on the national level; the others moved to lesser paid positions in larger states or to national or, less often, state volunteer positions. Of the national paid leadership, three-fifths had been state superintendents, and the same proportion had served in paid state positions below superintendent. Less than 20 percent served in voluntary national offices, and less than 10 percent in voluntary state positions. The occupants of national volunteer offices were recruited primarily from among the state volunteers, and a smaller but substantial

Table 7.2 Anti-Saloon League Officeholding

	National Paid Position	State Superin- tendent	Other State Paid Position	National Volunteer Position	State Volunteer Position
Additional service as (percentage):					
N	29	102	118	64	103
National paid position		17.6	15.2	7.8	1.9
State superintendency	62.1	—	53.4	34.4	13.6
Other state paid position	62.1	61.8	—	29.7	12.6
National volunteer position	17.2	21.6	16.1	—	33.0
State volunteer position	6.9	13.7	11.0	53.1	—
Number of positions held within same category (percentage):					
N	25	96	104	26	68
One	44.0	77.1	38.5	73.1	47.1
Two	40.0	15.6	35.6	19.2	35.3
Three or more	16.0	7.3	26.0	7.7	17.6
Years of service within same category (percentage):					
N	25	96	104	26	68
4 or less	24.0	40.6	29.8	15.3	14.7
4 years, one month to 8 years	8.0	21.9	19.2	23.1	13.2
More than 8	68.0	37.5	51.0	61.5	72.1
Date of birth (percentage):					
N	25	88	104	26	68
1810–64	48.0	53.4	49.0	61.6	67.7
1865–89	52.0	46.6	51.0	38.4	32.3
Date joined A.S.L. (percentage):					
N	25	89	104	22	57
1893–05	64.0	51.7	39.4	72.7	47.4
After 1905	36.0	48.3	60.6	27.3	52.6
Age joined A.S.L. (percentage):					
N	25	82	101	22	56
Younger than 42 years	76.0	53.7	58.5	45.4	32.1
42 years and older	24.0	46.3	41.5	54.6	67.9
Education (percentage):					
N	24	86	98	22	58
No college or professional training	8.4	8.1	10.1	18.1	10.3
College or professional training	91.6	91.9	89.9	81.9	89.7
Occupation (percentage):					
N	25	95	106	26	68
Clergy	60.0	71.6	66.0	42.3	54.4
Businessman	0.0	3.2	2.8	26.9	16.2
Lawyer	12.0	12.6	15.1	19.2	11.8
Temperance or social worker	20.0	6.3	11.3	11.5	4.4
Other	8.0	6.3	4.8	0.0	13.2

Source: Study data.

group came from among the state superintendents. State volunteers, if they changed positions at all, generally became holders of national voluntary offices. The Anti-Saloon League was not as specialized as it might have been, but its officers were considerably more specialized than their Prohibition Party counterparts.

Also, the League provided careers that could hold its able young men. The national paid officials typically served more than eight years in that category, and multiple officeholding, simultaneous or consecutive, was also the rule. In fact, they were more likely to change jobs within their own category than they were to slip into a voluntary position. The same was true of the paid state officials below superintendent. The superintendents were the bottleneck in the system, as they normally held only one position in that category, and that for more than four years. In fact, twice as many of them as party state chairmen served more than eight years in their category. This may have been the reason for the dispatch of a greater proportion of state superintendents than other paid officers into voluntary positions: to make room for proven young men. Among the volunteers, few positions and long tenure were the rule.

The youngest men were in the positions of greatest responsibility, in the national paid offices. The oldest men were in the positions of least responsibility, the state volunteers. This was undoubtedly in part because the national paid officials had come to the League at an earlier point in both their lives and that of the organization. Only the national volunteers could claim equal credit for steering the organization through its difficult early years. The state superintendents were the third largest group to come in during the early years, and that is undoubtedly why they were state superintendents, despite the fact that they were somewhat older than the national paid officials. Still, all classes of paid officials were younger than the volunteers, and all had joined the organization at a younger age. The old men set the policy, and the young men executed it—and maybe changed it a little along the way. This was the model of a modern reform organization.

Background and Experience

How can we explain the difference between the organizational structures of party and League? The possibility that the difference reflected the intrinsic natures of the two organizations, one a party, the other a pressure group, can be rejected fairly easily. The Prohibition Party certainly could have been organized more tightly. In fact, during the period 1900-04, under the national chairmanship of Oliver W. Stewart, the Prohibition Party did begin the process of reorganization. Through the formation of local party clubs, called Prohibition Alliances, appointment of paid representatives in several states, and sponsorship of the Intercollegiate Prohibition Association, the party tightened organizational bonds and improved recruitment and career opportunities. These beginnings came to nought after Stewart lost his position through an unrelated factional squabble in 1904, but they show that there was no intrinsic reason why the Prohibition Party could not have become much more thoroughly organized than it was. The Anti-Saloon League stabilized its organization only after a long and difficult struggle. It was not until the period 1905-09, for example, ten years after the creation of its national organization, that the League managed to lower the turnover rate among its state superintendents to a point below that for Prohibition Party state chairmen. [13] And one can certainly conceive of the League's continuing to conduct pressure-group politics, though not as effectively, in the unsystematic fashion of its early years. The Prohibition Party, in fact, could have turned itself into a pressure group with no significant change in its organizational structure or mode of operation.

We must turn then to the people who created the Anti-Saloon League. These people were on the average about ten years younger than their Prohibition Party counterparts. [14] Age and achievement, however, must be linked by experience. If the collective experience of the Anti-Saloon League leadership accustomed them to acting in a larger context than the Prohibition Party leadership, we might then infer that in response they developed more cosmopolitan attitudes than their older comrades. The League leadership's cosmopolitan experience and attitudes might then explain their greater ability and willingness to adopt a modern mode of organization. Four background variables allow us to measure range of experience: occupation, education, residence, and spatial mobility. Specifically, I assume that professional occupation, higher education, urban residence, and, most important, high spatial mobility suggest a more cosmopolitan orientation than do nonprofessional occupation, lower education, rural residence, and low mobility. None of these variables alone would afford a satisfactory indicator of cosmopolitanism; together they provide the best measure available.[15]

Nevertheless, our composite must be assembled piece by piece. The first test is professionalism. Professional groups can of course include both cosmopolitans and locals.[16] The use of occupation as a test of cosmopolitanism rests upon the assumption that a professional role, because of its greater opportunity for extralocal contact, would be more likely to give rise to cosmopolitan attitudes than would a nonprofessional role. As Table 7.3 shows, professional experience figured

Table 7.3 Occupations of Prohibition Party and Anti-Saloon League Leaders

	Party			League		
Occupations	N	Percentage	Clergy Excluded Percentage	N	Percentage	Clergy Excluded Percentage
Professionals						
Clergy	68	19.4	—	161	60.8	—
Lawyer	61	17.4	21.5	37	14.0	35.6
Teacher or professor	18	5.1	6.3	9	3.4	8.6
Physician	7	2.0	2.5	2	0.8	1.9
Total	154	43.9	30.4	209	78.9	46.1
Nonprofessionals						
Businessman	82	23.4	29.0	24	9.1	23.1
Temperance or social worker	33	9.4	11.7	20	7.5	19.2
Journalist	28	8.0	9.9	3	1.1	2.9
Farmer	21	6.0	7.4	2	0.8	1.9
Lecturer	19	5.4	6.7	4	1.5	3.8
Clerk or salesman	12	3.4	4.2	2	0.8	1.9
Skilled labor	2	0.6	0.7	1	0.4	1.0
Total	197	56.1	69.6	56	21.1	53.8
Total Professional and Nonprofessional	351	100.0	100.0	265	100.0	100.0

Source: Study data.

larger in the backgrounds of Anti-Saloon League leaders than it did for Prohibition Party leaders. Nearly twice as many leaders of the League came from professional backgrounds, and the correlation between Anti-Saloon League leadership and professional occupation (+.3522) is positive and significant.[17] The difference persists even when comparing leaders of the same age cohort. Clearly this is primarily due to the preponderance of clergymen in League ranks. When clergy are excluded from both groups only a weak difference remains: professional occupation and League leadership correlate at +.1469.[18] Yet both party and League clearly drew their leadership disproportionately from professional ranks: in 1900, only 3.4 percent of all male workers fell into the Census Bureau's generous definition of "professional, technical, and kindred workers."[19]

The preponderance of professionals among the League leadership was reflected in the amount of formal education received by both groups (Table 7.4).[20] Sixty-five percent of Prohibition Party leaders were exposed to college or professional training; 87 percent of League leaders were. This difference persists when age is controlled. The relationship between League leadership and college or professional education, while positive and significant, is weaker than that between League leadership and professional occupation: $\phi = +.2565$.[21] Excluding the clergymen with whom the League was so singularly blessed, however, reduces the disparity to the point of insignificance.[22] The League contained far fewer professionals without professional training than did the Party. Again, both Party and League drew from the most highly educated segment of the American population. In 1870, when the average Prohibition Party leader would have been enrolled in college, seminary, or law school, only 1.7 percent of the population of ages 18-21 years were similarly enrolled. By 1880, the comparable date for Anti-Saloon League leaders, the proportion of the general population had risen only to 2.7 percent. As of 1890, the maximum percentage of the white population over the age of 19 years who could have received college or advanced degrees during the previous two decades was less than one percent.[23]

Amount of education by itself is a crude indicator of cosmopolitanism. Especially for those trained in the widely varying educational institutions of the nineteenth century, it becomes important to assess the type and quality of formal education, insofar as they can be mea-

Table 7.4 Highest Educational Attainments of Prohibition Party and Anti-Saloon League Leaders

Education	Party			League		
	N	Percentage	Cumulative Percentage	N	Percentage	Cumulative Percentage
None	11	4.3	4.3	2	0.8	0.8
Grammar school	25	9.7	14.0	10	4.2	5.0
Secondary school	34	13.2	27.2	8	3.3	8.4
Academy	15	5.8	33.1	8	3.3	11.7
Trade school	5	2.0	35.0	3	1.3	13.0
Attended college	48	18.7	53.7	30	12.6	25.6
College graduate	39	15.2	68.9	26	10.9	36.5
Post-graduate study	26	10.1	79.0	42	17.6	54.1
Seminary	28	10.9	89.9	84	35.1	89.2
Law school	26	10.1	100.0	26	10.9	100.0
Total	257	100.0	—	239	100.0	—
No college (clergy excluded)	83	41.1		26	28.6	
College or professional (clergy excluded)	119	58.9		65	71.4	
Professionals (clergy, lawyers, teachers, physicians) without college or professional training	22/ 130	16.9		8/ 192	4.2	

Source: Study data.

sured. As Table 7.5 shows, the range of institutions was quite wide, extending from the most distinguished to the most obscure. Obviously no single set of similar institutions was responsible for forming the "dry mentality," if such a thing existed. The fact that some Party leaders and a lesser number of League leaders attended normal schools or colleges, together with the fact that some of both probably matriculated only in the preparatory departments of their colleges, dilutes the meaning of the "attended college" category of Table 7.4. More Prohibition Party leaders attended state universities, but more League leaders attended Ivy League schools. The differences in the educational quality of institutions attended by the two groups do not appear to be substantial. The single exception to this conclusion is the fact that, if "sectarian" can be equated with "narrow," then League leaders received a narrower education than did Party leaders. The pre-

Table 7.5 Post-Secondary Educational Institutions
          Attended by Prohibition Party and Anti-Saloon
          League Leaders

	Party			League		
		Enrollments				Enrollments
Institution	N	Percentage	Institution		N	Percentage
Colleges and Universities						
Enrolling 5 or more:			Enrolling 5 or more:			
Ohio Wesleyan University	7	4.2	Depauw University		9	4.4
Pa. State Normal College(s)	6	3.6	Ohio Wesleyan University		8	3.9
Wesleyan University (Conn.)	5	3.0	Oberlin College		6	2.9
University of Wisconsin	5	3.0	Yale University		5	2.4
Ivy League schools (5)	6	3.6	Other Ivy League schools (3)		5	2.4
Other state universities (12)	14	8.4	State universities (11)		14	6.8
Other private schools (76)	100	60.2	Other private schools (112)		150	73.2
Other normal schools (12)	12	7.2	Normal schools (8)		8	3.9
Unidentified	11	6.6	Unidentified		0	0.0
Total	166	100.0			205	100.0
Post-Graduate Institutions						
Enrolling 2:	12	27.9	Enrolling 3 or more:			
University of Denver			University of Chicago		5	6.0
Wesleyan University (Conn.)			University of Berlin		3	3.6
University of Chicago			Ohio Wesleyan University		3	3.6
University of Berlin			Boston University		3	3.6
University of Michigan			Northwestern University		3	3.6
University of Minnesota						
Other (31)	31	72.1	Other (59)		65	78.3
Unidentified	0	0.0	Unidentified		1	1.2
Total	43	100.0			83	100.0
Law Schools						
Enrolling more than 1:			Enrolling 2:		12	40.0
University of Michigan	5	20.0	University of Michigan			
University of Wisconsin	4	16.0	Western Reserve Law			
University of Virginia	2	8.0	School			
			Boston University			
			Cumberland University			
			(Tenn.)			
			Ohio Northern University			
			Georgetown University			
Other	12	48.0	Other		16	53.3
Unidentified	2	8.0	Unidentified		2	6.7
Total	25	100.0			30	100.0

Table 7.5 (continued)

	Seminaries				
Enrolling 2:	6	23.1	Enrolling 5 or more:		
Andover			Boston University	6	6.4
Auburn			Drew	5	5.3
Newton			Western (Pa.)	5	5.3
			Yale	5	5.3
Other	16	61.5	Other (48)	71	75.5
Unidentified	4	15.4	Unidentified	2	2.1
Total	26	100.0		94	100.0
	Colleges and Universities by Type				
Sectarian	80	48.2		126	61.5
Non-Sectarian	45	27.1		37	18.0
Foreign	2	1.2		5	2.4
College Unknown	11	6.6		0	0.0
Affiliation Unknown	28	16.9		37	18.1
Total	166	100.0		205	100.0
	Post-Graduate Institutions by Type				
Sectarian	18	41.9		49	59.0
Non-Sectarian	14	32.6		16	19.3
Foreign	2	4.6		6	7.2
Institution Unknown	0	0.0		1	1.2
Affiliation Unknown	9	20.9		11	13.2
Total	43	100.0		83	100.0

Sources: U.S. Dept. of the Interior, *Report of the Commissioner of Education for the Year 1882–83* (Washington, 1884), pp. 608–18; study data. This data was researched from notes and the original sources and is not included in the SPSS file.

ponderance of sectarianism among post-graduate institutions attended by League leaders, in particular, suggests that many of their M.A.'s were awarded by essentially undergraduate institutions to aspiring young ministers.

As Hays has pointed out, the community-society continuum is not the same as a rural-urban continuum. Urbanites can be localist, ruralites can be cosmopolitan. [24] Nevertheless, for these sons and daughters of the countryside, urban residence implied mobility and broadened perspectives. Table 7.6, then, presents the residence patterns for the two groups. [25] Although proportionately more League than Party leaders lived in the largest cities, the differences disappear

Table 7.6 Residence of Prohibition Party and Anti-Saloon League Leaders, by Population

Residence Size		Party			League	
	N	Percentage	Cumulative Percentage	N	Percentage	Cumulative Percentage
100,000 and over	101	33.8	33.8	79	44.6	44.6
25,000–99,999	56	18.7	52.5	21	11.9	56.5
10,000–24,999	35	11.7	64.2	24	13.6	70.1
5,000–9,999	27	9.0	73.2	9	5.1	75.1
2,500–4,999	27	9.0	82.3	12	6.8	81.9
Under 2,500	53	17.7	100.0	32	18.1	100.0
Total	299	100.0		177	100.0	

Source: Study data.

as one descends the urban hierarchy. At the lowest level, the difference vanishes altogether. Dichotomizing places of residence at 25,000 population produces a positive but very weak correlation between League leadership and residence size (+.0387).[26] Controlling for age and excluding clergy do not change the situation. The test of urbanism reveals no grounds for concluding that either Party or League leadership was likely to have been more cosmopolitan. Both Party and League leaders were far more concentrated in urban areas than the general adult, native-born, white population.

We move now to geographic mobility, a crucial question for the determination of cosmopolitanism. Unlike urban residence, a weak indicator, mobility is generally considered to be a necessary condition for cosmopolitanism.[27] It would seem to be essential in forming the broader perspectives on private and public affairs which characterize the cosmopolitan and thus provides a good standard of comparison when analyzing groups of the same social class.[28]

Geographic mobility can be measured in at least two ways, by frequency and extent. Table 7.7 compares the two groups of leaders by the number of discrete moves recorded in their biographical sketches. In all cases, the number should be regarded as a minimum.[29] Anti-

Saloon League leaders tended to move more frequently than Prohibition Party leaders, as 55 percent of the former, compared to 40 percent of the latter, made three or more moves. [30] When moves are dichotomized between two and three, Anti-Saloon League leadership correlates weakly but significantly with moves at +.1599. [31] The association between League leadership and frequency of moves is thus stronger than that between League leadership and urbanism, but weaker than those between League leadership on one hand and professional occupation and higher education on the other. No external comparison is possible.

The difference is, however, entirely attributable to the occupational variable discussed earlier. With minor exceptions, clergymen were the most frequent movers in both groups, and the League contained a significantly larger percentage of ministers. [32] Excluding clergy from both groups wipes out the difference and in fact leaves the Party leaders more frequently mobile (Table 7.7). [33]

Table 7.7 Recorded Moves of Prohibition Party and
Anti-Saloon League Leaders

Moves	Party			League		
	N	Percentage	Cumulative Percentage	N	Percentage	Cumulative Percentage
One or none	96	36.4	36.4	45	23.9	23.9
Two	66	25.0	61.4	40	21.3	45.2
Three or four	70	26.5	87.9	44	23.4	68.6
More than four	32	12.1	100.0	59	31.4	100.0
Total	264	100.0		188	100.0	
		Clergy	Excluded			
Two or less	146	67.0		56	73.7	
Three or more	72	33.0		20	26.3	
Total	218	100.0		76	100.0	

Source: Study data.

Finally, we can measure the comparative extent of League and party leaders' mobility by computing persistence rates, defined as the proportion of native-born resident in their communities and states of birth at the time of their death or biographical sketch. For the Prohibiton Party leaders, the community persistence rate is 7.6 percent; for the League, 3.5 percent. League leaders were thus less persistent in their communities than their party counterparts. Yet only a tiny percentage of each group were true locals in Merton's sense of life-long residence in their community. The persistence rate by state is virtually identical for the two groups: party, 40.34 percent; League, 40.37 percent. [34] There is no relationship whatsoever between out-of-state mobility and League leadership. [35] Thus, on the crucial question of mobility, in terms of both frequency and extent, differences substantial enough to suggest differing degrees of cosmopolitanism either do not exist or are explicable by occupation. Again, Party and League leaders represented the most mobile segment of the population: in 1910, 77.6 percent of native-born whites resided in their state of birth, and the rate was undoubtedly higher among the white-collar workers with whom the prohibitionist leaders should be compared. [36]

The combined effect of all the variables discussed so far can be judged by construction of a cumulative Index of Cosmopolitanism (IC). The IC scale has a range of 0 to 10 points, with two points awarded for professional occupation; two points for post-graduate, law, or seminary training, one for college attendance or degree; two points for residence size of 25,000 and over, one for residence size 2,500 to 24,999; two points for three or more moves, one for two; and two points for out-of-state mobility. [37]

The mean IC score for 159 Prohibition Party leaders was 5.7, with standard deviation of 2.3. Mean IC score for 124 Anti-Saloon League leaders was 7.2, with standard deviation of 2.2. [38] Despite the fact that the difference of means is statistically significant, I believe it is misleading. It reflects above all else the fact that the League leadership included a greater proportion of clergymen, most of whom were college- or seminary-trained. Indeed, when points are not awarded for clergy or seminary training, mean IC score for Party leaders becomes 5.2, for League leaders 5.3—a statistically insignificant difference.

Although it is clear that both Party and League leadership came from among the most cosmopolitan Americans, it would be unwise to conclude that the Anti-Saloon League leadership was more cosmopolitan than the Prohibition Party leadership. In urban residence they were not significantly different. The main factor differentiating the two groups was the League's far greater proportion of clergymen, which gave the League group some of the attributes of cosmopolitanism. They had more formal education, but in sectarian institutions. They moved more often, but ventured beyond state boundaries no more readily than the Party leaders.

Thus the hypothesis that modernization of the prohibition movement resulted from the more cosmopolitan experience of the Anti-Saloon League leadership must be abandoned. This negative demonstration strengthens the case I have made elsewhere that organizational changes in the prohibition movement constituted an incident in the general middle-class flight from radicalism during and after the crisis of the 1890s, not an autonomous development. [39] Centralization of control and creation of career-oriented professional positions answered the League's need to avoid the internal policy debates, spawned by general economic and political crisis, which had debilitated the Prohibition Party. Modernization by the Anti-Saloon League thus represented not the prohibition movement's adaptation to social change but rather its insulation against it. Recruitment of clergymen reflected one aspect of this insulating process, the League's decision to base its support among conservative middle-class Protestants.

These findings also add an intriguing dimension to the story of change in the prohibition movement at the turn of the century and help to explain historians' confusion over prohibitionist modernity. The Prohibition Party leaders stood out against their society: they were deviant not only in their political heresy but also in their social background, being drawn from the most cosmopolitan sector. But the Anti-Saloon League leadership, ten years younger on the average, presented not only a more conservative political policy but also a less cosmopolitan background *relative to their society*, which was more modern than that which faced the Party leaders. In other words, the Anti-Saloon League leaders were less cosmopolitan in relation to their contemporaries than were the Party leaders in relation to theirs, since the birth cohorts holding the largest numbers of League leaders can be assumed to have contained more professionals and to have been more urban and better educated than the cohorts containing the bulk of the Prohibition Party leaders. While the times changed, the prohibitionist leadership did not.

This fact may help to explain the confusion over prohibitionist modernity among historians. Those who see primarily the modern organizational structure of the League have rightly, but partially, emphasized prohibitionist modernity. At the same time, those who point out Anti-Saloon League provincialism also have a point, though still a partial one, in view of the fact that the most cosmopolitan reformers, of the sort who had earlier joined the Prohibition Party, now avoided the League. Let us not rehearse platitudes about blind men and elephants. Hopefully we can now abandon the simplicity of both approaches in order to understand a movement which not only changed over time, but did so in surprisingly complex ways.

Notes

1. Richard Hofstadter, *The Age of Reform* (New York, 1955), p. 289; Andrew Sinclair, *Era of Excess*, Harper Colophon edn. (New York, 1964), p. 5.

2. Robert H. Wiebe, *The Search for Order, 1877-1920* (New York, 1967), p. 301; Samuel P. Hays, "Political Parties and the Community-Society Continuum," in *The American Party Systems,* eds. W.N. Chambers and W.D. Burnham (New York, 1967), p. 174.

3. Joseph R. Gusfield, *Symbolic Crusade: Status Politics and the American Temperance Movement* (Urbana, Ill., 1963), p. 7; Peter H. Odegard, *Pressure Politics: The Story of the Anti-Saloon League* (New York, 1928), pp. 29-34.

4. Norman H. Clark, *The Dry Years: Prohibition and Social Change in Washington* (Seattle, 1965), pp. 126-27.

5. James H. Timberlake, *Prohibition and the Progressive Movement, 1900-1920* (Cambridge, Mass., 1963), p. 2; Paul A. Carter, *The Decline and Revival of the Social Gospel: Social and Political Liberalism in American Protestant Churches, 1920-40.* (Ithaca, N.Y., 1962), ch. 3; Lawrence W. Levine, *Defender of the Faith. William Jennings Bryan: The Last Decade, 1915-1925* (New York, 1965), pp. 103-05.

6. Ross E. Paulson, *Women's Suffrage and Prohibition: A Comparative Study of Equality and Social Control* (Glenview, Ill., 1973), p. 167.

7. For further explication of these terms, see Robert K. Merton, "Patterns of Influence: Local and Cosmopolitan Influentials," in *Social Theory*

and Social Structure, rev. ed. (New York, 1957), pp. 387-420; Hays, "Political Parties and the Community-Society Continuum," pp. 153-57; Ronald C. Tobey, "How Urbane Is the Urbanite? An Historical Model of the Urban Hierarchy and the Social Motivation of Service Classes," *Historical Methods Newsletter* 7 (September 1974): 259-75. For an analysis of modern grass-roots support for temperance using the community-society continuum, see John Wilson and Kenneth Manton, "Localism and Temperance," *Sociology and Social Research* 59 (January 1975): 121-35.

8. There is no suitable external baseline, since no one else has systematically studied leaders of Progressive-era organizations using the community-society continuum. For a review and critique of the literature, see Jerome M. Clubb and Howard W. Allen, "Collective Biography and the Progressive Movement: The 'Status Revolution' Revisited," *Social Science History* 1 (Summer 1977): 518-34.

9. *Pressure Politics,* p. 15.

10. Ernest H. Cherrington et al., eds., *Standard Encyclopedia of the Alcohol Problem,* 6 vols. (Westerville, O., 1924-30).

11. The data are contained in an SPSS file stored on magnetic tape at the Computing Centre, University of Western Ontario. Copies may be obtained at cost by writing to the author. For a profile of the entire group, both Anti-Saloon League and Prohibition Party leaders, see Jack S. Blocker Jr., *Retreat from Reform: The Prohibition Movement in the United States, 1890-1913* (Westport, Conn., 1976), pp. 8-13.

12. Timberlake, *Prohibition and the Progressive Movement,* pp. 124-48; Odegard, *Pressure Politics,* pp. 8-17.

13. Turnover rates were computed from lists in Anti-Saloon League of America, *Proceedings of the National Convention* for the years 1895-1909, and in D. Leigh Colvin, *Prohibition in the United States* (New York, 1926), pp. 643-57. The computations included changes in established positions and excluded new entries.

14. Mean birth year for the Anti-Saloon League leaders was 1860, median 1862, standard deviation 13 years. Mean and median birth year for the Prohibition Party leaders was 1850, standard deviation 14 years.

15. Historians should be aware that background variables are less than perfect indicators of attitudes. This has been shown by Lewis J. Edinger and Donald D. Searing, "Social Background Variables in Elite Analysis," *American Political Science Review* 61 (June 1967): 445. Nevertheless, in studying large groups there seems to be no better alternative. In particular, the concept of a community-society continuum would have little operational meaning if we could not define it in terms of background variables.

16. Alvin W. Gouldner, "Cosmopolitans and Locals: Toward an Analysis

of Latent Social Roles," *Administrative Science Quarterly* 2 (1957): 281-306, 444-80.

17. All correlation coefficients in this article are ϕ, computed from 2 x 2 tables using SPSS. With N = 616, chi-square is significant at the .001 level.

18. With N = 387, chi-square is significant at the .01 level.

19. U.S. Bureau of the Census, *Historical Statistics of the United States: Colonial Times to 1970* (Washington, D.C., 1975), p. 139.

20. For evidence of a positive relationship between education and cosmopolitanism, see Wilson and Manton, "Localism and Temperance," p. 126.

21. With N = 496, chi-square is significant at the .001 level.

22. With N = 293, ϕ = +.1198. Chi-square is not significant at the .05 level.

23. *Historical Statistics of the U.S.*, pp. 16, 386.

24. "Political Parties and the Community-Society Continuum," p. 156.

25. Place of residence was recorded as the last residence indicated in the biographical sketch for Party leaders and League leaders no longer in League service; as the last residence before joining the League for those still affiliated with the Anti-Saloon League. This was done so as to eliminate the effect of League service.

26. With N = 476, chi-square is not significant even at the .10 level.

27. Merton, "Patterns of Influence," pp. 395-96.

28. Hays discusses the centrality of widened perspectives in "Political Parties and the Community-Society Continuum," pp. 153-57, and "The Politics of Reform in Municipal Government in the Progressive Era," *Pacific Northwest Quarterly* 55 (October 1964): 161. Because of recent findings in mobility research demonstrating class differences in mobility, cosmopolitanism and mobility should not be linked when making cross-class comparisons.

29. For the Prohibition Party leaders, few of whom lived by their reform work, I tabulated all moves during their lifetime. For the Anti-Saloon League leaders, I counted moves only until they joined the League and after they left, so as to eliminate the influence of their often peripatetic professional prohibition work. Since the top category in the original tabulation (eight or more) was open-ended, it was unfeasible to calculate measures of dispersion or central tendency.

30. Two biases of unknown potency affect these results in opposite directions. The difference between the two organizations is diminished by the fact that Party leaders' moves were tabulated for their entire lives, while League leaders' moves did not include those attributable to League service. This excluded a portion of the latter's lives when they might have increased their total number of moves. The differences are increased, however, by the fact that 90 percent of the League biographies (as compared to 27 percent of the Party

biographies) came from the *Standard Encyclopedia of the Alcohol Problem*, which was generally more ample in its listings of moves than the periodical press.

31. With $N = 452$, chi-square is significant at the .001 level.

32. Only the five League teachers and the single League journalist moved more frequently than clergymen. Dichotomizing moves between two and three gives us a correlation with clergy of $+ .3911$; with $N = 433$, chi-square is significant at the .001 level. Neigher the relative youthfulness of the League leaders nor their greater proportion of *Methodist* clergymen contributed to the difference, since there is no significant correlation between age and moves, and Methodists, I found to my surprise, moved no more often than did other clergy. Education contributed to the difference primarily as it acted through occupation.

33. With clergy excluded, League leadership correlates with frequency of moves at only $+.0634$. With $N = 294$, chi-square is not significant at the .10 level.

34. This variable was tabulated so as to eliminate mobility due to League service wherever possible. Variance in state size and regional differences within states make this a crude measure of the extent and nature of mobility. I felt, however, that nineteenth-century political and social differences among the states were sufficient to make this a meaningful variable in measuring breadth of experience.

35. Out-of-state mobility and League leadership correlate at $-.0004$; $N = 503$.

36. U.S. Bureau of the Census, *Thirteenth Census, 1910, Vol. 1: Population* (Washington, D.C., 1913), p. 710.

37. Because of the importance of mobility in determining cosmopolitanism, and because they measure different dimensions of mobility, frequency and extent were given the same weight as each of the other three variables. We have already seen that their incidence was not equal in the two groups.

38. The relatively low observed frequencies (43 percent of party leaders, 46 percent of League leaders) result from missing values for one or more variables for many cases. A difference-of-means test produces a Student's t value of -5.0019, with 281 degrees of freedom, which is significant at the .001 level.

39. *Retreat from Reform.*

8. LARRY ENGELMANN

Organized Thirst: The Story of Repeal in Michigan

Prohibition has made nothing but trouble—trouble for all of us. Worst thing ever hit the country. Why, I tried to get into legitimate business two or three times, but they won't stand for it.

Al Capone

One thing I would like to emphaisze is that those working for the repeal of the Michigan dry law are not trying to make it easier to obtain liquor. We are trying to make it more difficult.

Mrs. Fred A. Alger

Scripture tells us that wine was for the disciples and water was drunk by the asses of the desert. The electorate should be afforded the opportunity of taking their choice.

Declaration of the Michigan Republican Party,1932

From the day of its adoption, it was generally assumed that the Eighteenth Amendment would never be repealed and that prohibition would remain part of the Constitution forever. Dry crusader Andrew Volstead told a national convention of the Anti-Saloon League in 1921 that there was no question at all in his mind regarding the permanency of prohibition. "They can never repeal it," he said. Senator Morris Sheppard of Texas asserted that "there is as much chance of repealing the Eighteenth Amendment as there is for a hummingbird to fly to the planet Mars with the Washington Monument tied to its tail." Evangelist Billy Sunday added his assurance and contended that there was no more chance of repealing the Eighteenth Amendment "than there is of repealing the Thirteenth Amendment and restoring slavery." No more chance, he said, "than you can dam Niagara Falls with toothpicks."[1]

But such assurances did not silence the expression of dissent regarding the Eighteenth Amendment. For ten years a number of critics called for revision of the Volstead Act and a redefinition of the term "intoxicating beverage," with the goal of legalizing beer and light wines. Not surprisingly, the U.S. Brewers' Association was one of the most outspoken champions of such revision. Spokesman for the organization, Hugh Fox, contended that beer containing 2.75 percent alcohol was not intoxicating. In a 1923 address Fox praised 2.75 beer as the salvation of the prohibition experiment. Dissatisfaction with prohibition was increasing, he asserted, and all indications were that prohibition in its bone-dry Volstead form was unenforceable. But bring back light beer and Americans would again have an inexpensive, palatable, and harmless beverage. This, Fox insisted, would subvert the illegal liquor business and result in greater compliance with the prohibition laws.[2]

Popular sentiment as registered in numerous public opinion polls in the 1920s seemed to favor some kind of revision of prohibition like that proposed by Fox. As early as the summer of 1922, in a national survey conducted by the *Literary Digest* which included more than one million responses from individuals listed in telephone directories throughout the country, 61.5 percent of those polled said they favored either modification or repeal of the Eighteenth Amendment. A separate poll of women showed them to be about 55 percent in favor of modification. A poll of workingmen indicated that they favored modification of the Volstead Act by more than nine to one.[3]

The portion of the *Literary Digest* poll conducted in Michigan indicated that 11,207 of those contacted favored the Volstead Act and the Eighteenth Amendment in their existing form but that 14,374 favored either the legalization of wine and beer or the outright repeal of the Eighteenth Amendment. A separate poll of Michigan women, however, indicated that a majority favored the dry laws as they stood. The poll of Michigan workingmen showed them to be in favor of modification by 16,251 to 13,390. Yet the proportion of Michigan workingmen in favor of revision was far less than the average for workingmen in the nation as a whole. [4]

A 1926 poll conducted in Michigan by members of the Newspaper Enterprise Association (NEA) indicated that the citizens of Michigan were strongly attracted to the idea of Volstead Act revision, as the following figures indicate: [5]

Newspaper	For Prohibition	For Repeal	For Modification
Ironwood *Globe*	221	105	731
Iron Mountain *News*	175	181	616
Sturgis *Journal*	555	20	216
Coldwater *Daily Reporter*	513	68	295
Alpena *News*	230	256	1239
Sault Ste. Marie *News*	883	210	1033
Marshall *Chronicle*	202	0	244
Three Rivers *Commercial*	397	9	78
Dowagiac *Daily News*	402	43	229
Big Rapids *Pioneer*	978	76	283
Albion *Evening Recorder*	477	30	138
Marquette *Mining Journal*	518	656	1301
TOTALS	5551	1654	6403

Rather than being persuaded by such surveys, outspoken drys went to great ends to discredit them. They were little more than part of a great deceptive charade aimed at destroying confidence in the Eighteenth Amendment, it was asserted. In 1926 the president of the Michigan WCTU summed up the prohibitionist position on the critical opinion polls by claiming, "The newspapers take straw votes and the wets vote early and often. We who believe that prohibition is the only solution to the liquor problem, who know that all of the talk about light wine and beer, all of the straw votes and the differently worded referendums submitted in the last election are simply entering wedges to pry the Eighteenth Amendment from the Constitution, are not blind to the fact that enforcement has been made a political football."[6]

It appeared that a turning point of sorts in public opinion toward prohibition came in 1923. In that year New York repealed its "Baby Volstead Act," and an increasing amount of criticism appeared in the mass media. In the fall of 1923 the *Detroit News* ran a series of articles describing crime and the illegal liquor business in Detroit and concluded that prohibition had produced at least as much crime and corruption as had the saloon before it. Many Detroit churches set aside Sunday, September 16, 1923, as a day for sermons and discussions on prohibition. The public learned on that day that even some of the leading clergymen in the city questioned prohibition and favored some kind of revision of the existing law.[7]

Then, in the spring of 1925 the *Detroit Free Press* came out in favor of revision. "Reluctantly," the editor observed, "this newspaper arrives at the conviction that the Eighteenth Amendment was a fearful error, and that the most pressing domestic problem before the U.S. today is how to get rid of prohibition in its present extreme form and substitute for it moderate but effective liquor legislation that will have the support of public sentiment."[8]

Yet the question remained as to how wide was the public support for such sentiments. If there really was an increasing public thirst for legal light alcoholic beverages, then why was it manifested only in opinion polls and not at the voting polls? Each passing state and national election returned larger dry majorities to Lansing and Washington. Where were the wets on election day? The answer, for those who embraced the prohibition cause intemperately, was quite obvious. The public opinion polls were either inaccurate in their sampling or fixed in their published results. And what about the critical press? As in the old saloon days, the newspapers were stirring up controversy and sensationalism at the cost of accuracy. In other words, why worry? Those who are not for us must be deluded.

Some of prohibition's critics, nevertheless, plunged ahead in efforts to organize public thirst and register it at the polls. For nearly a decade their failures made up part of the orthodox dry lexicon concerning public sentiment and prohibition.

The main outlet for anti-prohibition sentiment was the Association

Against the Prohibition Amendment, incorporated December 31, 1920, "for educational purposes and mutual improvement." By publicizing every failure of bone-dry prohibition the AAPA tried to keep the wet and dry controversy alive. Eventually, the AAPA hoped, the American public would see through the prohibition experiment and would vote to neutralize the excesses and successes of the Anti-Saloon League, the Woman's Christian Temperance Union, and their allies and fellow travelers.[9]

What inspired AAPA opposition to prohibition? AAPA spokesmen insisted that the promises of the prohibitionists had not been realized. In their fanaticism the drys had outrun both public opinion and common sense. Temperance was a good thing, a desirable virtue, AAPA speakers conceded. Even prohibition was good for some people. But prohibition and temperance did not necessarily mean the bone-dry type that triumphed with the passage of the Volstead Act. Because of the unreasonableness and the blindness of the leaders of the prohibition cause, the AAPA contended, the Eighteenth Amendment had produced a plague rather than a paradise.

The most intriguing facet of AAPA propaganda before 1930 was the way in which it aped earlier prohibition arguments. The successes of the anti-saloon and anti-liquor crusade apparently had made such an impact in America that even critics of the dry law dared couch their arguments only in anti-liquor phrases. Rather than favoring the right of an individual to drink, AAPA speakers called for revision of prohibition in order to decrease public consumption of alcohol. Ironically, they insisted that revision of prohibition was a temperance measure. The AAPA, they revealed, was the "real anti-saloon league" of America. Consequently, for nearly a decade, Americans who really wanted a strong legal shot had no champions speaking directly for them either in or out of Congress. Not even the anti-prohibitionists ventured to say a kind word about John Barleycorn.[10]

Not only were many of the arguments and promises of the prohibition crusade taken over by the anti-prohibitionists, but wet leadership was drawn more and more from the ranks of former drys who claimed to have seen the light and who no longer saw as through the bottom of a glass darkly. AAPA converts revealed that their disillusionment was with the alleged results of the Eighteenth Amendment and not with the social or economic ideals of the prohibitionists. And their publications tended to document that claim. One early AAPA broadside asserted, "Beer and Light Wines *Now*, But No Saloon Ever." And one of the first AAPA pamphlets listed as the ideals of prohibition modification: a contented citizenry, less drunkenness, less public graft, better and safer highways, and improved police protection for life and property. "We look forward now to the day when prohibition with its brood of speakeasies, home-brew kitchens, bootleggers, bomb throwers, and snoopers will follow the saloon system out of the nation's back door," Henry Curran of the AAPA said. [11]

AAPA officials also alleged that a primary fault of the Eighteenth Amendment was the way it led to a dangerous overextension of the power of the federal government and the consequent straining of the federal system. The traditional balance between the states and the central government and the built-in responsiveness to local conditions of a truly federal system had been breached by the passage of national prohibition. Whether this had occurred by accident or by deliberate design was debatable (many members of the AAPA, however, believed it was part of a conspiracy on the part of the Anti-Saloon League and the Methodists). AAPA officials warned that the overextension of government police power brought with it the certain destruction of American liberties. And the harder the government worked to enforce the prohibition laws, the greater the danger that individual freedoms other than that of choosing to drink, would be sacrificed. Modification, on the other hand, by making prohibition easier to enforce, would restore the true federal system, reduce the government bureaucracy, and restore the freer atmosphere of the prewar days.

In this argument, the anti-prohibitionists struck one of the most sensitive nerves of the dry establishment. For in general economic and political ideology, the prohibitionists and their critics shared a common conservative outlook. The promise of prohibition had included less expensive, simpler, less pervasive government and the realization of a free, productive, self-regulated economy. Saloons and saloon-related crimes and accidents created the need for big expensive police departments, prisons, hospitals, courts, revenue agents, and inspectors. The people employed in these fields, it was expected, would soon find more productive employment once prohibition went into effect. But it didn't happen. In fact, each year, much to their embarrassment, the prohibitionists saw the enforcement machinery increase in power, numbers, and budget. At first, such increases were viewed as temporary. But before long they were seen as ominous signs of things to come. A pervasive police state seemed to spring up where one was neither expected nor wanted. All agreed—wet and dry—on its dangers. Every prohibition agent, every border patrol boat in pursuit of illegal liquor, every federal attorney prosecuting rum runners, and every jail cell filled with a liquor-law offender was an argument that prohibition as it existed had outraced public sentiment. Each day such a law stayed on the books brought the American Way of Life into greater danger. [12]

The AAPA sought to save America from its well-intentioned dry subversives by supporting outspoken anti-prohibition candidates for public office. When elected, however, AAPA-blessed politicians were advised to cooperate with dry majorities. William Stayton, president of the AAPA for most of the 1920s, believed that the organization might undermine its own position if it supported obstructionist tactics and fought appropriations for prohibition enforcement. Stayton explained to Henry B. Joy that the drys would probably move more and more to the position of "give us twenty-five more years to try the experiment." "We, of course, do not want any such nonsensical thing," Stayton said, "but if we, the wets, throw any obstacles in the way of the drys so far as organization and appropriations are concerned, they will have some excuse and say that their law has not had a fair show and after consultation with a good many of our friends in Congress the Association has taken the attitude that we will not try to defeat at the present time any appropriations and that we will not object to any form of organization the drys ask for. We will give them, in short, all of the rope they want to take and we will be careful not to let them accuse us of obstructive politics." Of course, Stayton concluded, "when the time comes that we can win, we shall expect to give open battle." [13]

The Michigan chapter of the AAPA was organized in 1921. Under the direction of Dr. John Slevin, the Michigan branch worked throughout most of the 1920s to revise the state prohibition laws. Slevin declared that his organization hoped to secure the enactment of a law legalizing light wines and beer by "organizing the unorganized majority, by crystalizing the anti-prohibition sentiment and directing it into channels which will bring about the enactment of the law for which the majority clamor." He said that the principal activity of his organization would be voter education. No lobbies would be maintained by the state AAPA, he promised, and there would be no lavish expenditure of money, no bribery, and "no star chamber methods." Money was to be expended by the organization, Slevin explained, only to tell the public who was for and who against the AAPA programs. [14]

Despite its moderate program, the AAPA was fiercely denounced in Michigan by dry spokesmen. Congressman Louis Cramton described the organization as a group "opposed to law enforcement, promoting, thriving upon, and rejoicing at the triumph of crime and disorder over law and order. It brazenly proclaims by its title its opposition to a part of the Constitution of the United States, the fundamental law of the land." Cramton asserted that the country had little to fear from organized bootleggers and criminals, but a real danger was posed by men in high places, "fitted for and insisting upon leadership," who lent their names and their influence to a direct attack upon the Constitution and sought to justify its nullification. "Then lovers of law and order had better pay due regard," he warned. [15]

In his intemperate outburst, Cramton, like many other prohibitionists, misread the conservative nature of the AAPA. In Michigan the organization did not call for the repeal of the Eighteenth Amendment. It called simply for modification and state enforcement. It was against the Eighteenth Amendment as it was presently administered. And the organization never endorsed nullification of the Eighteenth Amendment or of any other law. In fact the AAPA was as strict on issues of law enforcement as was any dry organization. The primary difference between the law-and-order position of the wets and that of the drys in the mid-1920s lay in the fact that the AAPA believed bone-dry federal prohibition was unenforceable and consequently undermined all enforcement efforts and bred public disrespect for all law. Law and order could be established and maintained only when the law reflected true public sentiment. And state governments—which the AAPA believed should rule on and administer liquor laws—were more responsive to local sentiment. The drys, on the other hand, believed that law and order could be maintained only in a nation where there was no legal liquor traffic and where bone-dry prohibition was enforced uniformly throughout the nation by the federal government.

Eventually, critics of the anti-prohibition cause pointed to the great wealth enjoyed by many leaders of the AAPA and insisted that the primary motive of the organization was self-interest. It was charged that the AAPA believed that modification of the prohibition law would lower taxes significantly, and so they worked to change or abolish the Eighteenth Amendment because they were deluded into thinking it fiscally wise. But long before economic arguments became central to the anti-prohibition cause, many wealthy businessmen in Michigan joined the AAPA for conscience sake alone, they said. The Eighteenth Amendment weakened the social fabric to a greater degree than did the saloon, they believed, and it threatened the traditional American value system by bestowing wealth and prestige upon the lawbreaker, the bootlegger and the rum runner. The outspoken leaders of the AAPA believed that the Eighteenth Amendment, unlike the free enterprise system they idealized, rewarded hypocrisy and punished honesty and hard work, and this greatly disturbed them. It disturbed them enough, in fact, to work for whatever changes were necessary in the law to bring back what they saw as good and right and just in the American System.[16]

The AAPA's first efforts to modify the Michigan state prohibition law and to legalize the manufacture and sale of beer and light wine came in 1923. Robert Wardell of Detroit, secretary of the Michigan chapter of the AAPA and director of the Michigan Moderation League, led the fight for change. In the fall of 1923, Wardell sought to increase AAPA membership in the state in order to launch a massive campaign aimed at placing a prohibition referendum on the ballot. He placed advertisements in the leading Detroit newspapers asking readers to fill out AAPA membership applications and return them to him. Those who turned in the applications received a membership card, a membership button, and five additional cards to be issued to prospective members. In late September Wardell claimed that his organization included members in sixty-three of the state's eighty-three counties and had a total membership of nearly 27,000. He explained that this massive organization would not only support Senator James Couzens, a leading critic of bone-dry prohibition, but would launch a drive to place a modification proposal on the state ballot in November. Each of the 27,000 members was sent a petition with space for twenty-five names on it. Since only 63,000 signatures were required to place a referendum measure on the state ballot, if each of the AAPA members secured only three names, the measure could be placed before the voters of the state.

For the next several weeks the AAPA and the Michigan Moderation League gathered signatures to petitions requesting that the electorate be allowed to vote on a measure providing for the sale of alcoholic beverages that did not exceed legal U.S. Government standards, prohibiting the consumption of those beverages on the premises where the sale took place, taxing the production and sale of alcoholic beverages, and applying the resulting revenues to the retirement of the state's bonds and the construction and maintenance of county and state highways and institutions. In this effort Wardell combined a twin appeal that would eventually become central to the revisionist-repeal movement: the success of his measure would not only mean the return of legal mild booze, which was appealing to many voters, but also revenue for state and county treasuries would facilitate a reduction of taxes. [17]

Wardell gathered the necessary number of signatures for his petitions, but the state Anti-Saloon League raised the question of the petition's legality. The state constitution provided that every petition should include the full text of any amendment proposed for a statewide referendum, and Wardell's petition did not meet this requirement. The state Attorney General upheld the League's contention and informed Wardell that his measure could not be placed on the state ballot in November 1924. Wardell immediately petitioned the state Supreme Court for a reversal of the Attorney General's ruling, but the court refused to issue even an order to show cause, thereby bringing to an end the 1923-24 effort to modify the state prohibition law. [18]

In March 1927 Wardell introduced a resolution in the state legislature calling for a November 1928 referendum on an amendment to the state constitution providing for the sale, under state control, of beer and light wines for use in the home. Following the same legislative procedures that the drys used when they fought to secure statewide prohibition, Wardell promised that if the legislature would not act on his proposal, he would launch another petition drive and force the placement of his measure on the ballot. Wardell believed that the two major advantages of his 1927 bill were that it both insured against the return of the saloon in any form and that it would "terminate hypocrisy." His proposed resolution, however, was not reported out by the hostile House prohibition committee. [19]

As he had promised, Wardell set to work on another petition drive. A few days before the final deadline for presenting his petitions to the Secretary of State, Wardell filed 5,000 of the necessary 63,076 signatures. He promised to file the remainder later, but when the July 5, 1928, deadline passed, Wardell still had not filed them, and all chances for a referendum on prohibition in the fall of 1928 passed. Wardell offered no public explanation for his failure. Whether he found it impossible to gather the required number of signatures or whether he was convinced that such a measure would be easily defeated remained unknown. In the spring of 1929 Wardell again introduced a measure in the state House of Representatives to allow for the manufacture and sale of strong beer and light wine for home consumption, but once again his measure was not reported out by the House prohibition committee. [20]

As of late 1929 all but two of Michigan's congressmen were bone dry, the state legislature was dominated by the drys, and the greatest hope of the wets, the AAPA thought, lay in a revision of the state constitution to allow for the manufacture and sale of light wines and beer. Even if passed in Michigan, of course, such a measure would not go into effect until a similar revision had been made in the national dry law. There was outspoken criticism of bone-dry prohibition. But the drys remained securely in control. The idea that prohibition was a failure could not be registered on election day.

Then, suddenly, the entire situation shifted dramatically. The plans and expectations of both drys and wets were completely transformed.

"If you wish to be set down as the craziest of prophets by any of the men whom you have watched going about their affairs in the glaring sunlight of September 3, 1929, you would have only to tell them that within two months they were to witness the greatest financial panic in American history, and that it will usher in a prolonged and desperate economic crisis," Frederick Lewis Allen recorded in *Since Yesterday*, a study of America in the 1930s. Yet on that very day, the Great Bull Market peaked. The next day it declined, and by the end of October it was racing downward, destroying millions of dollars in investments. With the crash of the stock market in the last months of 1929 and with prosperity fleeing, "Americans were soon to find themselves living in an altered world which called for new adjustments, new ideas, new habits of thought, and a new order of values. The Post-war Decade had come to a close." Prohibition was an ideal and a dream of Americans in the good times of the 1920s. When the good times came to an end, prohibition was rapidly relegated to the scrapheap of outdated illusions. The depression destroyed prohibition. [21]

The deflation of the economy had an immediate impact in Michigan. Unemployment increased rapidly in the last three months of 1929; in September about 56,800 workers in the state were unemployed, but the number rose to 111,800 in October, 212,500 in November, and 249,400 in December. During the next three years unemployment in Michigan averaged 34 percent of the nonagricultural work force, as compared with 26 percent for the entire country. After only two years of depression, the number of dependents on Detroit's relief rolls was equal in size to the entire population of Grand Rapids. [22]

Numerous schemes were proposed for relieving the distress of the depression, ranging from the humanitarian to the absurd. One panacea that quickly gained public attention was the repeal of the Eighteenth Amendment. For many years, as a result of successful dry propaganda, prohibition had been associated closely with the economy. After 1919 prohibition's champions had attributed the nation's economic prosperity almost exclusively to the dry laws. Now with the dramatic collapse of the economy, all of prohibition's economic propaganda toppled over onto its proponents. Opponents of prohibition asked Americans to remember how many workers had been employed in the breweries before prohibition, how many had been employed as bartenders, how many had been employed in the allied trades of the liquor business, and how much money came into the government coffers as a result of the licensing and taxation of the alcoholic beverage business. The saloon need never return, the wets said, but if the production and sale of booze were once again legalized, more people could be put to work, the government would gain revenue, unemployment would be alleviated, and the depression could be ended. [23]

With public attention more and more fastened on the effects of the depression, the anti-prohibitionists began to place emphasis almost exclusively upon the economic advantages of repeal of the Eighteenth Amendment. Wet speakers argued not only that their measure would bring law and order, a restoration of the proper distribution of power between the federal government and local government, and true temperance, but also an end to the depression, the undermining of radical movements that had sprung up among the unemployed, and a new industrial Eden as perfect as that promised years earlier by the prohibitionists. For an American public searching for simple solutions to the depression, the wets provided very attractive answers.

The economic case for repeal was detailed carefully in Leslie Gordon's *The New Crusade*, in 1930. An introduction to Gordon's book by "S.R." stated that "before prosperity can return to this country the budgets of local and national governments must be balanced." The easiest way to accomplish this, the writer said, was to legalize liquor and then tax it. "If the liquor now sold by bootleggers was legally sold, regulated, and taxed, the excise income would pay the interest on the entire local and national bonded indebtedness and leave more than $200,000 for other urgently needed purposes. And while the government treasuries were being revived the power of the bootlegger would be broken and our country could once more become the law-abiding land of security that the forefathers of this country intended that it should be." With proper sharing of liquor revenues, "the tax assessments on the farms and on the small communities will be reduced to that point where the farmer, the small home owner and the small businessman will see daylight again." [24]

Addressing a crowd of 3,500 enthusiastic wets a short time before the election of 1932, Jouett Shouse of the AAPA explained the economic benefits of repeal. Under prohibition, Shouse claimed, the federal government had lost about $1,000,000 annually, an amount that could have been applied to the national debt throughout the twenties. If liquor were marketed under government supervision, Shouse contended, the resulting revenue would provide major relief for the individual taxpayer, who would also benefit because the government would no longer have to spend money to enforce prohibition since there would be greater respect for law and order and hence lower costs for law enforcement. [25]

In the depths of the depression the Detroit *Saturday Night* pointed to the economic results of liquor control in Quebec. In that Canadian province the liquor commission provided nearly $10 million annually in profits from the sale of liquor, much of it purchased by Americans visiting Canada. It followed, the *Saturday Night* reasoned, that if booze were legalized, the same profits could be realized in America. Establishing that repeal would yield an annual profit of not less than $800,000, the *Saturday Night* concluded that this "could relieve the pressure of the present depression and perhaps start a business revival that would crack it for keeps." [26]

Robert Wardell estimated that an excise tax on booze in Michigan would significantly decrease the real estate taxes which had become a serious burden in the depression. During pre-prohibition days, Wardell pointed out, Michigan levied about $15 million in taxes on real estate each year, but by 1930 that figure had doubled. Wardell predicted that an excise tax after repeal would restore the property taxes to their original level and reduce the state's deficit by $10 million. Wardell estimated that as much as $75 million spent annually on liquor by Michigan visitors to Canada could be returned to the domestic market, creating jobs and bringing a "general improvement in economic conditions." [27]

The economic benefits of repeal were given credence by the results of a state tax on malt passed in 1929 by the state legislature. In the closing days of the 1929 legislative session, legislators passed the malt-tax measure in the hope of returning over $2 million to the state treasury for the relief of depressed school districts. The statute provided for a tax of five cents per pound on malt syrup and extract and a small tax on wort, a basic ingredient of beer. Since these newly taxed products were used almost exclusively in the production of home-brewed beer, the state, for all practical purposes, had decided to tax the illegal booze traffic. In 1931 the legislature passed a similar measure over the veto of dry Governor Wilbur Brucker, who asserted that the taxation of an illegal product was "wrong in principle and vicious in practice." In a single year the tax raised over $500,000 in Detroit alone. Since the measure successfully produced a good deal of revenue, many people concluded that the anti-prohibitionists' economic arguments were sound. [28]

Mayor Frank Murphy of Detroit soon became an outspoken advocate of the economic benefits of repeal. Like other leading prohibition critics, Murphy was not opposed to the initial dry goals. "What was sought by prohibition is nothing but commendable," he wrote in reply to a dry inquiry in mid-1932. But an "unreasoning attitude crept into prohibition legislation and its enforcement," he contended, and "made it impractical in great areas of the country." "We both want the same thing," Murphy concluded, "good government and, as a consequence, a well-governed and happy people. There will have to be a correction in the prohibition law if this is to be brought about." [29]

Although he warned against making prohibition "a dump heap for all of our economic ills," he also pointed out that "we cannot avoid the fact that a reasonable tax on beer alone would bring $700,000,000 a year into the public treasury." Such a tax would also be equitable, Murphy asserted, since it was paid "only by those who chose to make themselves subject thereto." "Every citizen with the welfare of suffering humanity at heart, should give earnest consideration to the economic aspect of this proposal," Murphy suggested. [30]

In the spring of 1932 Mayor Murphy became a member of the Executive Committee of the Michigan Civic League Repeal Parade Committee in Detroit. The group organized a giant repeal parade and rally in Detroit. The slogans and banners carried in the parade testified once again to the miracle repeal was expected to bring. Among the slogans were: Better Business By Brewing; This Procession to End Depression; Bring Back Beer to Bear the Burden; Bring Back Beer and Better Business; Dry Failure or Wet Prosperity; Billions Spent or Billions Saved; Taxes Tell the Tale; Prohibition and Poverty or Beer and Business. The letterhead of the organization read, "Which shall it be, Poison Liquor or Everybody in Health and Happiness. Repeal the State Prohibition Law, Bringing Back Prosperity, Liberty, and Lower Taxes." [31]

But many people worried over the morality as well as the logic of the economic arguments for repeal. "I think 'Soup' comes ahead of beer," one man wrote to Murphy, "and I am opposed to weak minded men spending money for beer which should go for food and clothing for their families." "We are living in the days when the prophets foretold that satan would be doing his stuff," the writer warned, "but I do not propose to help him along with it, even if he would pay a tax for the privilege." [32]

Opponents of prohibition also rather blithely linked the dry law to the rise of radicalism during the depression and suggested that repeal would undermine this disturbing development. Before a special committee of the House Judiciary Committee in 1930, Congressman Robert Clancy warned that "this is a rather dangerous time, with the people in the cities, which hold 60 per cent of the population of this country, in great discontent because of prohibition and also in great discontent because of the unemployment situation." Clancy noted that just a few days previously a mob of unemployed in Cleveland had attacked city hall and battled the police. "They have announced meetings, the 'red' workers and the socialists and communists, to stir up discontent in Cleveland, and I now hold in my hand a 'red' placard, announcing the big meetings in Detroit sponsored by the communists, socialists and bolshevists, who are taking advantage of the unemployment situation, which is very serious. They issued a statement saying that there are 6,000,000 unemployed in the United States now, and that there will shortly be 10,000,000 unemployed." The radicals of Detroit demanded that the blacks be organized for the socialist and bolshevik cause, Clancy warned, and their appeal was being given a hearing because many blacks were unemployed and suffering. The Reds were also trying to organize the foreign-born, many of whom were also out of work. All of this was extremely dangerous, Clancy said, "because in my city 80 per cent of the population are very much dissatisfied with the government because of its stand on the dry question, and that is true in Cleveland, and as you know, in the large cities of the United States, and there is also quite a bit of discontent in the rural communities." Clancy assured the committee, nevertheless, that America would be "safe" as long as there were officials "who are fair and statesmanlike, and allow free discussion of grievous wrongs like the Eighteenth Amendment." [33]

Two years later, at a Senate hearing on the prohibition amendment, Matthew Woll, vice president of the American Federation of Labor, followed Clancy's lead and blamed radicalism in the United States on the Eighteenth Amendment. Former Governor Fred Green voiced concern over the violation of the Eighteenth Amendment and the continued existence of the United States as a free country. To Green, the very survival of the Republic hinged on nothing less than the immediate repeal of the Eighteenth Amendment. [34]

The repeal cause eventually marshalled an impressive array of sci-

entific statistics to its side just as the drys had done in their earlier prohibition campaign. Findings were published indicating that moderate
drinkers lived longer than total abstainers, alcohol was important in
treating disease, beer in the diet of pregnant women helped build
strong teeth in their children, and 4 percent beer was nonintoxicating.
All of these figures and more were circulated throughout the 1920s in
the middle-class-oriented magazines and were effectively used by the
AAPA and other repeal organizations. But the day of scientifically
gathered statistics swaying the public was passing, and now the public
was more interested, it seemed, in simple arguments, like those equa-
ting repeal with prosperity. If breweries and distilleries and liquor
stores could be opened, people would be put to work, thousands of
people, tens of thousands of people. That seemed simple logic. And
greatly appealing logic. [35]

The forces of repeal sought the endorsement of leading public figures in order to add luster and prestige to their cause. Before 1932 in
Michigan, however, they were disappointed in such efforts. Businessmen of national repute were reluctant to speak out on the repeal issue
in Michigan because of the policies of Alfred P. Sloan, Jr., of General
Motors and Henry Ford of the Ford Motor Company. When the wet-
and-dry debate intensified with the deepening of the depression,
Sloan forbade any member of the General Motors Corporation in
Michigan to express any opinion whatever on prohibition. Ford, on
the other hand, stood 100 percent behind prohibition and decreed
that no member of the Ford organization should speak out in behalf
of either modification or repeal. "The attitude of these two men,"
Henry Joy wrote, "sets the pace for the general businessmen, industrial leaders, and men in the banking world in our community. Bank-
ers will not speak out on either side for fear they may lose Ford deposits or General Motors deposits, or the deposits of those allied with
those respective companies. And so on down the line, throughout."
Joy said that many of Detroit's leading businessmen told him that
they would like to see the dry laws repealed but that they were opposed
to making "a public issue" out of the question. Some of them contributed anonymously to the repeal organizations, Joy claimed. [36]

A major breakthrough for the Michigan wets finally occurred in
June 1932 when Sloan announced that he favored repeal of the Eighteenth Amendment and strict government control of the liquor traf-

fic. Yet, like other wet converts, Sloan cautiously couched the reasons for his conversion in terms of his concern for true temperance. Sloan announced that he was "definitely content that the road toward greater temperance with a resulting better standard of ethics in our country is through repeal." He cited increases in the liquor traffic, lawlessness, and racketeering, as well as economic loss from prohibition as the main factors influencing his change in sentiment. Sloan asserted his belief that with repeal "lawlessness will no longer be subsidized and as a very important and vital economic consideration, industry will be relieved from part of the heavy burden of taxation through an increase in Government revenue made possible by placing the sale of liquor under governmental auspices instead of as now conducted. It is my belief," he concluded, "that our whole social and economic structure will in this manner be greatly strengthened and the real foundation built for renewed prosperity." [37]

While many leading businessmen and industrialists remained publicly uncommitted on the prohibition question, the wets won important endorsements from some major organizations. The American Federation of Labor had favored revision throughout the 1920s, and in early 1931 the Michigan Federation of Labor adopted a resolution demanding the total repeal of the Eighteenth Amendment. The principal reason given for the MFL's championship of repeal was that prohibition "had failed utterly in its avowed purpose and was largely responsible for the present economic conditions." [38]

The national convention of the American Legion met in Detroit in 1931, and members of the state's repeal organizations worked assiduously to secure from the Legionnaires a resolution favoring modification or repeal of the Eighteenth Amendment. Previously the Legion had avoided what it considered to be controversial political subjects, and at the national convention in 1930 the national commander had ruled out of order a resolution presented on the floor calling for the repeal of the Eighteenth Amendment. There was, however, outspoken sentiment at the 1931 convention in favor of repeal. The growth of anti-prohibition sentiment among the Legionnaires was striking in view of the fact that the strength of the Legion was concentrated in the small towns and rural districts of the country. The decline of sentiment for prohibition in the countryside was an extremely dangerous signal for the drys.

The repealists at the Legion convention, led by Col. Fred Alger of Detroit, were successful in securing a resolution stating that the Eighteenth Amendment "has created a condition endangering respect for law and the security of American institutions, therefore be it resolved that the American Legion in this thirteenth annual convention assembled favors the submission by Congress of the repeal or modification of the present prohibition laws to the several states with a request that each state submit this question to the voters thereof." The measure was reported out by the special resolutions committee after a prolonged session during which advocates of a declaration for outright repeal argued stubbornly with the prohibitionists, who sought to keep the issue from being submitted to the delegates at all. Alger wrote to Henry Joy during the convention, "In the whole history of the Legion there has never been such a bitter fight." The resolution was adopted by a vote of 1,008 to 394. [39]

Yet rapidly increasing anti-prohibition sentiment after 1929 did not bring a rush of new members into the AAPA. Ironically, the organization was in a very precarious situation in the fall of 1930. After financially overextending itself in crucial congressional campaigns the victorious state AAPA found itself over $120,000 in debt. [40]

The AAPA was laboring under such great difficulties in late 1930 that its directors decided that a major reorganization of the body was necessary. Henry Joy and Col. Alger were appointed by the national directors to consider how the state organization could be made more effective and more economical. The two men concluded that the AAPA should cooperate more closely with other repeal groups so that the finances of all could be closely coordinated and duplication of effort avoided. It was decided that the Michigan AAPA should not aim at a large membership as Wardell had done in the mid-1920s but should rather be composed of only about 150 or at most 300 "influential men" in the state. Ideally, this small membership was to be scattered throughout the key counties of Michigan, with a large nucleus in Wayne County, where Detroit was located. It was hoped that the AAPA could thus play a directing role for organization and provide financial management for the entire repeal movement. [41]

In early 1931 the state AAPA was further centralized and control of the organization passed into the hands of three directors—Joy, Alger, and Sidney T. Miller. These three were authorized by the organization's national leadership to make policy decisions without conferring with other members in the state because the others, according to Alger, were "not active, and are somewhat difficult to move." This triumvirate was tagged the Michigan Committee of the National Association Against the Prohibition Amendment. [42]

Following the reorganization Stayton informed Joy that it was necessary for the AAPA to counter the popular impression that the leading business executives and industrialists favored repeal simply for economic reasons that might be reduced to self-interest. Joy was accordingly authorized to recruit "men of large affairs to take a stand definitely and publicly on the prohibition issue" on other than economic grounds and to offer them membership in the AAPA in return for the use of their names. Names of prospective members were forwarded to Stayton, who then arranged to contact them through other prominent members of the AAPA. [43]

Despite the emergence of hundreds of grass-roots repeal groups and committees after 1929, effective leadership of the anti-prohibition movement remained in the hands of the AAPA and its two chief subsidiaries, the Crusaders and the Women's Organization for National Prohibition Reform (WONPR). The Crusaders were founded in Cleveland, Ohio, in 1929. The organization soon spread across the country by forming local chapters in major cities, its initial aim being to establish a chapter in every American city of over 25,000 population. Fred G. Clark, a Cleveland oil man, became the Crusaders' first commander-in-chief, and the first executive board consisted of fifty prominent citizens from the Northern and Eastern states. Despite efforts to recruit large numbers of members, however, the Crusaders, like the AAPA, ultimately depended upon the prestige and wealth of its membership rather than on its size. [44]

In 1930 the Crusaders began to organize divisions of young men under the age of thirty in Detroit. At that time one of the Michigan organizers explained to the *Free Press*, "We are a temperance, not a wet organization." The *Free Press* endorsed the calm approach of the Crusaders toward the liquor problem and described them as "a middle of the road movement, composed of reasonable and reasoning people who will look at facts as they are and proceed accordingly. If the Crusaders prove to be the pioneers of such a movement they will deserve the name they have adopted." [45]

Leslie Gordon's *The New Crusade* (1930) explained further both the concern of the members of the organization and their program of action. The book reads like a pre-1919 tract from the WCTU. The Crusaders, Gordon said, were insulted and outraged by the corruption in politics and law enforcement that accompanied the existing prohibition laws. The Crusader "warms under the collar when he hears the rumble of whiskey trucks on the highway and realizes that it is the neutrality of corrupted police officers that permits them to travel," an introduction to the book explained. Yet the Crusader understood that the blame for the flagrant law violation did not lie with the average police official. "He believes that under normal conditions all of these police agencies would take the bootlegger by the neck and vigorously give him his just desserts." But the power behind the police officer was the one corrupted by payoffs from liquor sellers. Echoing exactly the earlier dry propaganda, the Crusader recognized "the corrupt liason between the king botleggers and the ward heelers and leaders of local political machines is the most dangerous factor now facing the public. Ward heeling politicians protect ward-catering speakeasies and bootleggers." Corruption existed also when liquor was legal, and in both cases it was founded upon unscrupulously acquired profits from liquor sales. As a result, "the Crusader intends to use all his individual and organized strength to take the profit from the liquor traffic." [46]

According to Crusader founder Clark, members of the organization "interested in the salvation of society" believed that "actual temperance is so vitally necessary to the future welfare of this country that he is going to fight for it with every law-abiding power at his command." The Crusader, Clark wrote, "respects to the point of veneration the legions of silver-haired women and gray-haired men who gave the best part of their lives in placing the Eighteenth Amendment on the statute books. He thrills to the idealism that prompted the great temperance movement of fifty years ago, of thirty years ago, and twenty years ago." Clark assured those Americans who remembered the saloon that the Crusaders would fight hard to prevent that institution from ever being re-established. "He is determined that the licensed saloon must stay closed—the speakeasy saloon must be closed and the power of greed and profit must be removed from the traffic in alcoholic beverages." Clark concluded that the Crusader "believes that when sincere temperance people understand his motives, they will back his Crusade, since the principles he stands for are practically the same code of principles the WCTU adopted when present day gray-haired mothers were children in short dresses."[47]

At first the Crusaders operated in much the same way as the AAPA in Michigan and there was much duplication of effort by the two groups. Both organizations sent questionnaires to candidates for political office requesting information on their position regarding prohibition. Both sought to work through the electoral process to defeat dry candidates.[48]

The Crusaders soon changed from an organization of men under thirty to a group of men in their twenties, thirties, and forties who had either been too young to vote when the Eighteenth Amendment had been adopted or had been serving in the army at the time. These members, according to Clark, had come to believe that prohibition was responsible for "increasing hypocrisy, corruption and disregard for the law in the country." The goal of the new organization was "a solid, militant body determined to substitute true temperance for intemperance and prohibition." In Michigan the Crusaders announced that their members could be either wet or dry and had only to agree that existing conditions were intolerable. Clark described the group as "neither dreamers or fanatics," but as simply men who had "had enough lawlessness, bootlegging, highjacking, poison whiskey selling, shooting innocent citizens, gin parties attended by innocent high-school girls and boys and rum parties attended by dry agents and other hypocrites; of whisky flasks on the hips of college and high school men at gatherings of all kinds; ... of huge sums spent futilely in vain attempts to control men's appetites by legislation and of absolute disregard for the distinctions between drunkards and temperate users of liquor."[49]

Crusaders in Michigan were drawn almost without exception from the ranks of the Republican Party; and although the organization claimed nonpartisanship, it was almost exclusively Republican in its political activities. Indeed, what the AAPA, the Crusaders, and the WONPR hoped to accomplish before the fall of 1932 was to make the Republican party wet rather than to bring the already wet Democratic Party into power. Accordingly their principal political effort was to defeat dry candidates in Republican primaries.

The dilemma of the Republican wets was illustrated in 1930 when Alger, prominent in both the AAPA and the Crusaders, endorsed the dry Republican gubernatorial candidate, Wilbur M. Brucker, over the wet Democrat, William A. Comstock. In supporting Brucker, Alger rationalized his position by claiming that, if elected, Brucker would be "governed by the will of the people" with regard to prohibition. Frank A. Picard, Comstock's aide and one of the few leading Democratic Crusaders, protested that Alger was attempting to delude the electorate into believing that Brucker was potentially a wet. Picard pointed out to Alger, "You are not in favor of the State of Michigan being wet. You are in favor of the Republican Party being wet. If that will bring about prohibition in the state you are in favor of prohibition but you won't look at the big question because of your firm belief that if anything is to be done in this state the Democrats—though they help pay taxes, though they help support our government—cannot be expected to perform any political good." [50]

Two other Democratic congressional candidates complained bitterly about the failure of the Michigan branch of the AAPA to support Comstock in the gubernatorial race: Edward Frensdorf of Hudson and Michael J. Hart of Saginaw publicly criticized the two-faced policies of both the AAPA and the Crusaders. In response to an AAPA questionnaire, Frensdorf replied that he had concluded that "both wet and dry organizations in our state are strictly adjuncts of the Republican Party." Hart observed, "The general impression seems to be that the AAPA is the left wing of the Republican Party the same as the Anti-Saloon League is the right wing of the Republican Party. Just looking from the side lines," he wrote, "I would say that it is the purpose of this association to do just enough work, and create enough sentiment, and cause a change in the Republican party's attitude toward this question of prohibition and then join them." [51]

The third major repeal group was the WONPR, founded by Mrs. Charles Sabin in the spring of 1929 following meetings of several "society leaders" in New York and Chicago. The group first called itself the Women's Legion for True Temperance, but later changed its title to the WONPR. The first Michigan WONPR chapter was formed in Detroit in December 1929. A year later effective chapters were meeting in Kalamazoo and Battle Creek, and by the end of 1931 there were WONPR locals in nearly every sizeable community in the southern half of the lower peninsula. According to an early historian of the WONPR, the Michigan branch of the organization recruited most of its members by canvassing rural districts of the state. The leadership and membership list appearing in the papers at the time, however, included almost exclusively women from urban and suburban areas.[52]

The WONPR membership consisted of women from the upper social stratum, many of them wives of officers in the AAPA. The Michigan WONPR, headed by Mrs. Fred Alger, carried on a struggle for goals strikingly similar to those sought earlier by the WCTU. Mrs. Alger made this clear when she explained, "One thing I would like to emphasize is that those working for the repeal of the Michigan dry law are not trying to make it easier to obtain liquor. We are trying to make it more difficult; we are trying to regulate and control the sale of liquor; trying to wipe out the dives that infest Detroit and the rest of the state; trying to bring liquor from vile resorts that lure and ruin our young people into the sunlight where we can at least see what is going on and apply intensive restrictive measures." Mrs. Alger said she believed that the majority of people in the state accepted the view of the WONPR and favored true temperance, rather than prohibition, "which did nothing except cause intemperance." The pledge card for the organization read, "Because I believe that prohibition has increased crime, lawlessness, hypocrisy and corruption; because I believe that the cause of real temperance has been retarded and that sumptuary laws have no place in the Federal Constitution, I enroll as a member of this organization, which is working for some change in the law to bring about a sane solution of the problem without the return of the saloon."[53]

Because the WONPR drew to its ranks women from the upper social stratum who had not previously participated actively in political disputes, it was denounced by the drys for engaging in a controversy about which it knew next to nothing. Reverend Robert Atkins, pastor of the First Methodist Church of Birmingham, Michigan, claimed that "possibly no other group of women in America is less in touch with the common life or humanity." "It is notorious," he asserted, "that in their homes and clubs liquors are served with impunity and immunity and that there are drunkards in Bloomfield Hills whose debauches would disgrace a pagan social order." Atkins commented that the society women who belonged to the new organization were suffering from "an intellectual squint."[54]

Like the AAPA and the Crusaders, the WONPR was reluctant to practice the nonpartisanship that it preached. The women who made up the WONPR leadership were from wealthy Republican families; the Alger family itself was one of the leading Republican families in the state. Thus, when Democratic candidates endorsed repeal the WONPR was hesitant in supporting them. It required a heated seven-hour session in July 1932 for the national executive committee of the WONPR to produce a resolution "urging" members of the organization to support the national Democratic ticket, which was committed to outright repeal of the Eighteenth Amendment. The use of the word "urge" was significant—the vote of the members was not to be used as an acid test of their loyalty to the WONPR. Sixty-two prominent members of the WONPR repudiated the action of their executive committee by signing a statement that advised each member to vote for the presidential candidate "who is best qualified to lead the nation, regardless of the prohibition issue." "To make the position of the candidate towards control of the liquor traffic the sole test of his fitness for the office of president," the rebel group stated, "is the very negation of our responsibilities as citizens." Mrs. Alger ignored the rebels and, following the instructions of the national executive committee, urged the Michigan WONPR members to vote for Roosevelt and Garner because they were pledged to repeal. In the congressional races, Mrs. Alger said, "We will endorse any candidate who openly favors repeal of the Eighteenth Amendment, Republican or Democrat." WONPR regulars hoped to make it impossible for any political candidate in 1932 to straddle the repeal issue. "It has turned into a barbed wire fence between two camps," a WONPR member warned dry Congressman Earl Michener, "neither a safe nor a dignified seat for any candidate."[55]

In the fall of 1932, the AAPA, WONPR, and Crusaders formed the Michigan Repeal Fund Committee to coordinate the financing of all the major repeal organizations. The Committee set out to raise $70,000 to finance the campaigns of repeal candidates in the November election. The anti-prohibition campaign of the repeal groups came to a head in November 1932 in a final effort to repeal the prohibition amendment to the state constitution.[56]

In early 1931, Robert Wardell had initiated another petition drive to amend the state constitution and repeal prohibition. Wardell's 1931 initiative measure, like all his previous initiative petitions, provided simply for the legalization of light wine and beer under super-vision by the state. But after ten months and the gathering of only 22,000 signatures, Wardell gave up the drive. Then, in January 1932, the Crusaders and the WONPR began a new public petition drive— the Red, White and Blue Petition—which, unlike Wardell's propos-als, provided for the repeal of the state prohibition law and the estab-lishment of a state liquor control commission to regulate the alcohol-ic beverage traffic in the state and set the standards regarding legal percentage of alcohol in beverages. A major effort by the Crusaders and the WONPR resulted in the gathering of petitions containing 202,480 signatures by early April 1932. The petitions were presented to the Secretary of State on the steps of the state capitol building. [57]

In a last-ditch effort to block the repeal referendum the dry orga-nizations of Michigan formed a joint Board of Strategy. The executive secretary of the Board, Walter J. Hoshal, filed a petition with the state Supreme Court for the issuance of an order to prevent the proposed amendment from being placed before the voters. Hoshal's suit alleged that the state could not adopt the substitute amendment because it would violate the spirit and the letter of the Federal Constitution. Hoshal insisted at the same time that the drys were willing to go to the polls at any time to vote on an out-and-out wet-and-dry referendum that was legal. "We are fighting the present proposed amendment be-cause it is illegal and defies the Constitution of the United States," he explained. The state Supreme Court, however, refused to act on Hoshal's petition, which meant that the state electorate would be given the opportunity of expressing itself on the repeal issue in the fall election. [58]

As they prepared for the showdown with the forces of repeal, the state's leading dry organizations found themselves in an even more difficult situation than the repeal groups. Also, when the Anti-Saloon League and the WCTU sought to mobilize the voters of Michigan in defense of prohibition, it became apparent how much they had alienated many of their former supporters. The two organizations proved so ineffective in the emergency that special *ad hoc* campaign committees were organized to fill the power vacuum created by the de-cline of the established dry organizations.

The most dramatic loss of influence by a dry organization was that suffered by the Anti-Saloon League. Immediately following the passage of the Eighteenth Amendment there was a sharp decrease in the pledges to the national League, resulting, its officials concluded, from the common belief that the prohibition battle had been won once and for all. In the years after 1920, funds of the Anti-Saloon League of America decreased drastically until by the end of the decade the organization's financial position was desperate. When League fund raiser Howard H. Russell sought the usual large donation from Detroit businessman Joseph Boyer in 1928, he was turned down. Boyer's reasoning in the matter was not an uncommon one among former League patrons. "I am sorry to come to the conclusion that there is something incompatible with man's relation to prohibition," Boyer wrote at the time. "I am thoroughly discouraged over the outlook. I do not mean that you are on the wrong side, but it does appear to me that you are on the losing side, and what is the use of playing a losing game knowingly?" Three years later, Ernest Cherrington, a leading national officer of the League, wrote that he had been

hoping for weeks that . . . finances would improve, but our financial situation seems to be rapidly getting worse instead of better. . . . I have never found conditions quite as bad as they are and many of our best friends are in such position they cannot even pay their old subscriptions past due, to say nothing about giving any special help. . . . As you probably know, the salaries of many of the men . . . are back for several months. In some cases they are back for a year. . . . Frankly, I have never known a more difficult time from the financial point of view . . . and the prospects for the future are not very bright.[59]

Anti-Saloon League Superintendent R.N. Holsaple optimistically announced plans to restructure the state Anti-Saloon League to make it more effective in the final struggle with repealists. Yet, while he was publicly mouthing optimistic predictions, he was privately struggling to keep the state League solvent. In January 1931, Holsaple sent a confidential letter to various large contributors to the League stating that "the negative business situation has reacted disastrously to our work." He disclosed that over $100,000 was past due the League in unpaid pledges and that in December 1930, for the first time in the history of the League in Michigan, the organization had lacked the necessary funds to publish the monthly Michigan edition of *American Issue*, the official League newspaper. "We have gone to the limit in economizing," Holsaple warned. "Much needed workers have been let go and expenses cut wherever possible." Now, Holsaple said, "something heroic has to be done or the Michigan Anti-Saloon League will have to shut up shop." He asked those who had made pledges to pay them promptly. If the entire pledge could not be paid, he asked that at least some portion of it be forwarded immediately. "Nothing but the greatest need would prompt me to write this letter," he confided, "and I trust you will accept it in the spirit of helpfulness and generosity." [60]

About the time of Holsaple's appeal, F. Scott McBride, general superintendent of the Anti-Saloon League of America, told a League convention in Detroit that the growing popularity of the wet organizations had actually helped the dry cause by bringing many former members back into the fold. "Our organization finds itself in a better position today than ever before," he lied. "Despite the financial depression, our financial statement is favorable and in general we are in about the position we were just before prohibition was enacted." McBride predicted that in November, "if I'm any judge, we're going to win back every one of those lost districts and give the wets such an answer as will stand for all time." [61]

Yet the future for prohibition appeared very grim. Billy Sunday's 1932 Evangelistic Crusade in Detroit, instead of firing up voters in renewed enthusiasm for prohibition, simply demonstrated how enthusiasm and prestige had fled the dry camp. Sunday's 1916 crusade had been not only the high point of the prohibition drive but also one of the most exciting events in the city's history. In 1932, however, the mood of the city toward the evangelist had changed drastically. No large crowds greeted Sunday at the train depot in 1932, and no special tabernacle was built to house the meetings of the old-time preacher of the old-time gospel. A more restrained Sunday spoke at the Metropolitan Methodist Episcopal Church; his sermons lacked the fire and timeliness that had characterized them earlier, and the crowds were neither very large nor enthusiastic. Sunday reassured his listeners, nevertheless, that "the people of this country are going to knock the liquor traffic straight to hell, where it belongs." And he insisted that "you'll never see the Eighteenth Amendment repealed on God's earth. All we got to do is to hold twelve of our forty-eight states to keep America dry." That, he said, would be simple. The real trouble with prohibition, Sunday reasoned, was that "a bunch of low down crooks in official positions . . . don't want to enforce the law." He predicted that Hoover would be re-elected and would carry Michigan by a large majority. Sunday closed by calling the repealists "the worse crowd of God-Foresaken cut-throats this side of hell, and if I was God for half an hour they wouldn't be this side." But who was listening to this kind of rhetoric now? The evangelist's bullying made little impression in a depressed world, and his preaching illustrated that the prohibition cause was being buried by the illusions of its most outspoken support-ers. 62

The WCTU stood by the Anti-Saloon League and promised to fight the good fight for bone-dry prohibition. The organization, however, had lost both members and influence during the depression, and it no longer had the power or the prestige it had enjoyed before prohibition. The state president felt compelled to ask WCTU members in 1932 to "quit feeling poor and quit putting off subscribing to the *Michigan Union* and the *Union Signal.*" 63

The summer of 1931 witnessed the emergence of two new important dry organizations: the Allied Forces and the Allied Women. Leaders of these groups declared that they did not wish to divide the dry cru-sade but wanted simply to conduct a prohibition campaign along the lines they thought most effective. Some leaders of the Allied Forces were so confident that prohibition would win in a public referendum that they pushed for a showdown with the wets by endorsing the state referendum. Among the nationally prominent sponsors of the new movements were William G. McAdoo, Gifford Pinchot, Thomas A. Edison, and Jane Addams. 64

The most active and vibrant dry organization formed in the last months of the fight against repeal was the Michigan Youth Council on Prohibition, made up of students from high schools and junior high schools in the state. The Youth Council was formed by Mrs. Truman Newberry in early 1932 to aid in the November election. The Youth Council petitioned the Detroit Board of Education for a reintroduc-tion of textbooks that pointed out the physiological dangers of alco-holic consumption, but the Board refused even to consider the re-quest, explaining that the texts had been distorted in their presenta-tion of facts. In the fall of 1932 the Allied Youth held a mammoth rally on the steps of the state capitol in Lansing and pledged support for the

Constitution, the Eighteenth Amendment, and the prohibition laws. Over 7,000 members of the organization gathered in front of the capitol and took a temperance pledge administered by the prohibitionist lieutenant governor, Luren Dickinson. There was only one shortcoming to all of this youthful enthusiasm. The Allied Youth, unfortunately, contained not a single voter! [65]

In addition to revitalizing the old prohibition organizations and establishing new ones, the drys, like the wets, sought endorsement by leading influential public figures. The best known businessman to lend his prestige to prohibition in these hard times was Henry Ford. In an interview with Samuel Crowther of the *Ladies' Home Journal* in 1930, Ford contended that prohibition was a moral issue "because it is economically right. We know that anything which is economically right is also morally right," Ford reasoned in his sometimes peculiar manner. "There can be no conflict between good economics and good morals; in fact the one cannot exist without the other." Completely ignoring the fact that the illicit liquor industry was the second largest enterprise in the state, Ford restated the hackneyed dry argument that prosperity was built upon the abolition of the liquor traffic. "Our present industrial system simply cannot work with liquor," Ford said. "We must choose between drink and poverty on the one hand and prohibition and prosperity on the other." Ford seemed oblivious to the reality that the nation had prohibition with poverty in 1930. [66]

When Crowther appeared before a special House Judiciary Committee in the spring of 1930 he read messages from both Ford and Thomas Edison strongly supporting the Eighteenth Amendment. While Ford's statement predicted that "the sane people of the nation" would never let the Eighteenth Amendment be repealed or be weakened by "any dangerous modification," it was Edison's opinion that "prohibition is the greatest experiment yet made to benefit man. My observation is that its enforcement generally is at least 60 per cent and is gaining, notwithstanding the impression through false propaganda that it is a lower per cent. It is strange to me that some men of great ability and standing do not help remove the curse of alcohol." [67]

The Democratic state convention met in September 1930, two weeks after the primary elections in which two leading dry Republican congressmen had been unseated. Never before had it been so clear that public sentiment on the wet and dry issue was shifting. Prohibition was the issue upon which the Democrats might now ride to victory. With the promise of victory, the drys within the state party were silenced. The assembled delegates unanimously adopted a platform calling for a nation-wide referendum on the Eighteenth Amendment. "The Democratic party in Michigan," the plank stated, "recommends as a direction to Congress and the States a nationwide referendum on repeal of the Eighteenth Amendment in a separate election dealing with the question alone."[68]

The state Republican Party, on the other hand, remained staunchly behind the Eighteenth Amendment and the existing prohibition laws. The bone-dry state Attorney General, Wilbur Brucker, was nominated as the party's gubernatorial candidate. Fred Green told the party convention that prohibition was a social and not a political question and should therefore not be discussed by the party.[69]

After receiving the Democratic Party's gubernatorial nomination, William A. Comstock went beyond the party declaration in favor of a referendum and endorsed outright repeal of the Eighteenth Amendment. In an address before the Exchange Club of Warren, Comstock confessed that he had never been in favor of national prohibition, and he called for control of the liquor traffic by the states. "It is something that was put over on the people," Comstock said of national prohibition, "and should never have been permitted to get into the Constitution." Unlike state prohibition, he declared, national prohibition had been forced upon the people of Michigan after they had already eliminated the saloon by their own dry law. "The situation is ten times worse than it ever was in the wet days," he contended. "Yes, hundreds of times worse." Comstock promised, if elected, to request the legislature to memorialize Congress for repeal of the Eighteenth Amendment and to seek state and national referenda on the issue.[70]

In the general election in November, Comstock carried only three counties. Brucker was elected governor, and Luren Dickinson, the outstanding political prohibitionist in the state, was re-elected lieutenant governor.[71]

Yet the repealists continued their agitation and following the election dissident wet voices were heard even within the ranks of the victorious Republican Party. The Wayne County Women's Republican Club went on record in favor of the repeal of the Eighteenth Amendment, and a few weeks later the North End Republican Club of Detroit adopted a resolution favoring repeal of prohibition as an incentive to prosperity and a curb on crime. [72]

An increasing number of Michigan Republicans feared that the party would lose thousands of votes unless, at the very least, it endorsed a referendum on the question of prohibition. As a result, after months of debate and maneuvering and bargaining, in the spring of 1932 the state GOP endorsed a national referendum on the Eighteenth Amendment. [73]

Repeal sentiment continued to increase within the Democratic Party also. At the state party convention in Flint in 1931, the Democrats reaffirmed their 1930 stand in favor of a nationwide referendum on the prohibition issue. In December 1931 the Detroit Democratic Club unanimously endorsed a resolution assailing prohibition and adopted "Roosevelt and Repeal" as the club's slogan. [74]

The mid-summer national party conventions in 1932 added to the continuing drama of the wet and dry battle. The Democrats wrote a repeal plank into their platform and nominated Franklin D. Roosevelt of New York, a repealist. Following his nomination, candidate Roosevelt announced that "from this date on, the Eighteenth Amendment is doomed." The Republicans, on the other hand, endorsed a moist plank, calling for resubmission of the Eighteenth Amendment to the states and maintenance by the federal government of the power to protect dry territory and prevent the return of the saloon. The *Detroit Free Press* commented that the Republicans, at best, offered only a modified form of national prohibition. Despite their endorsement of a referendum on the prohibition question, the Michigan Republicans renominated bone-dry incumbent Brucker to oppose the wet William Comstock in the gubernatorial race. In the campaign of 1932, both nationally and locally, the Republicans were the party of the drys, and the Democrats the party of the wets. [75]

The election of November 8, 1932, resulted in a resounding victory for the Democratic Party and for the cause of repeal. For the first time since 1852 Michigan gave its electoral vote to the Democratic presidential candidate, and the entire Democratic slate for state office was swept into power. Lieutenant Governor Dickinson was defeated by the wet Allen E. Stebbins by nearly eight thousand votes. [76]

In the gubernatorial race, Comstock, who had joined the Crusaders in January 1931, and who had the endorsement of both the AAPA and the WONPR, triumphed over the incumbent Wilbur Brucker by 190,637 votes and carried forty-three counties to Brucker's forty. Comstock's victory came because of his majority in the most populous industrial counties of Wayne, Kent, Genesee, Saginaw, Oakland, St. Clair, and Macomb. In fact, Comstock's majority in Wayne County gave him the election: while Comstock carried Wayne County by 190,727 votes, Brucker carried the rest of the state by 90 votes. [77]

On the question of the establishment of a state liquor control commission and the repeal of state prohibition laws, Wayne County gave repeal a majority of 309,364, while the rest of the state voted repeal by a majority of 237,879, a total repeal majority of 547,243. As the repealists pointed out after the election, had Wayne County's vote not even been counted in 1932, repeal would still have carried Michigan. [78]

It is impossible to separate the influence of prohibition and depression upon the behavior of Michigan voters in 1932 or to draw any concrete conclusions regarding which of the two was more important in determining the outcome of the election. To do so would be to ignore the principal thrust of two and one-half years of repeal propaganda in the state. High employment, low taxes, and repeal had been welded together into a winning combination by the wets. A vote for repeal was a vote for recovery, a vote for a new deal in liquor as well as in politics. Try as they might, the drys had been unable to pry these issues apart or to invert the slogans of the wets.

Although Michigan voters responded to the presidential race (1,611,594 votes) and the gubernatorial race (1,584,607 votes) in greater numbers than they did to the repeal question (1,497,773 votes), they supported repeal more decisively (a majority of 1,022,508 votes) than they supported Roosevelt (a majority of 871,700 votes) or Comstock (a majority of 887,672 votes). A comparison of the total vote for the victorious gubernatorial candidate in each of Michigan's eighty-three counties with the repeal vote in each county reveals that repeal won more votes than either Comstock or Brucker in forty-four counties, while Comstock won more votes than Brucker and repeal in twenty counties and Brucker won more votes than Comstock and repeal in nineteen counties. Although many counties were unable to forgo their traditional Republican loyalties in 1932, they were by no means as reluctant to abandon prohibition. Voters in many counties were convinced that they could have the best of all possible worlds by repealing prohibition and maintaining the GOP in power. [79]

The countryside often cast as heavy a vote against prohibition in 1932 as did the city. The average vote for the entire state in favor of repeal was 69 percent. While Detroit (90 percent) and Flint (77 percent) cast a higher percentage of their vote in favor of repeal, the state's second largest city, Grand Rapids, cast only the same percentage of its vote in favor of repeal as did the rest of the state. An AAPA analysis of the 1932 vote found that repeal would have passed in Michigan even had the votes of the largest cities not been counted. [80]

In viewing the wreck of his beloved dry cause following the election, R.N. Holsaple of the Anti-Saloon League concluded that the drys had faced an impossible task. "All the psychology was against us," he said. "The voters were in an unreasonable and unreasoning state of mind. Whatever is, is wrong, was their slogan. That feeling defeated us," he insisted, "just as it defeated President Hoover and Governor Brucker." Holsaple contended that had the drys remained true to the bone-dry cause and refused to consider modification, they would have received more votes. Because many of them adopted a moderate position, he thought, the entire dry cause lost both respect and votes. Later, Holsaple remembered November 8, 1932, and concluded, "it was a sad day for the 'ins.' We were 'in,' therefore, we suffered." [81]

There was a good deal of truth in Holsaple's analysis. The main thrust of the repeal campaign had been economic in nature just like the prohibition campaign more than a decade earlier. A vote for repeal was a vote for a better economic future—just as a vote for prohibition in 1916 in Michigan had been a vote for a better economic future. In neither case, however, was the shape of that future tailored very precisely to its prophets' dreams.

Notes

1. Norman H. Dohn, "The History of the Anti-Saloon League" (Ph.D. diss., Ohio State University, 1959), p. 232; Henry Lee, *How Dry We Were: Prohibition Revisited* (Englewood Cliffs, N.J., 1963), p. 147; Herbert Asbury, *The Great Illusion: An Informal History of Prohibition* (Garden City, N.Y., 1950), p. 316.

2. Hugh Fox, "The Consumption of Alcoholic Beverages," in *Prohibition and Its Enforcement*, ed. T. Henry Walnut, The Annals of the American

Academy of Political and Social Science, vol. 109 (Philadelphia, 1923), pp. 143-44.

3. U.S., Congress, Senate, Subcommittee of the Committee on the Judiciary, *The National Prohibition Law*, 69th Cong., 1st sess., 1926, pp. 210-23; Charles Merz, *The Dry Decade* (Garden City, N.Y. 1931), p. 225.

4. Senate Subcommittee of the Committee on the Judiciary, *The National Prohibition Law*, pp. 210-23.

5. Ibid.

6. *Fifty-second Annual Report of the Michigan Woman's Christian Temperance Union* (1926), pp. 25-26; Leon Festinger, Henry W. Riecken, and Stanley Schachter, *When Prophecy Fails* (Minneapolis, 1956), p. 26.

7. *Detroit News*, September 17, 24, 1923; Detroit *Saturday Night*, September 22, 1923; William P. Lovett to "The Pastors of Detroit," September 29, 1923, Detroit Citizens League Papers, Correspondence Files, box 3, Burton Historical Collection, Detroit, Mich.; Lovett to "Dear Friend," October 2, 1923, op. cit., box 10.

8. *Detroit Free Press*, April 17, 1925; *New York Times*, April 17, 1925; Merz, *Dry Decade*, p. 214.

9. Dayton E. Heckman, "Prohibition Passes: The Story of the Association Against the Prohibition Amendment" (Ph.D. diss., Ohio State University, 1939), pp. 9-51.

10. Ibid., pp. 73-77; "Prohibition Pro and Con" (Washington, D.C., 1929), pp. 1-10, Association Against the Prohibition Amendment Papers, Library of Congress, Washington, D.C.; George Wolfskill, *The Revolt of the Conservatives: A History of the American Liberty League, 1934-1940* (Boston, 1962), pp. 40-41; U.S., Congress, Senate, Subcommittee of the Committee on the Judiciary, *Lobby Investigation*, 71st Cong., 1st sess., 1930, pp. 3832-59.

11. Senate Subcommittee of the Committee on the Judiciary, *Lobby Investigation*, pp. 3849-53; Heckman, "Prohibition Passes," p. 6.

12. "The Autobiography of Henry B. Joy," Joy Papers, Michigan Historical Collections, Ann Arbor, Mich.; Clarence Burton to Richard P. Joy, February 11, 1927, Clarence Burton Papers, Burton Historical Collection, Detroit, Mich.; Henry B. Joy to Arthur Vandenburg, February 6, 1928, Joy Papers, box 4, Michigan Historical Collections, Ann Arbor, Mich.; *Detroit News*, April 23, 1928.

13. William Stayton to Henry B. Joy, April 26, 1927, Joy Papers, Michigan Historical Collections, Ann Arbor, Mich.; Heckman, "Prohibition Passes," pp. 9-10.

14. Detroit *Saturday Night*, November 26, 1921, September 22, 1923; *Detroit News*, March 5, 1922, September 24, 1921; Senate Subcommittee of the Committee on the Judiciary, *Lobby Investigation*, p. 3847; Merz, *Dry Decade*,

p. 215; James Couzens to William Stayton, July 9, 1923, James Couzens Papers, Library of Congress, Washington, D.C.

15. MS of Cramton Speech, January 21, 1924, Louis Cramton Papers, box 1, Michigan Historical Collections, Ann Arbor, Mich.; *Forty-eighth Annual Report of the Michigan Woman's Christian Temperance Union* (1922), p. 24; *Fifty-second Annual Report of the Michigan Woman's Christian Temperance Union* (1926), p. 26.

16. *Detroit News*, April 23, 26, May 1, 1928, December 15, 1929.

17. *Christian Science Monitor*, September 27, 1923.

18. Ernest H. Cherrington et al., eds., *The Standard Encyclopedia of the Alcohol Problem*, 6 vols. (Westerville, O., 1924-30), Vol. 4, 1766; *The Anti-Saloon League Yearbook for 1924* (Westerville, O., 1924), pp. 108-09; for the complete text of the proposed amendment see Charles J. Deland to William P. Lovett, September 30, 1924, Detroit Citizens League Papers, Correspondence Files, box 11, Burton Historical Collection, Detroit, Mich.

19. *Detroit News*, March 11, 1927.

20. Ibid., March 11, 1927, July 6, 1928; "Prohibition Can Be Ended in 1928," Pamphlet of the Michigan Moderation League, Joy Papers, Michigan Historical Collections, Ann Arbor, Mich.

21. Frederick Lewis Allen, *Since Yesterday: The Nineteen-thirties in America* (New York, 1940), pp. 13-16, 24-25.

22. Frederick Lewis Allen, *Only Yesterday: An Informal History of the 1920s* (New York, 1930), p. 281; Richard T. Ortquist, Jr., "Depression Politics in Michigan, 1929-1933" (Ph.D. diss., University of Michigan, 1968), pp. 10, 126-27; Keith Sward, *The Legend of Henry Ford* (New York, 1968), p. 233; Reynold M. Wik, *Henry Ford and Grass Roots America* (Ann Arbor, 1972), p. 183.

23. Ortquist, "Depression Politics," pp. 149-52; *Detroit News*, November 19, 23, 1930; Detroit *Saturday Night*, December 20, 1930; Allen, *Since Yesterday*, p. 24; *Detroit Times*, January 27, 1929.

24. Leslie Gordon, *The New Crusade* (Cleveland, 1932), pp. xxi-xxii; H.A. Brink, *The Michigan Plan of Federal, State and Local Liquor Regulation, including State Internal Control* (Grand Rapids, 1932), passim.

25. *Detroit News*, October 30, 1932; Jimmie Lewis Franklin, *Born Sober: Prohibition in Oklahoma, 1907-1959* (Norman, 1971), p. 106; William Elliott West, "Dry Crusade: The Prohibition Movement in Colorado, 1858-1933" (Ph.D. diss., University of Colorado, 1971), p. 413; J.C. Burnham, "New Perspectives on the Prohibition 'Experiment' of the 1920's," *Journal of Social History* 2 (Fall 1968): 67.

26. Detroit *Saturday Night*, January 31, 1931, April 23, 1932.

27. *New York Times*, January 23, 1932. For similar arguments from repeal campaigns in other states see Gilman M. Ostrander, *The Prohibition Move-*

ment in California, 1848-1933 (Berkeley, 1957), p. 193, and Norman H. Clark, *The Dry Years: Prohibition and Social Change in Washington* (Seattle, 1965), pp. 219-21.

28. *Detroit News*, May 8, 1931, June 19, 1932; Detroit *Saturday Night*, September 5, 1931.

29. Frank Murphy to O.C. Davis, June 17, 1932, Mayors' Papers, 1932, box 8, Burton Historical Collection, Detroit, Mich.

30. Statement of Mayor Frank Murphy, 1932, Mayors' Papers, 1933, box 1, Burton Historical Collection, Detroit, Mich.

31. Larry Roskam to Murphy, April 29, 1932, Mayors' Papers, 1933, box 1, Burton Historical Collection, Detroit, Mich.; George P. Schudlich to Murphy, October 26, 1932, box 1, Burton Historical Collection, Detroit, Mich.

32. O.C. Davis to Murphy, April 30, 1932, box 1, Burton Historical Collection, Detroit, Mich.

33. U.S., Congress, House, Committee on the Judiciary, *The Prohibition Amendment*, 71st Cong., 1st sess., 1930, pp. 72-73.

34. U.S., Congress, Senate, Subcommittee of the Committee on the Judiciary, *Modification or Repeal of National Prohibition*, 1932, p. 62; Fred Green to Henry B. Joy, June 27, 1932, Joy Papers, box 17, Michigan Historical Collections, Ann Arbor, Mich.

35. Allen, *Since Yesterday*, p. 26.

36. Henry B. Joy to Stayton, April 28, 1931, Joy Papers, Michigan Historical Collections, Ann Arbor, Mich.

37. *Detroit News*, June 12, 1932.

38. Detroit *Saturday Night*, September 26, 1931; *Detroit News*, February 13, 1931.

39. Detroit *Saturday Night*, September 12, 26, 1931; Alger to Henry B. Joy, September 23, 1931, Joy Papers, box 14, Michigan Historical Collections, Ann Arbor, Mich.

40. *Annual Report to the Directors, Members and Friends of the Association Against the Prohibition Amendment Submitted by the Executive Committee of the Board of Directors for the Year 1931* (New York, 1931), Association Against the Prohibition Amendment Papers, Library of Congress. See also "421 Men You Should Know Who Are Directing the Fight for Repeal of the National Prohibition Amendment" (Washington, 1932), Joy Papers, Michigan Historical Collections, Ann Arbor, Mich.

41. Alger to Curran, November 24, 1930, Joy Papers, Michigan Historical Collections, Ann Arbor, Mich.

42. Alger to Curran, January 5, 1931, Joy Papers, Michigan Historical Collections, Ann Arbor, Mich.

43. Stayton to Henry B. Joy, April 22, 1931, Joy Papers, Michigan Historical Collections, Ann Arbor, Mich.

44. *Chicago Herald*, January 1, 1930; for Clark's obituary see *San Francisco Chronicle*, January 8, 1973. According to its Los Angeles Commander, the Crusaders were simply "organized thirst." Ostrander, *Prohibition in California*, p. 192.

45. *Detroit Free Press*, February 11, 1930; Benedict Crowell to Henry B. Joy, January 30, 1930, Joy Papers, Michigan Historical Collections, Ann Arbor, Mich.

46. Gordon, *New Crusade*, xvii.

47. Ibid., vii-viii.

48. John C. Graham to Earl C. Michener, October 20, 1931, Earl C. Michener Papers, box 13, Michigan Historical Collections, Ann Arbor, Mich.; Lewis L. Bredin to William A. Comstock, October 13, 1930, William A. Comstock Papers, Michigan Historical Collections, Ann Arbor, Mich.

49. Fred G. Clark, "The Crusaders and Their Purpose," pamphlet in the Joy Papers, box 1, Michigan Historical Collections, Ann Arbor, Mich.

50. Fred A. Picard to Alger, October 27, 1930, William A. Comstock Papers, Michigan Historical Collections, Ann Arbor, Mich.

51. *Detroit News*, October 30, 1930; Detroit *Saturday Night*, December 13, 1930; Michener to Earl Venable, November 1, 1932, Michener Papers, box 14, Michigan Historical Collections, Ann Arbor, Mich.; Comstock to Bredin, November 12, 1932, William A. Comstock Papers, Michigan Historical Collections, Ann Arbor, Mich.

52. Grace C. Root, *Women and Repeal: The Story of the Women's Organization for National Prohibition Reform* (New York, 1934), p. 25; *Detroit News*, June 28, 1930; Sidney T. Miller to Comstock, October 25, 1929, William A. Comstock Papers, Michigan Historical Collections, Ann Arbor, Mich.

53. *Detroit News*, June 20, 1930; Bulletin of the WONPR and the CRUSADERS, March 11, 1931, Joy Papers, box 14, Michigan Historical Collections, Ann Arbor, Mich.

54. *Detroit News*, June 30, 1930.

55. Detroit *Saturday Night*, July 16, 1932.

56. *Detroit News*, September 21, 1932; Joseph Standart to Joy, August 31, 1932, Joy Papers, Michigan Historical Collections, Ann Arbor, Mich.

57. *Detroit News*, July 29, September 14, 1932; *New York Times*, September 15, 1932.

58. *Detroit News*, July 29, September 14, 1932; *New York Times*, September 15, 1932.

59. Dohn, "History of the Anti-Saloon League," p. 260; Clark, *Dry Years*, p. 189; *New York Times*, October 25, December 17, 1929, February 7, 8, 1928.

60. Letter of R.N. Holsaple, January 14, 1931, Joy Papers, box 13, Michigan Historical Collections, Ann Arbor, Mich.; E.J. Quackenbush to Michener, April 18, 1932, Earl C. Michener Papers, box 14, Michigan Historical Collections, Ann Arbor, Mich.

61. *Detroit News*, April 27, 1931.

62. Ibid., November 11, 15, 1932.

63. *Fifty-sixth Annual Report of the Michigan Woman's Christian Temperance Union* (1930), p. 54; *Fifty-eighth Annual Report of the Michigan Woman's Christian Temperance Union* (1932), p. 25.

64. Detroit *Saturday Night*, June 13, 1931.

65. *Detroit News*, September 25, 30, November 5, 1932; Detroit *Saturday Night*, October 17, 1931.

66. Samuel Crowther, "Prohibition or Poverty: An Interview with Henry Ford," *Ladies Home Journal* 48 (April 1930): 225.

67. *Detroit News*, March 5, 1930; *New York Times*, March 25, 1930.

68. *New York Times*, September 21, 1930; Dewitt Robinson to Comstock, September 25, 1930, Comstock to Charles A. Goodwin, October 10, 1930, Comstock Papers, Michigan Historical Collections, Ann Arbor, Mich.

69. Ortquist, "Depression Politics," p. 66; Comstock to John K. Stack, Jr., October 10, 1930, Frank A. Picard to Comstock, October 29, 1930, William A. Comstock Papers, Michigan Historical Collections, Ann Arbor, Mich.

70. Comstock to *Detroit Evening News*, October 28, 1930, Comstock to Robert Rayburn, October 1, 1930, Comstock to William G. Simpson, October 1, 1930, Comstock to Brandes Randell, October 1, 1930, William A. Comstock Papers, Michigan Historical Collections, Ann Arbor, Mich.; Ortquist, "Depression Politics," pp. 43-44; *Detroit News*, October 10, 1930.

71. *Michigan Manual for 1931* (Lansing, 1931), pp. 238-39; *Fifty-sixth Annual Report of the Michigan Woman's Christian Temperance Union* (1930), p. 28; Comstock to Picard, November 4, 1930, Comstock Papers, Michigan Historical Collections, Ann Arbor, Mich.

72. *Detroit News*, November 11, 13, 1930, February 5, 1931.

73. "Declaration of the Michigan Republican Party," April 1932, Earl C. Michener Papers, box 14, Michigan Historical Collections, Ann Arbor, Mich.

74. *New York Times*, February 27, December 4, 1931; Detroit *Saturday Night*, April 16, 1932.

75. Ortquist, "Depression Politics," pp. 172-77, 180-84; *Detroit News*, October 9, 29, 1932; Andrew Sinclair, *Prohibition: Era of Excess* (New York, 1962), pp. 375-87; Root, *Women and Repeal*, pp. 81-83; Allen, *Since Yesterday*, p. 65. Joseph Lash, *Eleanor and Franklin: The Story of Their Relationship Based on Eleanor Roosevelt's Private Papers* (New York, 1971), pp. 346-62.

76. *Michigan Manual for 1933* (Lansing, 1933), pp. 246-48, 420-22.

77. Ibid., p. 270.

78. Detroit *Saturday Night*, November 12, 1932; *New York Times*, November 11, 1932.

79. *Michigan Manual for 1933*, pp. 270, 420-22, 246-48. It is also significant that with prohibition removed from state politics in 1934, the GOP swept back into power, capturing every major state office except that of state treasurer. Ortquist, "Depression Politics," p. 247.

80. *Annual Report to the Directors, Members and Friends of the Association Against the Prohibition Amendment, Submitted by the Executive Committee of the Board of Directors for the Year 1933* (New York, 1933), p. 25.

81. Joy to Vandenburg, February 9, 1933, Joy Papers, box 19, Michigan Historical Collections, Ann Arbor, Mich.; *Detroit News*, December 4, 1932, February 25, 1933; Burnham, "The Prohibition 'Experiment,'" pp. 65-67; Paul A. Carter, "Prohibition and Democracy: The Noble Experiment Reassessed," *Wisconsin Magazine of History*, 56 (Spring 1973): 198-99.

9.

DAVID E. KYVIG

Objection Sustained:
Prohibition Repeal and
the New Deal

Franklin D. Roosevelt, in his January 3, 1936, state of the union address, referred to conservative critics of the New Deal as "unscrupulous moneychangers" who "steal the livery of great national constitutional ideals to serve discredited special interests." These forces of "entrenched greed," FDR suggested, bore responsibility for the nation's economic collapse.[1] Six months later, as he accepted renomination, the president charged: "These economic royalists complain that we seek to overthrow the institutions of America. What they really complain of is that we seek to take away their power. In vain they seek to hide behind the Flag and the Constitution."[2] Roosevelt, usually given to charm, flattery, and compromise when dealing with political adversaries, used uncommonly harsh words. His unnamed target was clearly the American Liberty League. The American Liberty League at the time was regarded as the most powerful independent conservative political organization to arise since World War I and a serious threat to the Roosevelt administration. The league had attained this renown because of the individual stature of many of its supporters and because it had reconstituted the leadership of the extraordinary and recently successful crusade to repeal the Eighteenth Amendment to the Constitution, the national prohibition amendment.

During the winter of 1935-36, when FDR's popularity reached an all-time low, when severe criticism could be heard from both left and

right, and when a difficult re-election campaign appeared to lie
ahead, the president and his aides acted as if the Liberty League were
their principal foe. Other administration spokesmen, as well as the
president, often referred caustically to the league's motives.[3] Democratic National Chairman James Farley hired a full-time publicist to
do nothing but plan attacks on the league or, as he would label it,
"the millionaire's union." Throughout the 1936 campaign, the Roosevelt forces continued to flail away at the Liberty League.[4]

Meanwhile the Liberty League attacked the New Deal at least once
a week with a pamphlet, radio broadcast, leaflet, or bulletin. Statements by league leaders and reports from its staff attacked the administration for usurping congressional functions, placing legislative
power in bureaucratic structures within the executive branch, such as
the National Recovery Administration and Agricultural Adjustment
Administration, and creating huge, inflationary federal deficits. Roosevelt appeared intent on reshaping American constitutional government and building an omnipotent presidency, the league charged.[5]
The Liberty League hesitated to join the president's Republican opponents, however, preferring to try to influence the Democratic Party
to restrain its leader. This rather unusual political course proved
fruitless, but nevertheless continued through the Democratic convention of June 1936. Even afterwards, the Liberty League gave only luke-
warm support to Roosevelt's presidential opponent, Kansas Governor
Alfred E. Landon.

Historians have generally explained the Liberty League's behavior
in 1936 as the simple product of political naïveté. In contrast,
Roosevelt's attacks on the league have been regarded as a clever tactic
to embarrass the Republicans by describing an already unpopular
group as a powerful, dangerous influence within that party's ranks. In
retrospect this seems to make sense, for in the 1936 election FDR won
a better than sixty percent plurality, while the Liberty League, its efforts proven futile, simply faded away.

Such explanations, however, fail to take into account the previous
political history of those who formed the league, their prior relationship with Roosevelt, and FDR's resulting impression of the league's
power. Dismissing the league as FDR's straw man obscures the noteworthy fact that as long as it remained an active presence, Roosevelt
proved far more circumspect about governmental reform than he

would once the league departed. During his first term, when most of the New Deal's legislative programs to combat depression were being developed, the president appeared wary of conservative strength. This was obvious in early efforts to restore private enterprise through banking legislation and the National Recovery Act. It remained so in the so-called second New Deal of 1935-36 when FDR took a very conservative approach to financing and eligibility for Social Security, gave reluctant support to Senator Robert Wagner's National Labor Relations Act, and declined to fight for significant redistribution of tax burdens. [6] The president's own cautious reform philosophy in part explains the nature of his legislative efforts, but his political perceptions were also an important influence. Concern for the power of those to his right tempered FDR's response to the persistent demands of those to his left. To understand the American Liberty League's image and impact as well as its ideology and the paradox of its reluctance to sever its ties to the Democratic Party despite hostility to the New Deal, one must examine the league's background.

When the Liberty League was founded in the summer of 1934, it bore a remarkable resemblance to the recently disbanded Association Against the Prohibition Amendment. Jouett Shouse, the league's president, had also served as president of the AAPA. The founder and principal membership solicitor for the fifteen-year-old anti-prohibition association, William H. Stayton, became league secretary, while another former AAPA leader, New York financier Grayson Murphy, acted as treasurer. The seven-member executive committee directing the Liberty League's affairs contained three members of the AAPA's similar committee: Shouse, Irénée du Pont, and James W. Wadsworth, Jr. The committee also included Pauline Sabin, leader of the AAPA's female counterpart, the Women's Organization for National Prohibition Reform, and two former Democratic presidential nominees friendly to the AAPA, John W. Davis and Alfred E. Smith. The league's heaviest financial contributors, Pierre, Irénée and Lammot du Pont, and John J. Raskob, had also made among the largest donations to the AAPA. The league drew on AAPA and WONPR membership rolls to solicit members for a large national advisory board and for its general membership. Although some who joined the Liberty League had not been directly involved in the anti-prohibition crusade, nevertheless the league's leadership, membership, organizational structure, publicity techniques, and doctrines bore a striking similarity to the Association Against the Prohibition Amendment. [7]

Since the American Liberty League so obviously followed in the steps of the AAPA, the league cannot be fully understood without reference to the earlier organization and its struggles. In its fifteen-year fight to repeal national prohibition, the league's direct predecessor forged an identity which the Liberty League would carry into its battle with the New Deal. The only extended study of the Liberty League, published in 1962, devoted a chapter to the AAPA. However, forced to rely primarily on a sketchy and partisan 1930 congressional investigation and a few statements by Jouett Shouse, its author did not probe the anti-prohibition organization in depth. [8] Five years later an otherwise useful doctoral dissertation on the Liberty League made no reference whatsoever to its antecedents. [9] Subsequently, however, a number of large and rich manuscript collections have been opened to research, among them the papers of Pierre and Irénée du Pont, John J. Raskob, James W. Wadsworth, Jr., Jouett Shouse, and Joseph H. Choate, Jr. [10] They provide a picture of the AAPA and the entire anti-prohibition movement not previously available.

William H. Stayton, who founded the Association Against the Prohibition Amendment in November 1918, and persisted with his anti-prohibition activities despite completion of the Eighteenth Amendment's ratification only two months later, acted out of a fear that progressive reforms were altering the basic structure of American national government. A Delaware farm boy who won a competitive examination for appointment to the Naval Academy in 1877, later earned a law degree while serving in the Marines, and eventually became a successful admiralty lawyer and steamship company executive, Stayton drew on his own experience for his uncomplicated faith in the wisdom of traditional social and political structures. Stayton believed that the federal government should assure a strong national defense and otherwise avoid interfering with individual initiative and local decision making. Like many other former naval officers, Stayton became active in the Navy League of the United States early in the twentieth century. Through the Navy League he met many business leaders and, in a term as its executive secretary from 1916 to 1918, learned techniques of organizing campaigns to influence public policy. [11]

Trends in Wilsonian Washington, particularly agitation for a federal prohibition amendment, alarmed Stayton. [12] While prohibition accomplished worthwhile objectives, he contended, it should be dealt with locally "and not in violation of the fundamental principles of home rule under which our country has grown to greatness." [13] National prohibition appeared to Stayton only an entering wedge in an effort to alter traditional constitutional relationships. "This prohibition business is only a symptom of a disease," he asserted, "the desire of fanatics to meddle in the other man's affairs and to regulate the details of your lives and mine." [14] Stayton believed that the vital spirit of the Constitution was retention by individual states of power over their individual affairs. "This spirit," he wrote, "has been destroyed by the Eighteenth Amendment, under which the right of local self-government is torn from the individual states, whose people are made subject, even in the small routine affairs of their daily lives, to those living in far distant localities and under other conditions." [15] Those who joined Stayton's crusade in the early 1920s voiced similar views. [16] The AAPA showed little concern with alcoholic beverages themselves; indeed brewers and distillers were told to keep their distance. [17] The anti-prohibition organization began, and would continue, as a protest against the expanding activity and power of the federal government.

Stayton kept up his criticisms of national prohibition year after year despite few signs of progress and the widespread assumption that insurmountable obstacles stood in the way of the Eighteenth Amendment's repeal. After all, two-thirds of Congress and three-fourths of the states would have to approve any constitutional change. Since the Eighteenth Amendment had been ratified by more than those margins, repeal would involve a nearly total nationwide political reversal. Thirteen states could block any change in the constitutional liquor ban. Texas Senator Morris Sheppard, author of the Eighteenth Amendment, had reason to boast: "There is as much chance of repealing the Eighteenth Amendment as there is for a humming-bird to fly to the planet Mars with the Washington Monument tied to its tail." [18] Despite such bleak prospects, the AAPA enlisted more and more individuals who shared Stayton's views on government.

Several people who would subsequently play leading roles in the Liberty League joined Stayton's anti-prohibition organization early in its existence. Several explained their reasons for doing so. In an immediate sense, they feared for the health and safety of their society.

National prohibition, as it was put into practice, appeared to them to be so widely violated as to cause the growth of organized crime, corruption in government, lost respect for law in general, and a breakdown in morality, especially among the young. Most felt deeply threatened by the loss of local control over what they believed to be essentially a community matter, the establishment of standards of acceptable social behavior. Since most AAPA members were middle-class and upper-class persons prominent in their own communities, they undoubtedly worried about a personal loss of influence as decision making shifted to the national level. Some certainly saw prospects of increased federal involvement with private business. Men comfortable with past governmental arrangements came to regard prohibition as detrimental in itself and, if permitted to stand, an omen of other dreadful changes.

In many respects, of course, these anti-prohibitionists had much in common with the law's advocates. The two groups shared concerns for social health, safety, morality, and stability. Dry crusaders desired not only to uplift the unfortunate, they also wanted to defend traditional values and life styles and to protect government from corruption by saloon-based, urban political machines. Stayton and his supporters agreed with such goals but perceived the liquor ban as endangering them. Prohibitionists, who believed abolishing liquor both vital and possible, were willing, after local and state efforts failed, to employ federal power to achieve their ends. Their opponents, on the other hand, found this solution too costly in principle and consequences. Thus national prohibition reflected both the common bonds and the diversity of middle-class and upper-class thought in the early twentieth century. Desires for order, stability, and social betterment were widespread, as was a willingness to use government to achieve such ends; but opinions as to specific goals and the limits of government involvement varied considerably. Among those who had been willing before World War I to use federal power to reform certain economic, political, and social conditions were many who came to feel after the war that enough had been done.[19]

William Stayton reported meeting in Detroit in April 1926 with "a group of very serious businessmen, everyone of whom had been dry, had voted dry and had contributed to the Anti-Saloon League, and who had originally believed in National Prohibition." One manufacturer in the group asserted, "The people are not very much interested in the question of wet and dry, but they have become tremendously interested in the question of the form of government under which they shall live. They realize," he went on, "that prohibition is not a real disease, but merely a symptom of a very great and deep-seated disease—the disease of plutocracy, of centralization of government from Washington in public affairs that extends now into the home and to the dinner table." All those present nodded agreement.[20] A thirsty Detroit autoworker probably would not have come up with the same reasons for disliking prohibition, but other business and professional people to whom Stayton talked certainly did.

One of the first people Stayton tried to enlist for the AAPA in 1919 was John J. Raskob, treasurer of the E.I. du Pont de Nemours Company, who was soon to become treasurer of General Motors, having instigated the du Pont family's acquisition of controlling interest in the automobile firm. Raskob joined the AAPA in June 1922, and became a principal financial supporter.[21] Raskob, a devoted father of twelve, explained,

The thing that is giving me the greatest concern in connection with the rearing of these children and the future of our country is the fact that our children seem to be developing a thorough lack of respect for our laws and institutions, and there seems to be a growing feeling that nothing is wrong in life except getting caught. . . . What impressions are registering on the minds of my sons and daughters when they see thoroughly reputable and successful men and women drinking, talking about their bootleggers, the good "stuff" they get, expressing their contempt for the Volstead Law, etc. . . . what ideas are forming in their young and fertile brains with respect to law and order?[22]

Raskob, a devout Roman Catholic, also saw the law as an expression of religious intolerance, a regulation of conduct many more American Catholics than Protestants engaged in. Since drinking involved no moral wrong, government should no more prohibit it than deny religious freedom. To John Raskob then, prohibition represented an unwise federal intrusion into an area where it had no business and was producing distasteful social side effects.

Raskob's close friends and business associates, Pierre du Pont and his brothers Irénée and Lammot, also enlisted in Stayton's crusade against the Eighteenth Amendment, the latter two in 1922, and Pierre in 1925.[23] Irénée shared the concern with expanding federal power and felt that prohibition had increased liquor abuse, especially among young people, rather than furthering temperance. He seemed particularly upset that taxes and license fees which state and federal governments formerly received from the liquor industry now went entirely to bootleggers and supported the corruption of government officials. Why should legitimate business be taxed, Irénée asked, and the illegal liquor industry rewarded?[24] Growing intemperance and lawlessness, threats to property rights, and the loss of local decision-making power all worried Irénée's older brother, Pierre. He expressed particular concern that the Eighteenth Amendment had been adopted without the people having a direct opportunity to vote on it and that the federal government, in the name of social reform, had destroyed an industry without compensation. Pierre felt so strongly about national prohibition that for once he overcame his natural shyness to take a leading public role in the repeal campaign.[25]

Grayson Murphy, head of his own New York investment firm and a founder of the American Legion in 1919, also joined the AAPA in its early years. Murphy told a congressional committee that World War I accustomed him to rigid, centralized government and led him to expect the liquor ban to succeed. He joined Stayton's organization after concluding that the Eighteenth Amendment was "absolutely contrary to the spirit of the rest of the Constitution" and led the government in its enforcement efforts to engage in such unacceptable acts as wiretapping, bribery, and the careless shooting of innocent people by prohibition agents. Respect for the Constitution had been "materially weakened," Murphy sensed. Furthermore, prohibition generated crime and furnished the underworld a steady income. Finally, said Murphy, the law interfered with established social customs. The federal exercise of power dangerously unsettled American government and society.[26]

New York Senator James W. Wadsworth, Jr. had voted against the Eighteenth Amendment in 1917 and continued to oppose it. He came from a long line of politicians opposed to expanding federal power, from great-great-grand uncle General James Wadsworth who opposed ratification of the federal Constitution to his father who in 1906 lost his twenty-year House seat and agriculture committee chairmanship by opposing Theodore Roosevelt's federal meat inspection bill.

Nothing in his own secure, comfortable life caused Wadsworth to question, much less reject, his family's traditional viewpoint. [27] Referring to prohibition, he told a 1923 National Republican Club dinner, "I am sure we all dread the establishment, gradual though it may be, of a system of government in this nation which will sap the strength, initiative and sense of responsibility of the citizen and of the community in which he lives." [28]

In 1926, Wadsworth faced a tough reelection contest against Democrat Robert F. Wagner and an independent dry candidate. Throughout the campaign, Wadsworth talked of the dangers to traditional forms of government posed by national prohibition: centralization, threats to civil liberties, and an invasion of privacy. The liquor ban, he said, produced high enforcement costs, hypocrisy, corruption, and disregard for law. "Political and social morals are being poisoned to an extent never approached in the history of the country," the senator warned. [29] The dry candidate, running to punish Wadsworth for such views, drew more than enough normally Republican upstate votes to cause his narrow loss to Wagner. Stripped of senatorial rank and further convinced of the damaging influence of prohibition on American government, Wadsworth too began to devote a major portion of his time to the repeal crusade. [30]

These men and thousands of others became involved in agitating against national prohibition long before the onset of the Great Depression had generated arguments for repeal to create jobs, reduce taxes, cut government costs, and generate revenues. They shared an underlying belief that a fundamental change in the nature of the federal government had taken place, upsetting their stable, comfortable world and destroying a most satisfactory social and political structure. Many of these repeal advocates considered themselves self-made men. Whether from modest backgrounds, such as Stayton, Raskob, or Murphy, or comfortable families, like Wadsworth and the du Ponts, they believed they had created or significantly improved their elevated social and economic positions through personal effort. Understandably, these successful men believed strongly that the traditional American system of unrestrained individualism and circumscribed government worked well. Now, they felt, the federal government had gotten into an area beyond its responsibility and competence, thereby causing all sorts of turmoil. They clearly worried that if government could interfere in such unprecedented fashion in personal habits, it could also intrude more deeply into other matters, such as business affairs. Such power in the hands of a distant central government unconcerned with local conditions and impervious to local influence, such as they were used to exercising, alarmed them.

Many of these anti-prohibitionists would have criticized the law in principle even if it succeeded in ending the use of alcohol. But the failure of efforts to enforce the law caused even more dismay. The American system of government provided a combination of freedom and order which allowed them to acquire and preserve wealth and status. The prospect of a government strong enough to strip them of property and privileged position disturbed them, but so did the specter of a government too weak to defend them. When they talked about lost respect for law, they were genuinely concerned that widespread scoffing at prohibition might lead to other unchecked disobedience. Government's ability to enforce the law was in doubt. The Constitution had always symbolized the stability and limitations of government power, but a constitution provided little protection if it could be radically changed or its provisions could not be enforced. The AAPA became the vehicle for those to whom prohibition posed questions of constitutional stability.

The AAPA did not consist merely of a handful of millionaires, as its dry opponents charged. The association claimed 550,000 members in 1932.[31] A few dozen wealthy donors did contribute heavily to the AAPA. On the other hand, from 1928 through 1933 the AAPA averaged 10,000 contributions a year, the vast majority small. In the peak income year of 1930, for instance, 28 percent of the association's income came in gifts of less than $100, a total of 21,588 donations averaging $8.05.[32] AAPA leaders thus had reason to believe that their constantly reiterated constitutional arguments struck a responsive chord with a wide audience.

In January 1928 the AAPA reorganized, creating a small executive committee that included Stayton, Pierre and Irénée du Pont, Murphy, Wadsworth, and four others. Under this committee's guidance, the association conducted an intensive three-year publicity campaign, producing 1.1 million copies of thirteen pamphlets and generating extensive newspaper publicity.[33] Many signs appeared that opposition to the Eighteenth Amendment was growing, among them the emergence by 1929 of three important new repeal organizations: a New York-based attorneys' association called the Voluntary Committee of Lawyers, a young men's society known as the Crusaders, and a very active, influential women's group which claimed more than a million members, the Women's Organization for National Prohibition Reform. These organizations attacked prohibition for producing crime and corruption as well as for undermining traditional constitutional arrangements and respect for law. Although quite independent, these groups all accepted a degree of leadership from the AAPA.[34]

Repeal first became a partisan issue in 1928. Previously support for and opposition to national prohibition had cut quite evenly across party lines, and both Republican and Democratic platforms and candidates avoided the issue with pious statements about the need to enforce existing laws.[35] The AAPA played an important role in affixing a dry label on the Republicans and a wet label on the Democrats, despite continued divisions within each party. This proved crucial, for from 1928 on a Republican electoral triumph came increasingly to be seen as a renewed endorsement of prohibition, while a Democratic victory grew to be regarded as a mandate for repeal. Widespread public unhappiness with the liquor ban obviously mattered a great deal, but until circumstances arose in which such sentiments could be clearly demonstrated, they would have little political impact.

The AAPA appealed to both parties in 1928 to endorse repeal. The Republicans, as the party in power and therefore responsible for law enforcement, ignored the plea, while their nominee, Herbert Hoover, reinforced his long record of support for prohibition: "Our country has deliberately undertaken a great social and economic experiment, noble in motive and far reaching in purpose. It must be worked out constructively."[36] The Democrats' platform also supported law enforcement, but their candidate, New York Governor Alfred E. Smith, had for years shown hostility to prohibition. He quickly made clear his intention to work for a change if elected president.[37] As if to emphasize this, Smith appointed John J. Raskob Democratic National Chairman. About all the public knew about Raskob was that he was a millionaire businessman and a leader of the Association Against the Prohibition Amendment.[38] Smith and Raskob drew wet support to the Democrats but hardly enough to offset the popularity of Hoover and the Republicans in a period of prosperity. Nor could they counter-act anti-Catholic, anti-urban, and dry beliefs. The Happy Warrior and his repeal-minded backers were buried in an electoral land-slide.[39]

John Raskob, however, remained as Democratic National Chair-man, and during the following four years he worked hard to strength-en the Democratic wet image. Bitterly disappointed by Smith's defeat and determined to reverse the result, Raskob collected or contributed more money than the Democrats had ever had available and created the first full-time professional national headquarters in the party's history with former Congressman Jouett Shouse as executive director. Raskob privately told friends that prohibition represented the only big difference between the parties and that he became involved on the Democratic side because "there are few things more necesary or ex-pedient to the future welfare and well-being of our country" than a change in the liquor laws.[40] Raskob's continued connection with the AAPA publicly emphasized the Democratic chairman's wet lean-ings.[41] Even more visible were Raskob's efforts in 1931 and early 1932 to get the Democratic National Committee to support repeal. He paid little attention to other policy questions but relentlessly pursued his crusade to commit the party against prohibition, completing his term as chairman by appealing to the 1932 Democratic convention to endorse repeal.[42]

Raskob's concerns ran headlong into the quite contrary ideas of Franklin D. Roosevelt. The New York governor, seeking the 1932 Democratic presidential nomination, had always taken an ambiguous position on prohibition, worried that any definite stand would alien-ate either the dry South or the wet urban North. Both in March 1931 and January 1932 Roosevelt's forces, after intense behind-the-scene struggles, blocked Raskob's efforts to obtain a national committee declaration against prohibition. Furthermore, by a narrow margin, FDR's supporters frustrated Raskob's plans to have Shouse named temporary chairman of the 1932 convention. Both sides grew very sus-picious and unhappy with each other. But when the question of a plat-form statement on prohibition came before the convention, the Raskob position clearly was overwhelmingly popular with the dele-gates. At the last minute Roosevelt withdrew his opposition rather than suffer an embarrassing defeat which might cost him votes in his

contest against a field of other presidential candidates, each individually weaker than FDR but all wetter and perhaps able to unite
around such a cause. The 1932 Democratic platform called unequivo-
cally for repeal of the Eighteenth Amendment, a measure of rising
repeal sentiment within the party and the success of Raskob's effort to
overcome opposition from the party's eventual presidential nominee. [43]

Their positions on prohibition provided one of the noteworthy distinctions in 1932 between Republicans and Democrats, both of whom
were exceedingly vague about their plans for economic recovery. President Hoover had stuck to his defense of prohibition, ignoring both
wet appeals and the advice of a majority of members of a presidential
commission to change the law. [44] The Republican platform moved
from full-fledged support of enforcement to a willingness to allow voters to decide prohibition's fate, so long as the federal government retained power to ban saloons and protect dry states. The Republican
New York Herald Tribune called it a "wet-moist-dry plank," while
organized wets condemned it for seeking to continue the federal government's involvement in the liquor question. [45] Throughout the
campaign, the AAPA, the WONPR, and other wets made clear their
preference for the Democrats, although some remained leary of
Roosevelt. [46]

The 1932 Democratic landslide represented one of the most striking political reversals in American political history. Herbert Hoover,
who received 58.2 percent of the vote in 1928, now got only 39.6 percent. Congressional results were equally lopsided. Undoubtedly the
economic depression bore primary responsibility for the outcome, but
prohibition played a part as well. The number of wets in Congress rose
even more rapidly than the number of Democrats. Eleven state referendums on prohibition questions all produced wet majorities, most by
wide margins. [47] Whatever part repeal advocacy actually contributed
to the Democratic victory, politicians and other contemporary observ-
ers gave it major credit. When the old Congress met for a lame-duck
session in December, House leaders called the election a mandate for
immediate repeal. Their colleagues clearly agreed, for whereas nine
months earlier only 187 members voted for a repeal resolution, now on
the new session's first day 272 did. Only the votes of 81 lame ducks, 70
of them Republican, temporarily blocked the resolution. [48]

The AAPA and its allies kept pressing for immediate action, pointing all the while to the election results.[49] Within two and a half months, first the Senate and then the House approved by more than the necessary two-thirds vote a resolution drawn to AAPA specifications. These included unqualified repeal and submission of ratification to specially elected state conventions rather than the usual process of submission to state legislatures. The AAPA feared that drys would be overrepresented in rural-dominated legislatures. With AAPA and Voluntary Committee of Lawyers assistance, states quickly provided for such conventions. Slates of delegates pledged to support or oppose repeal gave voters a chance to express their opinion of prohibition. Between April and November, thirty-eight states chose delegates, and of nearly 21 million votes cast nationally, 73 percent favored repeal of the Eighteenth Amendment. By December 5, 1933, the fastest ratification ever of a constitutional amendment was completed, and national prohibition was abolished.[50]

Leaders of the Association Against the Prohibition Amendment shared a tremendous feeling of accomplishment and vindication. After being told throughout the 1920s that repeal was impossible, being rejected by the Republicans, and resisted by Franklin Roosevelt as he pursued the Democratic nomination, they had won successive victories in the Democratic convention, the Congress, and the repeal convention elections. Nearly three-quarters of the American electorate had supported repeal.

It was impossible, of course, to know which arguments against prohibition moved the voters. Probably many desired nothing more complicated than the right to take a legal drink. Nevertheless, time after time in the ratification conventions, delegates arose to condemn prohibition in the same terms the AAPA had long used, calling the Eighteenth Amendment a distortion of the Constitution which usurped each state's right to control its local affairs.[51] Jouett Shouse, who had become AAPA president in August 1932, summarized the association's view of itself: the AAPA had labored "through the long years of discouragement when the cause of repeal was unpopular, when the motives of those advocating it were maligned, when a successful result seemed well nigh impossible," and had "brought about the most remarkable change in national sentiment and the most far-reaching social reform thus far recorded in the evolution of the American people."⁵² Arthur Krock in the *New York Times* called the AAPA's repeal campaign "a constructive social task excellently performed."⁵³

Anti-prohibitionist leaders felt they had won because the American people shared their view that traditional constitutional arrangements, especially limited federal activity, ought to be continued. When all other issues were stripped away in the 1933 repeal convention elections, they believed, voters had overwhelmingly vindicated this principle. But with the Eighteenth Amendment barely laid to rest, they began to see the very thing they had fought—centralization in federal hands of authority to deal with local affairs—returning in the shape of Franklin Roosevelt's New Deal.⁵⁴ Roosevelt had never appreciated their objections to national prohibition, they felt, had sought to ignore them, and was now proceeding in a contrary direction. So repeal leaders quickly regrouped to call for "a return to the Constitution," establishing the American Liberty League in August 1934, on the pattern of the AAPA.⁵⁵ Shouse told Roosevelt to his face that the league was being formed

to defend and uphold the Constitution of the United states and to gather and disseminate information that (1) will teach the necessity of respect for the rights of persons and property as fundamental to every successful form of government, and (2) will teach the duty of governments to encourage and protect individual and group initiative and enterprise, to foster the right to work, earn, save and acquire property, and to preserve the ownership and lawful use of property when acquired.⁵⁶

Roosevelt immediately attacked the new league, dismissing its stated constitutional concerns and concentrating on its economic motives. The League's tenets, the president told reporters, seemed to be "love thy God but forget thy neighbor," and God in this case appeared to be property.⁵⁷ For the next two years, the Liberty League and the administration battled with vitriol and scorn, protestations of wounded virtue, and escalating criticism of the other side. James Wadsworth expressed a typical league view in 1935 when he wrote,

The common man is beginning to understand that these experiments launched, presumably, for his benefit have not only failed to benefit him financially but have resulted in robbing him of a large portion of that liberty which the Constitution seeks to guarantee to him. I feel very much about the issue as I did about the eighteenth amendment, except that I realize that it is far greater in the ramifications.[58]

Roosevelt and his aides treated the Liberty League as a serious threat, repeatedly questioning its ideas and motives. The White House knew, of course, that the league's leaders were the same people who had rallied so much support for prohibition repeal in the 1932 Democratic convention and the 1933 repeal elections. Using the same constitutional appeals against the New Deal that had proved so successful against prohibition, could they again mobilize support? Having seriously underestimated this group once, Roosevelt certainly did not want to make the same mistake twice.

The memory of the repeal episode not only helps explain FDR's uncharacteristically vocal and harsh response to his critics, it also provides a rationale for the Liberty League's rather unusual behavior in 1936. Despite great unhappiness with New Deal policies and the treatment they received from administration spokesmen, the league declined to officially sever all ties to the Democratic Party and openly make common cause with the Republicans. The league's former anti-prohibitionists easily recalled Republican lack of sympathy for their calls to revive traditional constitutional values and in contrast how much support surfaced in the Democratic Party between 1928 and 1932. Veterans of the repeal crusade remembered how earlier defeats at Democratic hands were followed, despite Roosevelt's opposition, by their great platform victory at the 1932 convention. League leaders made it clear that they believed the Democrats had temporarily fallen under the sway of an unrepresentative clique and might once again heed their voices of reason. On the eve of the 1936 Democratic convention, Al Smith and four other prominent leaguers appealed to the delegates to revive the economy by removing government's hand from business and balancing the budget, to preserve the constitutional separation of powers by preventing the president from making the Congress a rubber stamp or intimidating the judiciary, and to put aside Franklin D. Roosevelt and substitute "some genuine Democrat." [59] But 1936 was not 1932, and the league was no longer trying to lead in a direction the delegates wanted to go.

For all of Al Smith's celebrated talk at a January 1936 Liberty League dinner about "taking a walk" and well-publicized individual contributions to the Republican campaign by several prominent leaguers, including the du Pont brothers, the league could not bring itself to officially support the Landon-Knox ticket.[60] On August 5, the league declared it would endorse neither party nor candidate, specifying that "The League is neither an adjunct nor an ally of the Republican party." The league's principles, it announced, "harmonized" with the "excellent platform" adopted by the Democrats in 1932, but not "the New Deal party which for the moment has usurped control of the party of Jefferson, Jackson, Cleveland, and Wilson."[61]

Roosevelt's smashing reelection with over 60 percent of the popular vote and all but eight electoral votes completely shattered all illusions about Liberty League power. Whether or not leaguers understood that voters in 1932 and 1933 did not necessarily share their precise reasons for wanting prohibition repealed, they could easily see now that in a grave economic and social crisis their constitutional and economic ideas appealed to very few. The Liberty League sank quickly from view, and most of its leaders avoided politics thereafter. Roosevelt no longer felt inhibited by the presence of an apparently powerful organization which would rise to defend traditional constitutional arrangements. Within three months he proposed a more radical legislative step than anything initiated from the White House during his first term, his extraordinary plan to alter fundamentally the balance of power within the federal government by reorganizing the Supreme Court. The tone and thrust of the New Deal became more bold once Roosevelt's position was confirmed and the Liberty League definitely discredited. Constitutional arguments which FDR must have assumed were disposed of eventually helped frustrate the court-packing plan, although the Liberty League was no longer directly involved.

The rapid rise and fall of the American Liberty League provides a classic study of the overestimation of popular support for American conservatism. The AAPA skillfully—and with a measure of lucky timing—helped create circumstances in which a popular vote on national prohibition could be registered and thereby made a major contribution to the repeal of the Eighteenth Amendment. Thereafter, its leaders assumed, with insufficient evidence, that the landslide for repeal reflected their concern with constitutional principles, particularly the limits of federal authority, rather than a more simple and direct desire to end the liquor ban. From their generally secure and comfortable positions, they failed to see that to most people economic and social survival mattered far more than constitutional arrangements. They saw no need to offer new or different arguments to stimulate opposition to the New Deal. Unrealistically believing that the Democratic Party would again respond, the league failed to ally with the more like-minded Republicans until too late. Their own exaggerated self-image contributed to the conspicuous failure of the principal organized conservative opposition to the New Deal.

That Franklin Roosevelt took the Liberty League seriously demonstrates that he too overestimated conservative strength and political skill in the early 1930s as a result of prohibition's defeat. The extent to which the president's assessment of the political situation between 1933 and 1936 shaped his behavior and tempered his reform proposals cannot be measured precisely, but his confidence and boldness definitely increased once the 1936 verdict had been delivered. The repeal of the Eighteenth Amendment was important both in itself and because it later influenced both Roosevelt and his opponents. The national prohibition phenomenon helped shape both the concerns and strategies of interwar conservatism and the political course of the New Deal.

Notes

1. *The Public Papers and Addresses of Franklin D. Roosevelt*, vol. 5 (New York, 1938): 13-14.

2. Ibid., p. 234.

3. George Wolfskill, *The Revolt of the Conservatives: A History of the American Liberty League, 1934-1940* (Boston, 1962), pp. 30-33.

4. Ibid., pp. 212-19.

5. Jouett Shouse, *The Return to Democracy*, NBC radio speech, July 1, 1935, reprinted by the American Liberty League as a pamphlet (Washington, 1935), serves as an excellent example of the league's arguments. See also Wolfskill, *Revolt of the Conservatives*, pp. 65-67, 102-18; Frederick Rudolph, "The American Liberty League, 1934-1940," *American Historical Review* 56 (October 1950): 19-33. Robert J. Comerford, "The American Liberty League" (Ph.D. diss., St. John's University, 1967).

6. An excellent discussion of the limited nature of New Deal reform can

be found in Barton J. Bernstein, "The New Deal: The Conservative Achieve-ments of Liberal Reform," in *Towards a New Past: Dissenting Essays in American History* (New York, 1967), pp. 306-24.

7. American Liberty League Executive Committee and Board of Direc-tors minutes, August 23 to December 18, 1934, enclosed in William H. Stay-ton to Executive Committee, January 15, 1935; Jouett Shouse to James W. Wadsworth, Jr., June 18, 1935, James W. Wadsworth, Jr. Papers, Library of Congress, Washington, D.C.

8. Wolfskill, *Revolt of the Conservatives*, ch. 2.

9. Comerford, "The American Liberty League."

10. Pierre S. du Pont Papers, Irénée du Pont Papers, and John J. Raskob Papers, Eleutherian Mills Historical Library, Wilmington, Del.; James W. Wadsworth, Jr. Papers, Library of Congress, Washington, D.C.; Jouett Shouse Papers, University of Kentucky, Lexington; and Joseph H. Choate, Jr. file, Voluntary Committee of Lawyers Papers, Collection on Legal Change, Wesleyan University, Middletown, Conn.

11. "William H. Stayton," *Repeal Review* 7 (July-September 1942): 3; *Who Was Who in America* 2 (Chicago, 1950): 505; author's interviews with Stayton's two granddaughters, Mrs. Merle A. Roemer and Mrs. John H.C. Forbes, July 1973; Stayton Papers in possession of Mrs. Forbes; William H. Stayton service record, Records of the Bureau of Naval Personnel, Record Group 24, National Archives, Washington, D.C.; Armin Rappaport, *The Navy League of the United States* (Detroit, 1962), pp. 17, 76, 229n.

12. H.L. Mencken, "Man Who Really Busted Prohibition Gives All Credit to Opposite Sex," *Baltimore Sun*, October 30, 1932.

13. Stayton to John J. Raskob, October 2, 1919, John J. Raskob Papers, Eleutherian Mills Historical Library, Wilmington, Del.

14. *New York Times*, April 7, 1922.

15. Stayton, "Our Experiment in National Prohibition: What Progress Has It Made?" in *Prohibition and Its Enforcement*, ed. T. Henry Walnut, Annals of the American Academy of Political and Social Science 109 (1923): 26.

16. For example, Samuel Harden Church, "The Paradise of the Ostrich," *North American Review* 221 (1925): 626; Henry S. Priest, "The Eighteenth Amendment an Infringement of Liberty," *Prohibition and Its Enforcement*, ed. T. Henry Walnut, Annals of the American Academy of Political and So-cial Science 109 (1923): 40; Ransom H. Gillett, "Address to the Economic Club of Boston, March 6, 1923," *Consensus* 8 (April 1923): 3-32; Fabian Franklin, *What Prohibition Has Done to America* (New York, 1922).

17. Dudley Nichols, "Total Abstainer, Captain W.H. Stayton, Leads 726,000 People in Militant Fight against the Prohibition Amendment," *New*

York World, July 11, 1926; U.S., Senate, Special Committee Investigating Expenditures in Senatorial Primary and General Elections. *Senatorial Campaign Expenditures: Hearings*, 69th Cong., 1st sess., June 9 to July 7, 1926, pt. 1: 1223.

18. Associated Press dispatch, September 24, 1930, quoted in Charles Merz, *The Dry Decade* (Garden City, 1931), p. 297.

19. For the attitudes of prohibition's supporters, see James H. Timberlake, *Prohibition and the Progressive Movement, 1900-1920* (Cambridge, Mass., 1963). Both the shared beliefs and the diversity of early twentieth-century thought are well explored in Robert H. Wiebe, *Businessmen and Reform* (Cambridge, Mass., 1962), and *The Search for Order, 1877-1920* (New York, 1967).

20. Stayton to Halbert L. Hoard, May 8, 1926, Halbert L. Hoard Papers, Wisconsin State Historical Society, Madison.

21. Stayton to Raskob, October 2, 1919; Raskob AAPA membership card, June 26, 1922; unsigned handwritten memorandum of AAPA contributions, February 1926 through February 1930, John J. Raskob Papers, Eleutherian Mills Historical Library, Wilmington, Del.

22. Raskob to P.H. Callahan, June 4, 1928, John J. Raskob Papers, Eleutherian Mills Historical Library, Wilmington, Del.

23. Carter Field, "Captain Bill Stayton—Guiding Spirit of the 'Little Group of Millionaires'," *Life*, July 24, 1931; Irénée du Pont AAPA membership cards, 1922-1925, and Irénée du Pont to Stayton, March 31, 1925, Irénée du Pont Papers, Eleutherian Mills Historical Library, Wilmington, Del.

24. Irénée du Pont to Frank Haley, October 2, 1925, to William S. Prichett, February 9, 1926, to Dr. Layton Grier, June 3 and 9, 1926, to Rev. Philip Cook, June 21, 1926, to William Allen White, July 3, 1926, to Rev. J.H. Whedbee, July 28, 1926, and to G.C. Crawford, April 3, 1928, Irénée du Pont Papers, Eleutherian Mills Historical Library, Wilmington, Del.

25. Pierre S. du Pont to Mrs. Ella D. Cordray, March 16 and 20, 1925, Pierre S. du Pont Papers, Eleutherian Mills Historical Library, Wilmington, Del.; "Eighteenth Amendment Not a Remedy for the Drink Evil," *Current History* 28 (April 1928): 17-22; "Why I Am against Prohibition," *Liberty* 5 (November 13, 1928): 13-14; "A Business Man's View of Prohibition," NBC radio address, December 15, 1929, Association Against the Prohibition Amendment Papers, Library of Congress, Washington, D.C.

26. U.S., House, Committee on the Judiciary, *The Prohibition Amendment: Hearings*, 71st Cong., 2nd sess., 1930, serial 5, pp. 135-37.

27. Martin L. Fausold, *James W. Wadsworth, Jr.: The Gentleman from New York* (Syracuse, 1975), pp. 1-12.

28. Wadsworth, "Amending the Constitution," February 12, 1923, James W. Wadsworth, Jr. Papers, Library of Congress, Washington, D.C.

29. Wadsworth, campaign speech, September 4, 1926, Binghamton, New York, Wadsworth Papers. See also speech to Republican Businessmen's dinner, New York City, August 4, 1926, and speech at Madison Square Garden, October 30, 1926, James W. Wadsworth Papers, Library of Congress, Washington, D.C.

30. Wadsworth, "The Reminiscences of James W. Wadsworth," Oral History Research Office, Columbia University (New York, 1952), pp. 347, 362; Fausold, *Wadsworth*, pp. 182-99; J. Joseph Huthmacher, *Robert F. Wagner and the Rise of Urban Liberalism* (New York, 1968), pp. 50-53.

31. U.S., Senate, Committee on the Judiciary, *Modification or Repeal of National Prohibition: Hearings*, 72nd Cong., 1st sess., 1932, pt. 1:12-13.

32. Association Against the Prohibition Amendment, Cash Receipts and Expenditures, 1928-1933, Pierre S. du Pont Papers, Eleutherian Mills Historical Library, Wilmington, Del.

33. "An Analysis of the Work of the Research Department," and "An Analysis of the Publication and Information Service of the Association Against the Prohibition Amendment," Irénée du Pont Papers, Eleutherian Mills Historical Library, Wilmington, Del. The AAPA estimated that stories based on information from its pamphlets appeared in over 250 million copies of newspapers, an average of over 18,000,000 per pamphlet.

34. Clement E. Vose, *Constitutional Change: Amendment Politics and Supreme Court Litigation Since 1900* (Lexington, Mass., 1972), ch. 5; John C. Gebhart, "Movement against Prohibition," *Annals of the American Academy of Political and Social Science* 163 (September 1932): 177-78; "Prohibition: United Wets," *Time* 20 (November 7, 1932): 16; David E. Kyvig, "Women against Prohibition," *American Quarterly* 28 (Fall 1976): 465-82; *New York Times*, June 8, 1932.

35. When Congress approved the Eighteenth Amendment in 1917, partisanship was notably absent. In the Senate, 29 Republicans and 36 Democrats voted for the resolution, 8 Republicans and 12 Democrats against. In the House, 137 Republicans, 141 Democrats, and 4 independents supported the proposed amendment, while 62 Republicans, 64 Democrats, and 2 independents opposed it.

36. Herbert Hoover to William Borah, *New York Times*, February 24, 1928; "Address Accepting the Nomination," August 11, 1928, *Public Papers of the Presidents of the United States: Herbert Hoover 1929* (Washington, D.C., 1974), p. 511.

37. Alfred E. Smith, telegram to Democratic National Convention, *New York Times*, June 30, 1928.

38. Henry F. Pringle, "John J. Raskob: A Portrait," *Outlook* 149 (August 22, 1928): 645-49.

39. David Burner, *The Politics of Provincialism: The Democratic Party in*

Transition, 1918-1932 (New York, 1968), pp. 179-243; Don S. Kirschner, *City and Country: Rural Responses to Urbanization in the 1920s* (Westport, Conn., 1970), p. 50; Robert Moats Miller, *American Protestants and Social Issues, 1919-1939* (Chapel Hill, N.C., 1958), p. 51; Ruth Silva, *Rum, Religion and Votes: 1928 Re-examined* (University Park, Pa., 1962); Allan T. Lichtman, "Critical Election Theory and the Reality of American Presidential Politics, 1916-1940," *American Historical Review* 81 (April 1976): 317-51.

40. Raskob to Coleman du Pont, July 19, 1928, Defendants Trial Exhibit GM 20, *United States v. E.I. du Pont de Nemours and Company et al.*, Eleutherian Mills Historical Library, Wilmington, Del.

41. Senate Republicans called particular attention to Raskob's role in the AAPA during a 1930 investigation of lobbying. They hoped to divert attention from the revelation that their own party chairman was a paid lobbyist for the Tennessee River Improvement Association. *New York Times*, February 14, March 13, 14, 31, April 5, May 22, 1930; U.S., Senate, Committee on the Judiciary, *Lobbying and Lobbyists: Partial Report*, 71st Cong., 2nd sess., May 21, 1930, S.R. 43, pt. 8; and *Lobby Investigation: Hearing before a Subcommittee*, 71st Cong., 2nd sess., 1930, pp. 3676-96.

42. David E. Kyvig, "Raskob, Roosevelt, and Repeal," *Historian* 37 (May 1975): 469-87.

43. Ibid.

44. Prohibition correspondence, 1929-33, presidential subject file, Herbert Hoover Papers, Herbert Hoover Presidential Library, West Branch, Iowa; U.S., National Commission on Law Observance and Enforcement, *Report on the Enforcement of the Prohibition Laws of the United States*, 71st Cong., 3rd sess., 1931, H. doc. 722, pp. iv, 89-162.

45. *New York Herald Tribune*, June 16, 1932; *New York Times*, June 16, 1932.

46. *New York Times*, July 8, July 22, 1933; "Ladies at Roslyn," *Time* 20 (July 18, 1932): 9-10; Jouett Shouse, "How the Repeal of the Prohibition Amendment Will Improve Business," Address to the Advertising Club of Baltimore, September 14, 1932, Jouett Shouse Papers, University of Kentucky, Lexington; Association Against the Prohibition Amendment, *32 Reasons for Repeal* (Washington, D.C., 1932).

47. *New York Times*, November 10, 1932; [Jouett Shouse], *Annual Report of the President of the Association Against the Prohibition Amendment for the Year 1932* (Washington, D.C., 1933), pp. 8-12.

48. U.S., Congress, *Congressional Record*, 72nd Cong., 2nd sess., 1932, 76, pp. 6-13; *New York Times*, December 6, 1932. A resolution proposing a constitutional amendment required a two-thirds margin for passage, and the 272-144 vote of December 5 was six votes short.

49. [Jouett Shouse], *Annual Report of the President of the Association Against the Prohibition Amendment for the Year 1933* (Washington, D.C., 1934), pp. 12-16; AAPA press release, January 10, 1933, John J. Raskob Papers, Eleutherian Mills Historical Library, Wilmington, Del.; U.S., Congress, *Congressional Record*, 72nd Cong., 2nd sess., 76, 1622; Shouse, "The Status of Prohibition Repeal," speech of January 17, 1933, Louisville, Kentucky, AAPA Papers, Library of Congress, Washington, D.C.; *New York Times*, February 14, 1933.

50. David E. Kyvig, "Amending the U.S. Constitution: Ratification Controversies, 1917-1971," *Ohio History* 83 (Summer 1974): 166-68; Vose, *Constitutional Change*, pp. 111-26.

51. Everett Somerville Brown, comp., *Ratification of the Twenty-first Amendment to the Constitution of the United States: State Convention Records and Laws* (Ann Arbor, Mich., 1938), passim, especially pp. 69, 71, 112, 305.

52. Shouse, "The Repeal Victory," NBC radio address, November 7, 1933, Jouett Shouse Papers, University of Kentucky, Lexington.

53. *New York Times*, December 31, 1933.

54. [Shouse], *AAPA Report for 1933*, pp. 38-40; William H. Stayton to AAPA directors, November 27, 1933, Jouett Shouse to John J. Raskob, December 12, 1933, John J. Raskob Papers, Eleutherian Mills Historical Library, Wilmington, Del.; Repeal Associates, report, May 28, 1934, Pierre S. du Pont Papers, Eleutherian Mills Historical Library, Wilmington, Del.

55. Irénée du Pont to Pierre du Pont, July 10, 1934, Pierre du Pont to William H. Stayton, August 3, 1934, Pierre S. du Pont Papers, Eleutherian Mills Historical Library, Wilmington, Del.

56. Shouse, "Memorandum for the personal files of Jouett Shouse relating to the substance of conversation had with President Roosevelt at the White House, Wednesday afternoon, August 15, 1934," August 16, 1934, Jouett Shouse Papers, University of Kentucky, Lexington.

57. *New York Times*, August 29, 1934.

58. James W. Wadsworth, Jr. to William Cabell Bruce, March 30, 1935, James W. Wadsworth, Jr. Papers, Library of Congress, Washington, D.C.

59. *New York Times*, June 22, 1936.

60. Ibid., January 26, 1936; Wolfskill, *Revolt of the Conservatives*, pp. 206-07.

61. *New York Times*, August 6, 1936.

10.

The Wet War: American Liquor Control, 1941–1945

Historians frequently point to war as a major source of social change. Citing such factors as exaggerated patriotism, ethnic conflict, and increasing centralization, scholars have singled out war as the moving force behind numerous developments in the American past. The climax of the social justice movement, the emergence of the civil rights revolution, and the accelerated assimilation of certain immigrant groups are all seen as outgrowths of a wartime climate.[1] While emphasis on the pervasive impact of war generally sharpens scholarly focus, problems can crop up when historians indiscriminately use war as a catchall explanation for deep-rooted social phenomena.

Prohibition represents an obvious case in point. Accepting the version of events depicted by the repeal movement, traditional studies of the "noble experiment" argued that war was an essential factor in securing passage of the Eighteenth Amendment. Submitting that "tendencies in the state of war worked for the dry cause," Andrew Sinclair concluded that without "appeals to war psychology" temperance leaders could not have secured their desired goals.[2] More sympathetic to the temperance program, James Timberlake not only found war responsible for the "size and speed" of the dry victory but also for making a total abstinence amendment possible.[3] Not surprisingly, despite more recent scholarly refutation, the popular notion that prohibition originated during a movement of wartime madness persists.[4]

Is there a correlation between war and prohibition? Does a wartime climate necessarily lead to suppressive measures against drinking? Comparing liquor regulation in a number of belligerent nations during World War I, Ross Evans Paulson concluded that no apparent relationship existed between war and the enactment of permanent prohibition. He observed that countries faced with the most serious wartime threats often seemed least willing to adopt tough anti-liquor restrictions.[5] While Paulson examined wartime liquor regulation in a cross-cultural setting, efforts to equate war and prohibition in America are similarly unwarranted.

Writing in 1944, the Reverend Sam Morris, a fiery temperance advocate, pointed out a startling contrast in the history of American liquor control. "In the last World War," he observed, "the drinking of alcoholic beverages was not only discouraged, but it was specifically forbidden and outlawed. In this war it is promoted and encouraged."[6] Deeply disappointed with the liquor control policies that emerged out of World War II, Morris characteristically overstated his views. Yet the point he made, when stripped of its rhetoric, was essentially accurate. Sharp differences clearly marked the federal liquor control policies during America's two world wars.

Strict curbs on alcoholic beverages characterized the World War I experience. Faced with a wartime emergency, Congress enacted a series of laws in 1917 designed to restrict sharply the hated "liquor traffic." Seeking to protect the health, morals, and proficiency of newly conscripted American troops, lawmakers legislated rigid bans on military drinking. The Selective Service Act of May 1917 established dry zones around military camps throughout the United States and prohibited individuals from selling or serving alcoholic beverages to members of the armed forces—even in private homes. Focusing on the need to conserve food for overseas relief efforts, Congress curtailed liquor manufacturing as well. In August 1917, the Lever Food and Fuel Control Act banned the use of foodstuffs in the manufacture of distilled spirits, effectively ending legal production of hard liquor in the United States for the duration of the war emergency. Cutbacks on liquor production and restrictions on wartime sales led inexorably to a hoped for "final solution" to the alcohol problem—national prohibition. In December 1917, Congress submitted the Eighteenth Amendment to the states for ratification. Prohibition was to be America's lingering legacy of the Great War.[7]

Markedly different liquor control policies, however, accompanied World War II. Seeking to avoid any repetition of the World War I experience, lawmakers ignored dry demands for renewed curbs on alcohol. Far from enacting bans on drinking, federal officials enlisted the liquor industry in the war effort in order to raise revenue, provide vital combat materials, and boost military and civilian morale.

Anticipating a far different government response, liquor manufacturers and temperance leaders alike were surprised by the contrasting wartime policies. Industry leaders initially had feared a resurgence of prohibitionist sentiment during the war. As early as 1936, dire warnings had been issued to industry leaders by Repeal Associates, a group established to succeed the Association Against the Prohibition Amendment in maintaining vigilance against drys. Repeal Associates predicted that "if some national emergency (war, for example) developed into national hysteria," drys would again take advantage of the situation.[8] Between 1939 and 1941, industry trade journals viewed war prospects with great interest and frequent hints of alarm.[9]

Temperance groups expected war to provide special opportunities for prohibition. Forecasting renewed efforts to suppress alcohol consumption, a leading dry spokesman warned in 1939 that "the full force of dry pressure would once again be brought to bear on Congress" if the United States entered the war.[10] *Christian Century*, a liberal Protestant weekly with a long record of support for the temperance cause, theorized that war was no friend to "John Barleycorn." Recalling that World War I had provided the "impetus for prohibition in the United States," the journal predicted promising times ahead.[11]

Hoping to take advantage of the national emergency, prohibitionists pushed for federal controls on liquor similar to those enacted in 1917. Top priority was once again given to insuring military sobriety. Seeking to restrict drinking in and around training camps, dry leaders urged the War Department to rescind post-repeal regulations permitting the sale of 3.2 beer on domestic and overseas military bases. Rejecting the view of beer as a beverage of moderation, dry spokesmen denied claims by military leaders that the presence of beer in controlled surroundings encouraged temperate drinking. Rather than representing a policy of lesser evils, beer sold in military canteens under government auspices posed a particular danger to impressionable young men, drys warned. "I would rather have a sober son in a concentration camp in Germany than in a service camp in America," remarked the editor of a temperance monthly, "if that son should become the victim of the drink habit."[12]

Faced with the refusal of military leaders to alter the canteen arrangement, temperance groups demanded Congressional action. Dusting off familiar arguments, dry spokesmen added new twists. Prohibitionists lamented the burden alcohol imposed on national strength. Representative Joseph R. Bryson of South Carolina told an Anti-Saloon League gathering in 1941 that alcohol "is no friend to national defense." Charging that high liquor consumption was in large measure to blame for the fall of France to strongly disciplined, sober German forces, Bryson asked, "Will tomorrow find America softened by alcohol for the same sort of moral collapse?"[13] *Christian Century* brooked no excuses from opponents of military liquor curbs. "One does not need to favor the return of national prohibition," the weekly argued, "to advocate the removal of liquor from the camps in which the nation's young men are compelled to live."[14]

Sympathetic congressmen began introducing a host of so-called military protective bills in 1941 soon after lawmakers had approved Selective Service legislation. Senate Bill 860, sponsored by Texas Democrat Morris Sheppard, a long-time prohibition advocate, gained the most notoriety. Sheppard's bill called for bans on the sale and possession of alcoholic beverages "including beer, ale, or wine," at all American military bases and authorized the Secretaries of War and the Navy to create dry zones in the vicinity of camps that required them. Seeking broad support for the legislation, Sheppard included vice restrictions in his bill. Emphasizing the moderation of the proposed curbs, the Texas Democrat observed that under his bill, in contrast to the World War I statutes, servicemen could still lawfully buy liquor wherever it was legally available. Senate Bill 860, he argued, would "simply remove liquor from the workshop of the American Army, Navy and Air Force."[15]

Military drinking, however, though a special concern in 1917, prompted little Congressional action during World War II. Ignoring the pleas of church and temperance groups to re-enact earlier controls, Congress instead chose to accept the advice offered by the many critics of Senate Bill 860. War Department officials voiced strong opposition to the proposal. Secretary of War Henry Stimson wrote the Senate Committee on Military Affairs urging defeat for the first three sections of the bill, dealing with alcoholic beverages, and support for the fourth section, on prostitution. Convinced that "temperance cannot be attained by prohibition," Stimson regarded existing laws permitting the sale of beer and light wine on military bases as the best alternative. "This policy," he argued, "has caused a degree of temperance among Army personnel which is not approachable in civil communities now." The Secretary believed that War Department regulations encouraged American soldiers "to remain on the reservation (their home) and enjoy refreshment under conditions conducive of temperance." [16]

Senate Bill 860 faced forceful attacks from other sources as well. Newspapers gave wide dissemination to a survey of Army camp conditions conducted by the Office of War Information (OWI) in the fall of 1942. OWI reporters found troops not engaged in excessive drinking, 3.2 beer sales a positive factor, and Army officers preferring wet communities to dry. "Bootleggers cannot be regulated," the report concluded, "legal dispensers can." Seeking to calm rumors of military debauchery, the survey informed American mothers that the "best-selling beverages around Army camps are coffee, milk, malted milk, and bottled soft drinks." [17] The head of a Pennsylvania liquor control study group warned that taking beer from canteens would create intense resentment among soldiers. "We believe our men have the maturity to face the enemy successfully," he observed. "Shall we add, 'but you haven't got enough of what it takes to face a drink?'" [18]

Mounting public criticism and limited Congressional support caused most military prohibition bills to die in House or Senate committees. [19] Preferring to rely on army regulations to enforce sobriety among the troops, legislators adopted no special bans on liquor sales to soldiers and established no new dry zones around military training camps where state and local laws had not already mandated them. Despite the entreaties of religious and temperance leaders to curtail alcohol consumption among servicemen, only beer drinking aboard Navy ships remained expressly forbidden during the war—ostensibly because of "storage problems." [20]

If federal inaction on alcohol consumption by servicemen upset drys, government policies pursued during the war proved even more disconcerting. Not only were soldiers permitted to consume beer under military auspices, but government agencies seemed determined to make it easy for them to do so. A Food Distribution Administration order, issued in 1943, required brewers to set aside 15 percent of total annual beer production for use by the armed forces. [21] The War Production Board (WPB), in banning continued use of nonreturnable beer cans and bottles, specifically exempted supplies destined for overseas military shipment. [22] Local draft boards were authorized to grant deferments to highly skilled, irreplaceable brewery workers. [23] In January 1945, the War Labor Board ordered Teamsters to end a strike against Minneapolis breweries because beer manufacturing was considered an essential industry. [24] That same year, army leaders made plans to operate recently recaptured French breweries to insure adequate supplies would be available to troops. [25]

Dry leaders strongly protested the turnabout in wartime alcohol policy. Edward Blake, Prohibition Party national chairman, telegrammed Secretary Stimson to voice indignation over the brewery plan. "It seems incredible that money loaned the government by self-sacrificing bond buyers should be used to create a beer-drinking habit among soldiers," Blake complained. [26] A dry editor wondered aloud if Americans were fighting "[t]o make the world safe for the liquor traffic?" [27] Picking up on the theme, Bishop James Cannon sadly observed that "[t]he contrast between the efforts of the Wilson administration to protect our armed forces from liquor . . . and that of the present Administration . . . is startling indeed." [28]

Faced with far less severe liquor control measures during World War II, GIs nonetheless confronted a few restrictions. In 1942, military authorities imposed curfews on sales to members of the armed forces in eight western states. From time to time, similar curfews were put into effect elsewhere. [29] Seeking compliance with a turn-of-the-century law, the War Department also banned the sale of distilled spirits in officers' clubs on military reservations. [30] Such policies, however, offered little solace to drys.

Along with efforts to curb drinking by GIs, temperance groups pressed for other wartime changes as well. Citing a need to conserve grain, sugar, and other raw materials, dry leaders rekindled demands for restrictions on liquor manufacturing. Urging a cessation of wartime liquor production and a redistillation of stored liquor for salvaging purposes, *Christian Century* asked, with limitations "being placed on automobiles, refrigerators, articles of clothing, certain kinds of food, why should booze be promised immunity from making sacrifices?"[31]

Having failed to achieve curbs in military drinking during the war, however, drys fared only slightly better in efforts to restrict liquor manufacturing. Although the arguments advanced by temperance leaders carried little weight with federal officials, the WPB nonetheless ordered a halt to distilled spirits production in October 1942. Hardly intending to ostracize distillers in issuing the ban, government agencies assigned liquor manufacturers a major wartime role—providing vast quantities of industrial alcohol for such vital war materials as explosives, antifreeze, and synthetic rubber.[32]

Hoping to avoid the adversary relationship which had existed during World War I, wartime administrators worked to secure the cooperation of the liquor industry in converting distillery operations. Industry representatives joined government agencies in policy-making capacities.[33] The WPB offered distillers a cost-plus, fixed-profit allowance for producing war alcohol with conversion costs to be fully borne by the government. Distilleries were converted on a voluntary basis at first with full-scale conversion coming only as war orders and lend-lease requirements surged forward. In addition, beer, wine, rum, and brandy manufacturing—less suited for industrial alcohol production—were not affected by the government order.[34]

Sharply critical of the World War I production cutoff, distillers generally welcomed the World War II ban. Confident that the curb would prove temporary and presaged no prohibitionist assault, liquor manufacturers hailed the opportunity to display their patriotism and avoid a recurrence of postwar problems.[35] Envisioning no efforts to curb liquor sales and hoping to solve longstanding overproduction problems, distillers expected to meet wartime demand with the estimated five-year supply of whiskey aging in government warehouses.[36] The Distilled Spirits Institute, an industry trade association, observed in 1942 that "[n]either the War Production Board nor any other government agency has given any indication that its actions are intended to place restrictions on the use of alcoholic beverages by reason of the social problems involved." Noting that the curbs were designed solely to further the war effort, the Institute cautioned Americans to be thankful that Prohibition had ended before the wartime crisis occurred. [37]

If distillers harbored any secret doubts about government intentions during the war, the removal of production curbs for a brief time in 1944 and 1945 served to reassure them further. Fearing a drain on industry resources as a result of sky-rocketing wartime consumption, liquor manufacturers reduced the amount of whiskey supplied to wholesalers by 30 percent in late 1942. Convinced of the possibility of a liquor shortage after the war—when the lifting of government price ceilings would make sales even more lucrative—industry representatives permitted whiskey to join the already long list of scarce wartime consumer goods. [38] By mid-1943, liquor stores commonly limited package sales to regular customers, often on a tie-in basis—requiring them to buy a stipulated amount of gin and rum in order to obtain the more desirable whiskies. Hard-pressed state monopoly systems were forced to institute strict liquor rationing. Even bootleggers and a revived black market proved largely unable to satisfy stepped-up consumer demand during the war because of difficulties in obtaining rationed raw materials in sufficient quantity at reasonable cost. [39]

Sparking a national controversy, distillers appealed for federal assistance in solving supply problems. In 1943, the Senate established a special subcommittee to investigate ways of increasing the available whiskey supply. Blaming the shortage on monopolistic industry trade practices, Senate investigators nonetheless rejected the idea of forcing distillers to sell off all whiskey stored in government warehouses longer than four years. [40]

By late 1943, distillers were privately urging lawmakers to grant a "liquor holiday"—a furlough during which the production of beverage alcohol might be resumed. Reluctant to plead openly at first, fearing possible repercussions, liquor manufacturers enlisted support from influential members of the administration, most notably Treasury Secretary Henry Morgenthau, as well as beleaguered state liquor officials. Proponents argued that current stocks of industrial alcohol were more than adequate for the war effort and that a liquor holiday would guarantee a continued flow of much-needed tax revenue for the duration and immediate aftermath of the war. [41] In 1944, the WPB permitted three plants to manufacture an experimental quantity of spirits made from surplus and waste potatoes and skins. While test marketing in New York City proved surprisingly brisk, the measure did little to ease the shortage.[42]

Convinced that existing alcohol reserves insured the nation against any and all contingencies, federal officials finally acceded to industry requests for a "liquor holiday" in August 1944. Distillers asked for and received two additional holiday periods in January and July 1945. During these months the WPB also permitted industrial alcohol plants to manufacture liquor.[43]

Not surprisingly, dry spokesmen decried the "liquor holidays." "If there is sufficient synthetic rubber on hand," a group of petitioners wondered, "why cannot civilians get tires?"[44] Rep. Clifford Hope of Kansas demanded that Congress investigate the planned policy changes, contending that farmers had not gone all out in producing grain "for the purpose of making possible a whiskey holiday."[45] Stunned by the move, dry leaders nonetheless proved unable to save a policy they had no role in making.

Faced with mild wartime restrictions, liquor manufacturers celebrated long-awaited good times. From repeal until the war years beer consumption had hovered well below the pre-prohibition high of 66 million barrels reached in 1914 (see Table 10.1). Distressed by the low sales, brewers blamed the depression economy, high taxation, and the lingering effects of the noble experiment for their plight.[46] Limited restrictions, military procurement policies, and increased consumer spending during wartime, however, pushed beer consumption to record levels after 1943. Forecasting even better prospects ahead, *Brewers Digest* provided ammunition for drys in 1941 by candidly viewing the establishment of army camps as "a chance for brewers to cultivate a taste for beer in millions of young men who will eventually constitute the largest beer-consuming section of our population."[47] Distilled spirits sales also registered large gains (see Table 10.2). Between 1941 and 1942 total apparent consumption of hard liquor grew by more than 20 percent.

While generally encouraged by the favorable business climate, liquor manufacturers nonetheless faced a number of vexing wartime problems. A few federal agency heads continued to regard liquor as something of a pariah during the war. Federal regulations barred the industry from touting GI alcohol consumption or in any way using military themes in ad campaigns.[48] Army leaders also sought to play

Table 10.1 Total and Per Capita Consumption of Malt
Beverages in the United States, 1934–45

Calendar Year	Total Consumption (in barrels)	Per Capita Consumption (in gallons)
1934	35,862,145	8.8
1935	41,476,658	10.1
1936	48,928,871	11.8
1937	52,193,605	12.6
1938	50,385,365	12.0
1939	52,308,044	12.4
1940	51,244,274	12.1
1941	56,971,239	13.3
1942	62,967,617	14.6
1943	70,367,841	16.2
1944	76,490,083	17.8
1945	79,753,005	18.7

Source: United States Brewers Foundation, *The Brewing Industry in the United States: Brewers Almanac* (New York: United States Brewers Foundation, Inc., 1954), pp. 52, 54.

Note: A barrel of beer contains 31 gallons. Per capita consumption figures are based on total population, not merely those of drinking age.

down GI drinking—temperate or otherwise.[49] Serious manufacturing and distribution snags proved even more troublesome. Railway tie-ups on the West Coast led the WPB to insist that national brewers discontinue deliveries there.[50] Military priorities led government agencies to restrict use of various agricultural and packaging materials.[51] Yet in nearly all cases, federal officials treated liquor manufacturing like any other U.S. industry in applying wartime controls. *Modern Brewery Age* observed that "the changes made necessary by wartime restrictions need not prove particularly injurious and may well prove a blessing in disguise."[52] Dry leaders angrily agreed. The Woman's Christian Temperance Union complained that when the matter of "priorities has been under consideration, it has been with great reluctance that any restrictions were placed on the alcoholic beverage industry and these have only taken effect after the industry has been permitted to well stock itself . . . not only to maintain its status quo but actually to expand."[53] Decrying the deference shown

Table 10.2 Total and Per Capita Consumption of Distilled
Spirits in the United States, 1934–45

Calendar Year	Total Consumption (in gallons)	Per Capita Consumption (in gallons)
1934	57,964,788	0.65
1935	89,670,446	0.82
1936	122,117,965	1.08
1937	135,362,692	1.16
1938	126,892,827	1.05
1939	134,653,694	1.08
1940	144,991,927	1.16
1941	158,156,921	1.26
1942	190,248,257	1.52
1943	145,529,454	1.16
1944	166,679,635	1.38
1945	190,130,760	1.51

Source: Distilled Spirits Institute, *Apparent Consumption of Distilled Spirits, 1934–1948* (Washington, D.C.: Distilled Spirits Institute, Inc., 1949), p. 2.
Note: Per capita consumption figures are based on total population, not merely those of drinking age. This table includes consumption in wet states only.

the liquor industry, *Christian Century* suggested that "something has happened to the American mind with respect to liquor which prevents us from dealing with it according to the pressing needs of the hour." [54]

Stymied in attempts to achieve limited goals, dry leaders pressed for even wider restrictions. By late 1942, church and temperance groups were demanding that Congress completely prohibit the manufacture and sale of alcoholic beverages for at least the duration of the conflict. [55] Failure to adopt a stern wartime temperance program, drys warned, would greatly lessen Allied chances for victory. "Our enemies . . . are notably progressive in anti-alcoholic military measures," advised Kansas Representative U.S. Guyer, "but the United States still lags behind." [56]

Pearl Harbor provided drys with a case in point. Finding ready explanations for Japanese successes, temperance publicists regarded the timing of the Sunday morning attack as no accident. A typical Saturday night of "strong drink rendered the island helpless, befuddled, off-guard, and at the mercy of the heartless Japs," one claimed.[57] A booklet entitled *What Really Happened at Pearl Harbor?* informed readers in 1943 that local Japanese saloonkeepers—notified of the impending attack—made sure that U.S. troops were well supplied with alcohol the night before.[58] George Barton Cutten, president of Colgate University, complained that a ban on intoxicants in Honolulu since the attack was a case of too little, too late. Rejecting the findings of the Roberts Commission, which found no evidence of excessive drunkenness among defending forces, Cutten told a 1942 Northern Baptist convention that "77 days of prohibition at Pearl Harbor before December 7, instead of 77 days afterward, might have saved us from the worst naval defeat [in our nation's] history."[59] Citing absenteeism among defense workers, possible "loose" speech by government personnel, and the wasting of precious raw materials on liquor, drys nonetheless met with little success in their endeavors.[60] Congress remained adamant in opposing any return to World War I controls.

What factors accounted for the sharp change in federal policy? Reduced voter support for the temperance cause played the largest role. Dry leaders simply lacked a strong base from which to press for federal liquor bans during the war. In 1917, as a result of decades of temperance agitation, more than half the states were already dry. As early as 1914, voters elected a Congress pledged to support prohibition. Statewide referenda, editorial opinion, and pressure from business, civic, and religious leaders all indicated deep and widespread backing for the temperance cause. As one historian has observed, U.S. entry into World War I at most transformed a Congressional majority for prohibition into an overwhelming mandate.[61]

Prohibitionists, however, faced a far more difficult task during World War II. In 1941, no state completely barred the sale of beer, while only three—Mississippi, Kansas, and Oklahoma—continued to prohibit hard liquor. Only a small number of Congressmen, largely from southern and plains states, vocally backed the dry cause. In addition, pollsters revealed strong voter opposition to wartime liquor curbs. The Gallup Poll reported that between 34 and 37 percent of the electorate supported prohibition—a figure consistent with responses during the immediate post-repeal years.[62] Suggesting fourteen different kinds of sacrifices which the government might require in the event of war, a pre-war *Fortune* survey rated a new national prohibition law least acceptable.[63] Only one state considered the question of prohibition during the war years. Nebraska voters rejected a statewide liquor ban by more than three to one.[64] Drys managed only minor gains in wartime local option balloting as well.[65] (See Table 10.3).

Failing to approach pre-World War II strength, temperance groups also confronted a more sophisticated and formidable opponent in the post-repeal liquor industry. During World War II wets capitalized on the pervasive negative image of the Volstead years. Liquor lobbyists held up the specter of bootlegging, corruption, and poison whiskey in asserting that any steps taken to restrict wartime liquor sales might once again lead the nation back to national prohibition. In addition, industry officials urged a moratorium on wartime local option elections. Suggesting that Americans forgo such potential divisiveness, *Spirits* magazine chided drys for seeking referenda on the liquor question while millions of American servicemen were out of the country and unable to vote.[66]

Massive advertising and public relations campaigns also bolstered

Table 10.3 Results of Local Option Elections on Distilled Spirits Sales, 1940–45

Calendar Year	Net Dry Gain (in geographic units)	Net Dry Gain (in population)	Total Percent Dry
1940	14	70,880	18.3
1941	104	255,271	17.5
1942	119	689,114	18.4
1943	116	646,962	18.9
1944	−10	229,609	19.3
1945	44	311,293	18.9

Source: Distilled Spirits Institute, *Annual Report of the Distilled Spirits Institute, Inc.* (Washington, D.C.: Distilled Spirits Institute, Inc., 1940–46).

Note: Geographic units in local option elections vary according to state law. Some states mandate that balloting take place on a county level. Others provide for elections in cities or towns. Southern states with traditionally large dry populations accounted for nearly all the wartime dry gains. Among the states exhibiting the strongest anti-liquor sentiment during the war were Kentucky, Alabama, Texas, Arkansas, and Virginia.

industry efforts to maintain a favorable climate during the war. The Brewing Industry Foundation, claiming "Morale is a Lot of the Little Things," touted beer drinking as a natural and essential part of the wartime scene. Anheuser-Busch, the nation's largest brewery, launched a major advertising campaign in 1942 boosting the company's production of war-related products other than beer. [67] War bonds work also kept industry public relations executives busy. Typical was a 1943 advertisement by the Standard Wine and Liquor Company, New York City wholesalers. Assigning forty-five salesmen to war bonds work at the height of the liquor shortage, company officials boasted, "Who Says There's Nothing to Sell!" [68] A whiskey advertisement exhorted consumers, "Don't Buy Liquor, Buy United States Defense Bonds." [69] Occasionally, liquor manufacturers promoted public relations clean-up campaigns, like the brewing industry's Nebraska Plan, in an effort to correct abuses at the retail level and to counter dry support. [70]

Wets also gave full exposure to GIs' anti-prohibition sentiment. Both in word and deed, American servicemen expressed strong and damaging opposition to wartime temperance proposals. Ernie Pyle, the war correspondent, reported that:

There is a great deal more talk along the line of "Those Bluenoses back home better not try to put prohibition over on us while we're away this time" than you hear about bills and resolutions looking toward the postwar world. [71]

A *Stars and Stripes* editorial voiced alarm at "the growing political strength of the anti-liquor crowd" back home. Recalling the days of prohibition, editors demanded that dry leaders "wait until we return before initiating any further legislation on liquor control." [72] At its 1942 convention, the American Legion urged Congress to insure that "all questions of prohibition . . . be deferred until the end of the present war." [73] A poll conducted among American servicemen overseas by the British Institute of Public Opinion recorded 85 percent wet, 9 percent dry, and 6 percent undecided. [74]

Widespread GI drinking—even under the most adverse wartime conditions—further bolstered the wet cause. Many Americans came to realize that the question was not whether American servicemen would drink but simply what they would drink. On her trip to the Pacific theater in 1943, Eleanor Roosevelt sadly reported the absence of wine and beer on one of the islands. "Last night four men died from drinking distilled shellac," she lamented. [75] In 1945, the Army disclosed that 188 GIs had died in France and Germany between January 1 and July 10 from consuming bootleg methyl (wood) alcohol. [76] Herbert Charles, president of the United States Brewers Foundation, saw a lesson in the tragedy. "It is bad enough that many American young men have had to die or be maimed in the war itself," he told a New York gathering of sales executives. "Is it not far better that they are able to get a bottle or can of clean, pure, wholesome beer wherever it can be made available to them?" [77]

Forrest Harrison, a naval medical officer, voiced concern over the ban on shipboard drinking. An alcoholic confined at sea, he observed, was likely to "drink vanilla extract, hair tonic, bay rum or anything else containing alcohol that he can lay his hands on." Nonetheless Harrison contended that alcohol did "not constitute a serious problem in the Navy," serving as "an excellent aid in quickly releasing tension, dispelling hostilities, and . . . acting as a sedative or soporific" during liberty ashore. Reflecting changes promoted by civilian research agencies, Harrison recommended increased educational and alcoholism treatment programs as far more effective and desirable in dealing with excessive drinking in the Navy than prohibitory legislation. [78]

Other factors also limited dry gains. During World War I temperance leaders capitalized on widespread anti-German sentiment. New revelations about the activities of the brewing industry fueled the dry cause. In 1916 a number of breweries and trade associations faced election law violations. That same year the *New York World* published letters and documents linking several prominent brewing families with pro-German lobbying efforts. [79]

Ethnic antagonisms, however, failed to play into dry hands during World War II. Throughout the pre-war years, brewers for the most part carefully avoided any identification with Hitler's Germany. [80] Moreover, Japanese, not German-Americans, bore the brunt of the ethnic backlash during World War II. [81] With a high representation of Jews among distillers, the liquor industry proved hardly more susceptible to serious fifth-column charges. [82]

While liquor manufacturers seemed immune to any complaints of wartime disloyalty, drys themselves were not. Critics decried temperance advocates as "unwitting tools of enemy propaganda." Unknowingly, one observer recalled, drys "fell in with the German plan of fomenting dissension among the American people."[83] In 1942, Repeal Associates reported "a strong probability of collaboration between German agents and leaders of the Prohibition movement in the United States." Admitting that no concrete documentation existed, directors cited the "great deal of circumstantial evidence available."[84] On at least several occasions, however, inept dry leaders did manage to get the temperance cause identified with Edward Page Gaston, an apparent fascist admirer serving as U.S. director of the World Prohibition Federation.[85] Critics also seized on Pearl Harbor drunkenness stories, charges of dissipation among the troops, and pre-war praise for Adolph Hitler, himself a teetotaler, as examples of questionable allegiance by anti-liquor forces.[86]

If federal officials needed an additional reason to ignore dry demands, the critical tax revenues derived from liquor clearly provided one. Seeking to protect a valued revenue source, lawmakers championed continuing liquor tax collections during the war. Throughout the New Deal era, liquor taxes comprised between 9 and 13 percent of yearly federal revenue. While stiff increases in the income tax reduced that figure to between 4 and 8 percent during the war years, the total volume of liquor revenue reached unprecedented levels (see Table 10.4). Liquor taxes amounted to more than $2.3 billion in fiscal year 1945 compared with just $440 million in fiscal year 1918. Regarding the liquor tax as a fairly painless, easily obtainable source of revenue, Congress increased the excise rate on distilled spirits from $3.00 per proof gallon in 1940 to $4.00 in 1941, $6.00 in 1942, and $9.00 in 1944. Taxes on beer jumped from $6.00 per barrel in 1940 to $7.00 in 1942 and $8.00 in 1944.[87] While drys downplayed the importance of liquor taxes, wet leaders recognized yet another tangible barrier to wartime prohibition. "So long as such enormous sums are needed," a representative of National Distillers Products Corporation told a convention of liquor dealers in 1942, "I doubt if we need indulge in any misgivings" about the future of the industry.[88]

Far from providing special opportunities for prohibition, World War II—like World War I—merely accentuated already existing social trends. Just as strong support for prohibition in the years before 1917 had translated into major efforts to restrict liquor consumption during World War I, World War II control measures reflected a decade of growing disenchantment with the temperance cause. Sensing

Table 10.4 Internal Revenue Collections on Alcoholic
Beverages in the United States, 1934–45

Fiscal Year	Revenue from Alcoholic Beverages	Percent of Total Tax Revenue
1934	$ 258,911,332	8.67
1935	411,021,772	11.28
1936	505,464,037	12.93
1937	594,245,086	11.56
1938	564,978,601	9.44
1939	587,799,701	10.68
1940	624,253,156	10.97
1941	820,056,178	10.56
1942	1,048,516,706	7.80
1943	1,423,646,457	6.27
1944	1,618,775,156	3.99
1945	2,309,865,790	5.23

Source: Tun Yuan Hu, *The Liquor Tax in the United States: A History of the Internal Revenue Taxes Imposed on Distilled Spirits by the Federal Government* (New York: Columbia University Graduate School of Business, 1950), pp. 160–61.

Note: Approximately two-thirds of wartime liquor revenue stemmed from distilled spirits sales. Another third derived from taxes on beer. Wine taxes amounted to less than 3 percent of the total.

widespread acceptance of the post-repeal role of alcohol in American society, federal officials opted for exceedingly lenient wartime controls. In sharp contrast to World War I policies, government actions during World War II only confirmed what repeal had already signaled—an end to decades of serious national conflict over the temperance issue. Mortally wounded by repeal and unable to make any real comeback during the war years, the dry movement faced further decline after 1945. Rising alcohol consumption and the end of the prohibitionist threat, however, insured a far different fate for the postwar liquor industry.

Notes

1. For a good introduction to the literature on war and social change in the United States, see Keith L. Nelson, ed., *The Impact of War on American Life: The Twentieth Century Experience* (New York, 1971). Allen F. Davis,

"Welfare, Reform, and World War I," *American Quarterly* 19 (Fall 1967): 122-29, discusses the social justice movement. See Richard M. Dalfiume, "The 'Forgotten Years' of the Negro Revolution," *Journal of American History* 55 (June 1968): 90-106, on the civil rights movement during World War II. German-American acculturation patterns are explored in Frederick C. Luebke, *Bonds of Loyalty: German-Americans and World War I* (DeKalb, Ill., 1974).

2. Andrew Sinclair, *Prohibition: The Era of Excess* (Boston, 1962), pp. 116-26.

3. James M. Timberlake, *Prohibition and the Progressive Movement, 1900-1920* (Cambridge, Mass., 1963), p. 178.

4. Recent studies downplaying the influence of World War I on prohibition include Ross E. Paulson, *Women's Suffrage and Prohibition: A Comparative Study of Equality and Social Control* (Glenview, Ill., 1973); Norman H. Clark, *Deliver Us from Evil: An Interpretation of American Prohibition* (New York, 1976); and Jack S. Blocker Jr., *Retreat from Reform: The Prohibition Movement in the United States, 1890-1913* (Westport, Conn., 1976).

5. Paulson, *Women's Suffrage and Prohibition*, pp. 160-68.

6. Sam Morris, *Booze and the War* (Grand Rapids, Mich., 1944), p. 17.

7. Sinclair, *Prohibition*, pp. 156-66; Timberlake, *Prohibition and the Progressive Movement*, pp. 173-76; Clark, *Deliver Us from Evil*, pp. 122-29.

8. "Specific Program of Repeal Associates for 1937," *Repeal Review* 1 (December 1936): 8.

9. Most articles, however, tended to reassure liquor manufacturers that the industry would survive any renewed conflict. For example, see Arnold Kruckman, "Brewing Industry Place in Huge National Defense Plan," *American Brewer* 71 (December 1938): 66-70; Paul P. Walsh, "What Will Happen to Brewing Industry if War Comes?" *American Brewer* 72 (September 1939): 46, 48; "Business at Full Blitz! United Kingdom's Industry Retains Perspective under Wartime Stress," *American Wine and Liquor Journal* 9 (February 1942): 11-12.

10. Stanley High, "The Drys Return to the Wars," *Saturday Evening Post* 212 (November 25, 1939): 8-9, 32, 34-35, 37.

11. "Canadians Seek Liquor Curbs," *Christian Century* 57 (August 14, 1940): 489.

12. Eugene V. Rostow, "Recent Proposals for Federal Legislation Controlling the Use of Liquor," *Quarterly Journal of Studies on Alcohol* 3 (September 1942): 230-35.

13. U.S., Congress, *Congressional Record*, 77th Cong., 2nd sess., p. 8508.

14. "Was American Youth Drafted for This?" *Christian Century* 58 (July 9, 1941): 875-76.

15. U.S., Congress, *Congressional Record*, 77th Cong., 2nd sess., pp. 418-

24; Rostow, "Recent Proposals," pp. 230-35.

16. Randolph Childs, *Making Repeal Work* (Philadelphia, Pa., 1947), p. 244; Rostow, "Recent Proposals," pp. 231-33. Stimson's views underwent no change after Pearl Harbor. See U.S., Congress, *Congressional Record*, 77th Cong., 2nd sess., p. 2319.

17. Office of War Information, *Coast to Coast Survey of Drinking Conditions in and around Army Camps*, Office of War Information Report no. 1 (Washington, D.C., 1943); Childs, *Making Repeal Work,* pp. 245-47; *New York Times*, December 31, 1942. Drys derided the OWI survey as wet propaganda. See, for example, the remarks of Senator W. Lee O'Daniel of Texas, U.S., Congress, *Congressional Record*, 78th Cong., 1st sess., pp. 203-04.

18. Childs, *Making Repeal Work*, p. 245.

19. The one major exception was the so-called Lee Amendment, which came to a vote on October 22, 1942. Sponsored by Oklahoma Democrat Josh Lee, the amendment was proposed as a rider to the bill drafting eighteen- and nineteen-year-olds. A motion to refer Lee's proposal back to the Senate Committee on Military Affairs, where it would face a certain death, was approved by a vote of 49 to 25. No other piece of legislation initiated by drys ever again received a formal House or Senate vote. U.S., Congress, *Congressional Record*, 77th Cong., 2nd sess., pp. 8524-45; Childs, *Making Repeal Work*, pp. 244-45.

20. Stanley Baron, *Brewed in America: A History of Beer and Ale in the United States* (Boston, 1962), pp. 332-34; William L. Downard, *The Cincinnati Brewing Industry: A Social and Economic History* (Athens, O., 1973), p. 138; Alvin Griesedieck, *The Falstaff Story* (St. Louis, Mo., 1951), pp. 199-200; "Navy Still Bars Beer," *Brewers Digest* 19 (June 1944): 53.

21. "Food Distribution Order 66," *Brewers Digest* 18 (August 1943): 17. Government favoritism toward big business, prevalent in the awarding of most war contracts, was reflected in beer allocation procedures as well. Because small brewers faced difficulties meeting the requirements of Army officials, the large national brewers received a disproportionate share of military business. "Embattled Beer," *Business Week* (November 24, 1945), pp. 42-45; U.S., Congress, *Congressional Record*, 78th Cong., 3rd sess., pp. 204-05.

22. Baron, *Brewed in America*, p. 334; Richard R. Lingeman, *Don't You Know There's a War On? The American Home Front, 1941-1945* (New York, 1970), p. 253; "War Production Board Bans Beer in Cans." *American Brewer* 75 (February 1942): 42.

23. Baron, *Brewed in America*, p. 335.

24. *New York Times*, January 24, 1945.

25. "Sales Executives Given Review of Brewing Industry Since Repeal," *Brewers Digest* 20 (August 1945): 38.

26. Ibid.

27. U.S., Congress, *Congressional Record*, 77th Cong., 2nd sess., p. A1670.

28. James Cannon Jr., *Hornet or Bee Sting—Which Is Worse?* (Richmond, Va., 1943), p. 2.

29. Childs, *Making Repeal Work*, p. 247.

30. *New York Times*, February 4, 1943.

31. "Why Not Wartime Prohibition?" *Christian Century* 59 (January 14, 1942): 37.

32. Civilian Production Administration, Bureau of Demobilization, *Alcohol Policies of the War Production Board and Predecessor Agencies, May 1940 to January 1945*, Historical Reports on War Administration, War Production Board, Special Study no. 16, Prepared under the supervision of James W. Fesler, War Production Board Historian, by Virginia Turrell (Washington, D.C., 1945), pp. 4-5, 25, 41; Licensed Beverage Industries, Inc., *Beverage Distilling Industry Facts and Figures, 1934-1945* (New York, 1946), p. 45.

33. M.J. McNamara, vice-president of National Distillers Products Corporation and the Distilled Spirits Institute, was appointed to the WPB in early 1942. Other industry leaders served in the Office of Price Administration. U.S., Senate, *Liquor Industry*, Hearings before a Subcommittee of the Committee on the Judiciary on S. Res. 206, 78th Cong., 1st sess., 1944, p. 534.

34. Civilian Production Administration, *Alcohol Policies of the War Production Board*, pp. 49, 62. Despite the exemption, numerous beer and wine manufacturers also sought to share in the conversion program. Civilian Production Administration, *Alcohol Policies of the War Production Board*, pp. 16, 31-32, 81.

35. *New York Times*, January 14, 1942; "History's Greatest Conversion Job," *Spirits* 9 (December 1942): 34-43; Civilian Production Administration, *Alcohol Policies of the War Production Board*, p. 5.

36. "Whiskey Drafted," *Business Week* (May 9, 1942), pp. 48-50; "Distillers Status," *Business Week* (October 17, 1942), pp. 30-32; Civilian Production Administration, *Alcohol Policies of the War Production Board*, pp. 5, 61.

37. Distilled Spirits Institute, Inc., *War Record of the Distilled Spirits Industry* (Washington, D.C., 1942), p. 6.

38. Lingeman, *Don't You Know There's a War On?* p. 253; Tun Yuan Hu, *The Liquor Tax in the United States: A History of the Internal Revenue Taxes Imposed on Distilled Spirits by the Federal Government* (New York, 1950), pp. 112-13; "Blame It on Thirst," *Business Week* (June 12, 1943), p. 93.

39. Childs, *Making Repeal Work*, pp. 190, 200-01, 233-37; M. Nelson McGeary, *Pennsylvania and the Liquor Business: A Study of the Pennsylvania Liquor Control Board* (State College, Pa., 1948), pp. 28-29; Memorandum, Robert E. Hannegan to Henry Morgenthau Jr., November 10, 1943,

Morgenthau Diaries, vol. 675, pp. 22-24, Franklin D. Roosevelt Library, Hyde Park, N.Y.

40. U.S., Senate, Committee on the Judiciary, Investigation of the Alcoholic Beverage Industry, Partial Report no. 2, *Congressional Record*, 78th Cong., 2nd sess., pp. 6738-6743; Childs, *Making Repeal Work*, pp. 233-37.

41. "Whiskey in Sight," *Business Week* (May 6, 1944), pp. 21-23; Hu, *The Liquor Tax in the United States*, pp. 112-13.

42. Civilian Production Administration, *Alcohol Policies of the War Production Board*, p. 110; Donald Rogers, *Since You Went Away* (New Rochelle, N.Y., 1973), p. 20; Lingeman, *Don't You Know There's a War On?* p. 124.

43. "Distillers Get War Alky Furlough," *Business Week* (June 24, 1944), p. 17; "Six Month Oasis," *Business Week* (September 9, 1944), pp. 31-32; Childs, *Making Repeal Work*, pp. 237-38; Hu, *The Liquor Tax in the United States*, pp. 112-13; Licensed Beverage Industries, *Facts and Figures*, p. 25. After announcing plans for the first holiday, the WPB learned that increased military operations in France threatened the alcohol supply picture. Nevertheless, the holiday was allowed to proceed because to "cancel it would have caused too much disruption of the industry." Civilian Production Administration, *Alcohol Policies of the War Production Board*, pp. 111-12.

44. U.S., Congress, *Congressional Record*, 78th Cong., 2nd sess., p. A3756.

45. Ibid., 79th Cong., 1st sess., pp. A2599-2600.

46. Baron, *Brewed in America*, pp. 323-24, 338; Downard, *Cincinnati Brewing Industry*, p. 137.

47. "Beer in the Army Camps," *Brewers Digest* 16 (May 1941): 19; "Was American Youth Drafted for This?" *Christian Century* 58 (July 9, 1941): 875-76.

48. "Relax Army Beer Ad Ban," *Modern Brewery Age* 33 (March 1945): 21; "Rules of Advertising," *American Brewer* 77 (September 1944): 44. Treasury Secretary Morgenthau complained about industry advertising practices at a departmental meeting in 1940. "When I saw 'Serve Army and Navy Rye Whiskey'" ads, he noted, "I thought it meant to serve it to them." He ordered a review of previously approved spirits, wine, and beer labels. Transcript, December 12, 1940, Morgenthau Diaries, vol. 339, pp. 21-28; Memorandum, Stewart Berkshire to Morgenthau, December 13, 1940, Morgenthau Diaries, vol. 339, p. 403. Franklin D. Roosevelt Library, Hyde Park, N.Y.

49. "Armed Forces in Brewer Ads," *American Brewer* 78 (March 1945): 49.

50. "To Ship or Not Ship," *American Brewer* 76 (February 1943): 9.

51. Childs, *Making Repeal Work*, pp. 240-41; Baron, *Brewed in America*, pp. 334-35; "Bottlecap Blues," *Business Week* (June 6, 1942), pp. 50, 54; "Beer Bottlenecks," *Business Week* (May 2, 1942), pp. 19-20.

52. "The Changing Scene," *Modern Brewery Age* 28 (August 1942), pp. 9-10.

53. U.S., Congress, *Congressional Record*, 78th Cong., 1st sess., p. A1400.

54. M.V. Oggel, "Liquor: A Case of National Paralysis," *Christian Century* 60 (June 16, 1943): 717-18.

55. The Woman's Christian Temperance Union reported the following church groups on record in support of wartime prohibition: Northern Baptist, Southern Baptist, Methodist, Disciples of Christ, Presbyterian, United Presbyterian, Reformed Church, Lutheran Church (Norwegian), and Evangelical Church (Augustana Synod). "The Voice of the Church," *Union Signal* 69 (April 24, 1943): 4, 10. The object of their support was a House bill introduced by Rep. Joseph R. Bryson. Not all drys, however, enthusiastically endorsed the measure. The Anti-Saloon League and Bishop James Cannon, Jr. ridiculed the effort as a waste of time. Regarding Congressional passage as most unlikely, dry critics argued that FDR would not enforce the measure in any event. Childs, *Making Repeal Work*, pp. 220, 222; U.S., Congress, *Congressional Record*, 78th Cong., 2nd sess., pp. A1695-96.

56. U.S., Congress, *Congressional Record*, 77th Cong., 1st sess., pp. A5633-34.

57. Morris, *Booze and the War*, p. 9.

58. Dan Gilbert, *What Really Happened at Pearl Harbor?* (Grand Rapids, Mich., 1943), pp. 9-12.

59. "Baptists Ask Ban on War Liquor," *Christian Century* 59 (June 10, 1942): 762. Investigating the attack on Pearl Harbor, the Roberts Commission, headed by Supreme Court Justice Owen Roberts, found that conditions on the night of December 6 with regard to drunkenness among servicemen compared closely with conditions during the previous months. U.S., Senate, *Attack Upon Pearl Harbor by Japanese Armed Forces*, Report of the Commission Appointed by the President of the United States to Investigate and Report the Facts Relating to the Attack Made by Japanese Armed Forces Upon Pearl Harbor in the Territory of Hawaii on December 7, 1941, 77th Cong., 2nd sess., 1942, pp. 13-14.

60. Richard Polenberg, *War and Society: The United States, 1941-1945* (Philadelphia, 1972), pp. 152-53; Childs, *Making Repeal Work*, pp. 224-25; "Have We a Liquor-Sodden Capital?" *Christian Century* 59 (May 27, 1942): 636; "Are We Saving Tin for the Brewers?" *Christian Century* 59 (October 14, 1942): 1243-44; Claude A. Watson, *Repeal Has Succeeded* (Winona Lake, Ind., 1945), pp. 33-39, 90-99.

61. "The Drys Talk It Over," *Repeal Review* 6 (January-March 1944): 17-18; Blocker, *Retreat from Reform*, pp. 235-46.

62. George H. Gallup, ed., *The Gallup Poll: Public Opinion, 1935-1971*, 3

vols. (New York, 1972), vol. 1, pp. 43-44, 90, 129-30, 203-04, 251-52, 322-23, 356, 403, 430, 549.

63. Cited in Elizabeth Livingston, *Report on Conditions Relating to the Campaign for National Prohibition* (Washington, D.C., 1941), p. 3.

64. U.S. Brewers Association, *The Brewing Industry in the United States: Brewers Almanac* (Washington, D.C., 1975), pp. 114-16.

65. Some states did show noticeable dry advances in local option balloting. The number of wet counties in Alabama, for example, declined from 25 in 1939 to 17 in 1943. The fact that many of these counties quickly reversed themselves after the war has led one scholar to contend that residents were not so much voting against liquor as against the presence of off-duty military personnel. William H. Stewart, Jr., *Government and Alcohol: The ABC System in Alabama* (University, Ala., 1973), p. 38.

66. "Whose Option?" *Spirits* 9 (December 1942): 55-57.

67. Roland Krebs, in collaboration with Percy J. Orthwein, *Making Friends Is Our Business: 100 Years of Anheuser-Busch* (St. Louis, Mo., 1953), pp. 345-71. Distillers stressed ancillary scientific activities as well. Karl Morrison, "The State and the Marketing of Alcoholic Beverages in the United States" (Ph.D. diss., University of Texas at Austin, 1948), pp. 239-40.

68. Krebs, *Making Friends Is Our Business*, p. 225; Calvert Distillers Corporation, *Looking Ahead: An Analysis of Liquor Wholesaling with Suggestions for Wartime Operations* (New York, 1943), p. 48.

69. *St. Louis Post-Dispatch*, January 4, 1942.

70. Griesedieck, *The Falstaff Story*, pp. 192-95; Alvin Griesedieck, "Beer and Brewing in a Nation at War," *Quarterly Journal of Studies on Alcohol* 3 (September 1942): 293-301; Carl W. Badenhausen, "Self-Regulation in the Brewing Industry," *Law and Contemporary Problems* 7 (Autumn 1940): 689-95; Carl W. Badenhausen, "The Brewing Industry's Program of Action," *Public Opinion Quarterly* 4 (December 1940): 657-63; "Clean Teamwork," *Spirits* 9 (December 1942): 74-79.

71. Ernie Pyle, *Here Is Your War* (New York, 1943), p. 300.

72. *Stars and Stripes*, May 20, 1943. Quoted in Childs, *Making Repeal Work*, pp. 248-49.

73. U.S., Congress, *Congressional Record*, 77th Cong., 2nd sess., p. 8508.

74. *New York Times*, October 19, 1943.

75. Joseph P. Lash, *Eleanor and Franklin* (New York, 1971), p. 683.

76. *New York Times,* July 24, 1945. Graphic descriptions of GI drinking practices can be found in Bill Mauldin, *Up Front* (New York, 1945), pp. 84-92, and Norman Longmate, *The G.I.'s: The Americans in Britain, 1942-1945* (London, 1975), pp. 206-16.

77. "Sales Executives Given Review of Brewing Industry Since Repeal,"

Brewers Digest 20 (August 1945): 38.

78. Forrest M. Harrison, "The Alcohol Problem in the Navy," *Quarterly Journal of Studies on Alcohol* 5 (December 1944): 413-25.

79. Timberlake, *Prohibition and the Progressive Movement*, pp. 164-65; Sinclair, *Prohibition*, pp. 119-21.

80. This observation is based on extensive reading of brewing industry trade publications between 1933 and 1941. Among the periodicals examined were: *American Brewer, Brewers Digest, Brewers Journal-Western Brewer, Brewers Technical Review, Modern Brewer, Modern Brewery,* and *Modern Brewery Age.*

81. Polenberg, *War and Society*, pp. 37-72; John Morton Blum, *V Was for Victory: Politics and American Culture during World War II* (New York, 1976), pp. 45-52, 147-67.

82. Leading distillers with Jewish backgrounds included Lewis Rosensteil of Schenley Distillers Corporation and Samuel Bronfman of Distillers Corporation-Seagrams Ltd. The fact that Jews played so significant a role in the industry did not go unnoticed by drys. See, for example, the anti-Semitic overtones of Ernest Gordon, *The Wrecking of the Eighteenth Amendment* (Francestown, N.H., 1943), pp. 157-58.

83. Childs, *Making Repeal Work*, pp. 225-26.

84. "Who Dictates Prohibition Policies?" *Repeal Review* 7 (July-September 1942): 7-10; "If You Were Hitler?" *Repeal Review* 6 (July-September 1941): 21-23.

85. John Carlson, *Under Cover: My Four Years in the Nazi Underworld of America* (New York, 1943), pp. 516-17; U.S., Congress, *Congressional Record,* 77th Cong., 2nd sess., pp. 1645-46.

86. Alfred McClung Lee, "Techniques of Social Reform: An Analysis of the New Prohibition Drive," *American Sociological Review* 9 (February 1944): 72. For examples of pre-war praise for Hitler, see "Hitler Attitude toward Alcohol," *Scientific Temperance Journal* 42 (Spring 1933): 18; U.S., House, Foreign Affairs Committee, *World Woman's Christian Temperance Union,* Hearings before the Committee on Foreign Affairs, House of Representatives, 74th Cong., 2nd sess., on S. 3950 to Aid in Defraying the Expenses of the Sixteenth Triennial Convention of the World W.C.T.U. to be held in this Country in June 1937, 1936, pp. 6-7; U.S., Congress, *Congressional Record,* 76th Cong., 1st sess., pp. 2295-96; U.E. Harding, *Liquor Mad America* (Grand Rapids, Mich., 1940), pp. 52-53.

87. Hu, *The Liquor Tax in the United States*, pp. 138-40.

88. "The Alcoholic Beverage Industry Goes to War," *Spirits* 18 (January 1942): 9.

JACQUIE JESSUP

The Liquor Issue in American History: A Bibliography

This is a bibliography of secondary sources dealing with the use of beverage alcohol and social response to that use throughout American history. It does not include anthropological and sociological studies of drinking. For guides to such studies, see: the notes to the Whitehead and Frankel essay, this volume; Michael W. Everett, Jack O. Waddell, and Dwight B. Heath, *Cross-Cultural Approaches to the Study of Alcohol: An Interdisciplinary Perspective* (Paris, 1976); and the abstracts published annually by the *Journal of Studies on Alcohol*. The line between primary and secondary sources has not always been easy to draw, "participant histories" of the liquor industry or temperance movement being particularly difficult to classify. Generally such histories have been included when they seemed to be more than simply polemical in nature and contained retrospective material not available elsewhere or significant statistical or biographical data.

Books

Additon, Lucia H. Faxon. *Twenty Eventful Years of the Oregon Woman's Christian Temperance Union, 1880-1900*. Portland, Ore.: Gotshall Printing Co., 1904.

Ade, George. *The Old-Time Saloon: Not Wet—Nor Dry—Just History*. New York: Richard R. Smith, 1931.

Allsop, Kenneth. *The Bootleggers*. London: Hutchinson, 1961.

Ansley, Lula Barnes. *History of the Georgia Woman's Christian Temperance Union from Its Organization, 1883 to 1907*. Columbus, Ga.: Gilbert Printing Co., 1914.

Appleton, Jean. *La prohibition de L'alcool aux Etats-Unis.* Paris: Editions du "Progrescivique," 1922.

Armstrong, Lebbeus. *The Temperance Reformation: Its History from the Organization of the First Temperance Society to the Adoption of the Liquor Law of Maine, 1851; and the Consequent Influence of the Promulgation of That Law on the State of New York, 1852. . . .* New York: Fowler & Wells, 1853.

Arnold, John Paul, and Penman, F. *History of the Brewing Industry & Brewing Science in America.* Chicago: n.p., 1933.

Asbury, Herbert. *Carry Nation: The Woman with the Hatchet.* New York: Alfred A. Knopf, 1929.

———. *The Great Illusion: An Informal History of Prohibition.* Garden City, N.Y.: Doubleday and Co., 1950.

Austin, Benjamin Fish, ed. *Prohibition Leaders of America.* St. Thomas, Ont.: n.p., 1895.

Baird, R. *Histoire des sociétés de temperance des Etats-Unis d'Amerique, avec quelques détails sur celles de l'Angleterre, de la Suède et autres contreés.* Paris: Hachette, 1836.

The Bancroft Library, Regional Oral History Office. *The California Wine Industry Oral History Project.* 19 vols. Berkeley, Cal.: The Bancroft Library, 1971-1976.

Bandy, William. *Commentary on Intoxicating Liquor Laws in Oklahoma.* St. Paul, Minn.: West Publishing Co., 1953.

Banks, Louis Albert. *The Lincoln Legion: The Story of Its Founder and Forerunners.* New York: Mershon Co., 1903.

Barker, John M. *Saloon Problem and Social Reform.* Boston: Everett Press, 1905.

Baron, Stanley. *Brewed in America: A History of Beer and Ale in the United States.* Boston: Little Brown & Co., 1962.

Beals, Carleton. *Cyclone Carry: The Story of Carry Nation.* Philadelphia: Chilton, 1962.

Beard, Mattie Carson Duncan. *The Woman's Christian Temperance Union in the Volunteer State.* Kingsport, Tenn.: Kingsport Press, 1962.

Beman, Lamar T. *Prohibition: Modification of the Volstead Law.* New York: H.W. Wilson Co., 1924.

———. *Selected Articles on Prohibition of the Liquor Traffic.* 2nd rev. ed. New York: H.W. Wilson Co., 1917.

Black, James. *Brief History of Prohibition and the Prohibition Reform Party.* New York: National Committee of the Prohibition Reform Party, 1880.

Blakey, Leonard Scott. *The Sale of Liquor in the South.* Studies in History,

Economics and Public Law, vol. 51. New York: Columbia University Press, 1912.

Bland, Joan. *Hibernian Crusade: The Story of the Catholic Total Abstinence Union of America.* Washington, D.C.: Catholic University of America Press, 1951.

Blocker, Jack S. Jr. *Retreat from Reform: The Prohibition Movement in the United States, 1890-1913.* Westport, Conn.: Greenwood Press, 1976.

Bossard, James H.S., and Sellin, Thorstein, eds. *Prohibition: A National Experiment.* The Annals of the American Academy of Political and Social Science, vol. 162. Philadelphia: American Academy of Political and Social Science, 1932.

Bradford, S.B. *Prohibition in Kansas and the Kansas Prohibitory Law.* Topeka, Kansas: G.W. Crane Pub. Co., 1889.

Breuere, Martha B. *Does Prohibition Work?* New York: Harper, 1926.

Byrne, Frank L. *Prophet of Prohibition: Neal Dow and His Crusade.* Madison: State Historical Society of Wisconsin, 1961.

Carosso, Vincent P. *The California Wine Industry: A Study of the Formative Years, 1830-1895.* Berkeley: University of California Press, 1951.

Carpenter, Charles K. *The Origin of the Women's Crusade and the WCTU.* N.p.: Mines Press, 1949.

Carter, Paul A. *The Decline and Revival of the Social Gospel: Social and Political Liberalism in American Protestant Churches, 1920-40.* Ithaca, N.Y.: Cornell University Press, 1962.

Catlin, George E. *Liquor Control.* New York: H. Holt & Co., 1931.

Chalfant, Harry Malcolm. *Father Penn and John Barleycorn.* Harrisburg, Pa.: Evangelical Press, 1920.

Chapin, Clara Christiana Morgan, ed. *Thumb Nail Sketches of White Ribbon Women.* Chicago: Women's Temperance Publishing Association, 1895.

Cherrington, Ernest H. *The Evolution of Prohibition in the United States.* Westerville, O.: American Issue Pub. Co., 1920.

————. *History of the Anti-Saloon League.* Westerville, O.: American Issue Pub. Co., 1913.

Cherrington, Ernest H. et al., eds. *Standard Encyclopedia of the Alcohol Problem.* 6 vols. Westerville, O.: American Issue Pub. Co., 1924-30.

Clark, George Faber, *History of the Temperance Reform in Massachusetts, 1813-1883.* Boston: Clark & Carruth, 1883.

Clark, Norman H. *Deliver Us from Evil: An Interpretation of American Prohibition.* New York: Norton, 1976.

————. *The Dry Years: Prohibition and Social Change in Washington.* Seattle: University of Washington Press, 1965.

Clubb, Henry S. *The Maine Liquor Law . . . Including a Life of Hon. Neal Dow*. New York: Fowler & Wells, 1856.

Cochran, Thomas C. *The Pabst Brewing Company: The History of an American Business*. New York: New York University Press, 1948.

Colvin, D. Leigh. *Prohibition in the United States: A History of the Prohibition Party and of the Prohibition Movement*. New York: G.H. Doran Co., 1926.

Committee of Fifty. *Economic Aspects of the Liquor Problem*. Boston: Houghton Mifflin Co., 1899.

————. *The Liquor Problem: A Summary of the Investigations Conducted by the Committee of Fifty, 1893-1903*. Boston: Houghton Mifflin Co., 1905.

————. *Liquor Problem in Its Legislative Aspects*. Boston: Houghton Mifflin Co., 1897.

————. *Physiological Aspects of the Liquor Problem*. Boston: Houghton Mifflin Co., 1903.

————. *Substitutes for the Saloon*. Boston: Houghton Mifflin Co., 1901.

Cyclopaedia of Temperance and Prohibition. New York: Funk & Wagnalls, 1891.

Dabney, Virginius. *Dry Messiah: The Life of Bishop Cannon*. New York: Alfred A. Knopf, 1949.

Daniels, W.H., ed. *The Temperance Reform and Its Great Reformers*. New York: Nelson & Phillips, 1878.

Dobyns, Fletcher. *The Amazing Story of Repeal: An Exposé of the Power of Propaganda*. New York: Willett, Clark and Co., 1940.

Dorchester, Daniel. *The Liquor Problem in All Ages*. New York: Phillips & Hunt, 1884.

Downard, William L. *The Cincinnati Brewing Industry: A Social and Economic History*. Athens: Ohio University Press, 1973.

Dunford, Edward B. *The History of the Temperance Movement*. Washington, D.C.: Tem Press, 1943.

Dykstra, Robert R. *The Cattle Towns*. New York: Alfred A. Knopf, 1968.

Earhart, Mary. *Frances Willard: From Prayers to Politics*. Chicago: University of Chicago Press, 1944.

Eastman, Mary F. *Biography of Dio Lewis, A.M., M.D.* New York: Fowler & Wells, 1891.

Engelmann, Larry D. *Intemperance: The Lost War Against Liquor*. New York: Macmillan Co., 1979.

Ervin, Mary B. *History of the Ohio Woman's Christian Temperance Union*. Columbus: Ohio Woman's Christian Temperance Union, 1949.

Eubanks, John Evans. *Ben Tillman's Baby: The Dispensary in South Carolina, 1892-1915*. Augusta, Ga.: privately published, 1950.

Fanshawe, E.L. *Liquor Legislation in the United States and Canada.* London: Cassell, 1892.

Fehlandt, August F. *A Century of Drink Reform in the United States.* Cincinnati, O.: Jennings and Graham, 1904.

Feldman, Herman. *Prohibition: Its Economic and Industrial Aspects.* New York: D. Appleton & Co., 1927.

Filstead, William J., Rossi, Jean J., and Keller, Mark, eds. *Alcohol and Alcohol Problems: New Thinking and New Directions.* Cambridge, Mass.: Ballinger Pub. Co., 1976.

Finch, Frances E., and Sibley, Frank J. *John B. Finch: His Life and Work.* New York: Funk & Wagnalls, 1888.

Franklin, Jimmie Lewis. *Born Sober: Prohibition in Oklahoma, 1907-1959.* Norman: University of Oklahoma Press, 1971.

Furnas, J.C. *The Life and Times of the Late Demon Rum.* New York: G.P. Putnam's Sons, 1965.

Gordon, Anna. *The Beautiful Life of Frances E. Willard.* Chicago: Woman's Temperance Publishing Association, 1898.

Gordon, Elizabeth Putnam. *Women Torchbearers: The Story of the Women's Christian Temperance Union.* Evanston, Ill.: NWCTU Publishing House, 1924.

Gould, Lewis L. *Progressives and Prohibitionists: Texas Democrats in the Wilson Era.* Austin: University of Texas Press, 1973.

Grose, George Richmond. *James W. Bashford: Pastor, Educator, Bishop.* New York: Methodist Book Concern, 1922.

Gusfield, Joseph R. *Symbolic Crusade: Status Politics and the American Temperance Movement.* Urbana: University of Illinois Press, 1963.

Hammell, George M. *The Passing of the Saloon.* Cincinnati, O.: Tower Press, 1908.

Hays, Agnes Dubbs. *Heritage of Dedication: One Hundred Years of the National Woman's Christian Temperance Union, 1874-1974.* Evanston, Ill.: Signal Press, 1973.

————. *The White Ribbon in the Sunflower State; A Biography of Courageous Conviction, 1878-1953.* Topeka: WCTU of Kansas, 1953.

Hendrickson, Frances. *Hoosier Heritage, 1874-1974: Woman's Christian Temperance Union.* Indianapolis: n.p., 1974.

Hiatt, James M. *The Ribbon Workers.* Chicago: J.W. Goodspeed, 1878.

Hillerman, Abbie B. *History of the Woman's Christian Temperance Union of the Indian Territory, Oklahoma Territory and the State of Oklahoma.* Sapulpa, Okla.: Jennings Printing and Stationery Co., 1925.

Hills, Aaron M. *The Life and Labors of Mary A. Woodbridge.* Ravenna, O.: F.W. Woodbridge, 1895.

Historical Sketch of the Woman's Christian Temperance Union [of Littleton,

N.H.], *1881-1896*. Littleton, N.H.: Courier Publishing Co., 1897.

History of the Woman's Temperance Crusade and Allegheny County Woman's Christian Temperance Union, 1874-1930. N.p.: Allegheny County WCTU, n.d.

Hu, Tun Yuan. *The Liquor Tax in the United States: A History of the Internal Revenue Taxes Imposed on Distilled Spirits by the Federal Government.* New York: Columbia University Graduate School of Business, 1950.

Hunt, Rockwell D. *John Bidwell, Prince of California Pioneers.* Caldwell, Idaho: Caxton Printers, 1942.

Ironmonger, Elizabeth Hogg, and Phillips, Pauline L. *History of the Woman's Christian Temperance Union of Virginia.* Richmond, Va.: Cavalier Press, 1958.

Isaac, Paul E. *Prohibition and Politics: Turbulent Decades in Tennessee 1885-1920.* Knoxville: University of Tennessee Press, 1965.

Jensen, Richard J. *The Winning of the Midwest: Social and Political Conflict, 1888-1896.* Chicago: University of Chicago Press, 1971.

Kleppner, Paul. *The Cross of Culture: A Social Analysis of Midwestern Politics, 1850-1900.* New York: Free Press, 1970.

Kobler, John. *Ardent Spirits: The Rise and Fall of Prohibition.* New York: G.P. Putnam's Sons, 1973.

————. *Capone: The Life and World of Al Capone.* New York: G.P. Putnam's Sons, 1971.

Krout, John A. *The Origins of Prohibition.* New York: Alfred A. Knopf, 1925.

Lathrop, Elise L. *Early American Inns and Taverns.* New York: Tudor Publishing Co., 1935.

Lee, Henry. *How Dry We Were: Prohibition Revisited.* Englewood Cliffs, N.J.: Prentice-Hall, 1963.

Lyle, John H. *The Dry and Lawless Years.* Englewood Cliffs, N.J.: Prentice-Hall, 1960.

McCarthy, Justin. *Prohibitory Legislation in the United States.* N.p.: Tinsley Bros., 1872.

McGeary, M. Nelson. *Pennsylvania and the Liquor Business: A Study of the Pennsylvania Liquor Control Board.* State College, Pa.: Penn Valley Publishers, 1948.

McKenzie, Frederick A. *"Pussyfoot" Johnson, Crusader—Reformer—A Man among Men.* New York: Fleming H. Revell & Co., 1920.

Malin, James C. *A Concern About Humanity: Notes on Reform 1872-1912, at the National and Kansas Levels of Thought.* Lawrence, Kansas: privately published, 1964.

Marshall, Jim. *Swinging Doors.* Seattle, Wash.: Frank McCaffrey, 1949.

Marshall, Thomas K. *The First Six Months of Prohibition in Arizona and Its Effect Upon Industry, Savings and Municipal Government.* Tucson, Arizona: Tucson Printing & Publishing Co., 1915.

Massachusetts. *Drunkenness in Massachusetts; Conditions and Remedies. Special Report of the Board of Trustees of the Foxborough State Hospital.* Boston: Wright & Potter, State Printers, 1910.

————. *Report of the Commission to Investigate Drunkenness in Massachusetts.* Boston: Wright & Potter, State Printers, 1914.

Merz, Charles. *The Dry Decade.* Garden City, N.Y.: Doubleday, Doran and Co., 1931.

Miller, Robert M. *American Protestantism and Social Issues.* Chapel Hill: University of North Carolina Press, 1958.

Odegard, Peter H. *Pressure Politics: The Story of the Anti-Saloon League.* New York: Columbia University Press, 1928.

One Hundred Years of Brewing. Chicago: H.S. Rich & Co., 1903.

Ostrander, Gilman M. *The Prohibition Movement in California, 1848-1933.* Berkeley: University of California Press, 1957.

Parker, T.F. *History of the Independent Order of Good Templars.* New York: Phillips & Hunt, 1882.

Paulson, Ross E. *Women's Suffrage and Prohibition: A Comparative Study of Equality and Social Control.* Glenview, Ill.: Scott, Foresman & Co., 1973.

Pearson, C.C., and Hendricks, J. Edwin. *Liquor and Anti-Liquor in Virginia, 1619-1919.* Durham, N.C.: Duke University Press, 1967.

Pickering, Clarence R. *The Early Days of Prohibition.* New York: Vantage Press, 1964.

Pierce, I. Newton. *The History of the Independent Order of Good Templars.* Philadelphia: Daughaday and Becker, 1869.

Pierce, P.R.L. *A History of the Order of the Sons of Temperance in Ohio.* Cincinnati: Geo. M. Young & Co., 1849.

Quinn, Larry D. *Politicians in Business: A History of the Liquor Control System in Montana.* Missoula: University of Montana Press, 1970.

Root, Grace C. *Women and Repeal: The Story of the Women's Organization for National Prohibition Reform.* New York: Harper & Bros., 1934.

Ross, Ishbel. *Crusades and Crinolines: The Life and Times of Ellen Curtis Demorest and William Jennings Demorest.* New York: Harper & Row, 1963.

Rowntree, Joseph, and Sherwell, Arthur. *The Temperance Problem and Social Reform.* New York: Thomas Whittaker, 1899.

Ruff, Donald G., and Becker, Kurt. *Bottling and Canning of Beer.* Chicago: Siebel Publishing Co., 1955.

Schmeckebier, Laurence F. *The Bureau of Prohibition.* Washington, D.C.: Brookings Institute, 1929.

Schluter, Herman. *The Brewing Industry and the Brewing Workers in America.* Cincinnati, O.: n.p., 1910.

Scomp, Henry Anselm. *King Alcohol in the Realm of King Cotton, or, A History of the Liquor Traffic and of the Temperance Movement in Georgia from 1733 to 1887....* Chicago: Press of the Blakeley Printing Co., 1888.

Scovell, Bessie Lathe. *A Brief History of the Minnesota Woman's Christian Temperance Union, 1877 to 1939.* St. Paul: Bruce Publishing Co., 1939.

Sellers, James Benson. *The Prohibition Movement in Alabama, 1702 to 1943.* Chapel Hill: University of North Carolina Press, 1943.

Sinclair, Andrew. *Prohibition: The Era of Excess.* Boston: Little Brown & Co., 1962.

Steuart, Justin. *Wayne Wheeler, Dry Boss: An Uncensored Biography of Wayne B. Wheeler.* New York: Fleming H. Revell & Co., 1928.

Stewart, William H., Jr. *Government and Alcohol: The ABC System in Alabama.* University, Ala.: Bureau of Public Administration, 1973.

Stinness, J.H. *Rhode Island Legislation against Strong Drink.* Providence, R.I.: n.p., 1919.

Stivers, Richard. *A Hair of the Dog: Irish Drinking and American Stereotype.* University Park: Pennsylvania State University Press, 1976.

Storms, Roger C. *Partisan Prophets: A History of the Prohibition Party, 1854-1972.* Denver: National Prohibition Foundation, 1972.

Stout, Charles Taber. *The Eighteenth Amendment and the Part Played by Organized Medicine.* New York: Mitchell Kennerley, 1921.

Taussig, Charles William. *Rum, Romance and Rebellion.* New York: Minton, Balach & Co., 1928.

Taylor, Robert Lewis. *Vessel of Wrath: The Life and Times of Carry Nation.* New York: New American Library, 1966.

Thomann, G. *Liquor Laws of the United States: Their Spirit and Effect.* New York: United States Brewers' Association, 1887.

Timberlake, James H. *Prohibition and the Progressive Movement, 1900-1920.* Cambridge: Harvard University Press, 1963.

Tyler, Alice Felt. *Freedom's Ferment: Phases of American Social History from the Colonial Period to the Outbreak of the Civil War.* New York: Harper & Row, 1962.

Tyler, Helen E. *Where Prayer and Purpose Meet: The WCTU Story, 1874-1949.* Evanston, Ill.: Signal Press, 1949.

Tyrrell, Ian R. *Sobering Up: From Temperance to Prohibition in Antebellum America, 1800-1860.* Westport, Conn.: Greenwood Press, 1979.

United States Brewers' Association. *Documentary History of the U.S.B.A.*
New York: United States Brewers' Association, 1896-98.

Van Meter, Harriet F. *First Quarter Century of the Woman's Christian Temperance Union, Salem, N.J.* Salem, N.J.: n.p., 1909.

Van Norman, Louis E., ed. *An Album of Representative Prohibitionists.* New York: Funk & Wagnalls, 1895.

Walker, Robert S., and Patterson, Samuel C. *Oklahoma Goes Wet: The Repeal of Prohibition.* New Brunswick, N.J.: Rutgers University Press, 1960.

Walnut, T. Henry, ed. *Prohibition and Its Enforcement.* The Annals of the American Academy of Political and Social Science, vol. 109. Philadelphia: American Academy of Political and Social Science, 1923.

Warburton, Clark. *The Economic Results of Prohibition.* New York: Columbia University Press, 1932.

Ward, Harold Wesley. *The Administration of Liquor Control in Virginia.* Charlottesville: Division of Publications, Bureau of Public Administration, University of Virginia, 1946.

Wheeler, Henry. *Methodism and the Temperance Reformation.* Cincinnati, O.: Walden and Stowe, 1882.

Whipple, Sidney B. *Noble Experiment.* London: Methuen & Co., 1934.

Whitener, Daniel Jay. *Prohibition in North Carolina, 1715-1945.* Chapel Hill: University of North Carolina Press, 1945.

Willard, Frances E. *Woman and Temperance.* Hartford, Conn.: Park Publishing Co., 1883.

Willoughby, Malcolm F. *Rum War at Sea.* Washington, D.C.: Treasury Department, United States Coast Guard, 1964.

Wittenmyer, Annie, *History of the Woman's Temperance Crusade.* Boston: J.H. Earle, 1882.

Woodbury, Nathan Franklin. *Prohibition in Maine.* Lewiston, Me.: Journal Printshop and Bindery, 1920.

Woollen, W.W., and Thornton, W.W. *Intoxicating Liquors: The Law Relating to the Traffic in Intoxicating Liquors and Drunkenness.* 2 vols. Cincinnati, O.: W.H. Anderson Co., 1910.

Woolley, John G., and Johnson, William E. *Temperance Progress in the Nineteenth Century.* Philadelphia: Linscott Publishing Co., 1903.

Theses and Dissertations

Adrian, Frederick Wayne. "The Political Significance of the Prohibition Party." Ph.D., Ohio State University, 1942.

Alexander, Ellen. "The South Carolina Dispensary System." M.A., Duke University, 1940.

Baluyut, Fernando de Lara. "Anheuser-Busch—A Study in Firm Growth." M.A., St. Louis University, 1961.

Barnett, Redmond J. "From Philanthropy to Reform: Poverty, Drunkenness, and the Social Order in Massachusetts, 1780-1825." Ph.D., Harvard University, 1973.

Beattie, Donald W. "Sons of Temperance: Pioneers in Total Abstinence and 'Constitutional' Prohibition." Ph.D., Boston University, 1966.

Beauchamp, Dan Edward. "Precarious Politics: Alcoholism and Public Policy." Ph.D., Johns Hopkins University, 1973.

Benson, Ronald Morris. "American Workers and Temperance Reform, 1866-1933." Ph.D., University of Notre Dame, 1974.

Blanks, James B. "Social Control by Baptists in Virginia and North Carolina, 1775-1928." M.A., Wake Forest College, 1929.

Boocks, G. Clifford. "Experiment in Municipal Reform: The Prohibition Party in Norfolk Politics, 1892-1896." M.A., Old Dominion College, 1967.

Brook, Susan Mary. "The World League against Alcoholism: An Attempt to Export an American Experience." M.A., University of Western Ontario, 1972.

Coffey, John Joseph. "A Political History of the Temperance Movement in New York State, 1808-1920." Ph.D., Pennsylvania State University, 1976.

Cory, Earl Wallace. "Temperance and Prohibition in Ante-Bellum Georgia." Ph.D., University of Georgia, 1961.

Davis, William Graham. "Attacking 'The Matchless Evil': Temperance and Prohibition in Mississippi, 1817-1908." Ph.D., Mississippi State University, 1975.

DePew, Kathryn Mehl. "The Temperance Movement in Territorial Colorado." M.A., University of Colorado, 1953.

Dohn, Norman H. "The History of the Anti-Saloon League." Ph.D., Ohio State University, 1959.

Drescher, Nuala McGann. "The Opposition to Prohibition, 1900-1919: A Social and Institutional Study." Ph.D., University of Delaware, 1964.

Duis, Perry R. "The Saloon and the Public City: Chicago and Boston, 1880-1920." Ph.D., University of Chicago, 1975.

Dwyer, Ellen. "The Rhetoric of Reform: A Study of Verbal Persuasion and Belief Systems in the Anti-Masonic and Temperance Movements 1825-1860." Ph.D., Yale University, 1977.

Engelmann, Larry D. "O Whiskey: The History of Prohibition in Michigan." Ph.D., University of Michigan, 1971.

Forth, William Stuart. "Wesley L. Jones: A Political Biography." Ph.D., University of Washington, 1962.

Frederickson, Edna Tutt. "John P. St. John, The Father of Constitutional Prohibition." Ph.D., University of Kansas, 1930.

Frederickson, Otto F. "The Liquor Question in Kansas before Constitutional Prohibition." Ph.D., University of Kansas, 1931.

French, Warren G. "Timothy Shay Arthur Views His Times." Ph.D., University of Texas, 1954.

Gemmer, H. Robert. "The Contribution of the Prohibition Party." B.D., Chicago Theological Seminary, 1947.

Giele, Janet Zollinger. "Social Change and the Feminine Role: A Comparison of Woman's Suffrage and Woman's Temperance, 1870-1920." Ph.D., Radcliffe College, 1961.

Hall, Alvin LeRoy. "The Prohibition Movement in Virginia, 1826-1916." M.A., University of Virginia, 1964.

Hanson, James E. III. "A Study of Prohibition in Denver." M.A., University of Denver, 1965.

Hayner, Norman S. "The Effect of Prohibition in Packingtown." M.A., University of Chicago, 1921.

Heckman, Dayton E. "Prohibition Passes: The Story of the Association Against the Prohibition Amendment." Ph.D., Ohio State University, 1939.

Hohner, Robert A. "The Anti-Saloon League in Virginia, 1901-1910; Prelude to Prohibition." M.A., Duke University. 1963.

Hohner, Robert A. "Prohibition and Virginia Politics, 1901-1916." Ph.D., Duke University, 1965.

Isetts, Charles A. "The Women's Temperance Crusade of Southern Ohio." M.A., Miami University (Ohio), 1971.

Jackson, William John. "Prohibition as an Issue in New York State Politics, 1836-1933." Ph.D., Columbia University, 1974.

Jones, Bartlett C. "The Debate Over National Prohibition, 1920-1933." Ph.D., Emory University, 1961.

Kaylor, Earl C., Jr. "The Prohibition Movement in Pennsylvania, 1865-1920." Ph.D., Pennsylvania State University, 1963.

Kline, Lawrence Oliver. "H.L. Mencken's Controversy with the Methodists with Special Reference to the Issue of Prohibition." Ph.D., Duke University, 1976.

Krause, Mary Lou. "Prohibition and the Reform Tradition in the Washington State Senatorial Election of 1922." M.A., University of Washington, 1963.

Kyvig, David Edward. "In Revolt Against Prohibition: The Association Against the Prohibition Amendment and the Movement for Repeal, 1919-1933." Ph.D. Northwestern University, 1971.

Langston, Edward Lonnie. "The Impact of Prohibition on the Mexican

United States Border: The El Paso-Ciudad Juarez Case." Ph.D., Texas Tech University, 1974.

Lawrence, Joseph John. "Alcohol and Socioeconomic Statutes in the State of Washington." M.A., Washington State University, 1955.

Lindhurst, James. "History of the Brewing Industry in St. Louis, 1804-1860." M.A., Washington University, 1939.

McCuskey, Wilfrid S. "The Political Campaign of 1883 in Ohio." M.A., Ohio State University, 1948.

Maxwell, Lora E. "History of Liquor Legislation in the State of Washington." Honors, Washington State University, 1917.

Medley, Steven James. "Men Must Live Straight if They Would Shoot Straight: The Campaign to Protect the Morals of American Servicemen in World War I." M.A., University of Western Ontario, 1970.

Mertz, Paul. "Oklahoma and the Year of Repeal, 1933." M.A., University of Oklahoma, 1958.

Mezvinsky, Norton H. "The White Ribbon Reform, 1874-1920." Ph.D., University of Wisconsin, 1959.

Morrison, Karl. "The State and the Marketing of Alcoholic Beverages in the United States." Ph.D., University of Texas at Austin, 1948.

Murray, Sean Collins. "Texas Prohibition Politics, 1887-1914." M.A., University of Houston, 1968.

Murrell, Daniel R. "Prelude to Prohibition: The Anti-Saloon League and the Webb-Kenyon Act of 1913." M.A., University of Western Ontario, 1974.

Nordsieck, Joseph E. "The Prohibition Crusade in Cincinnati." M.A., University of Cincinnati, 1970.

Otis, Delos S. "The Rise of National Prohibition, 1865-1919." Ph.D., University of Wisconsin, 1919.

Pearlin, Leonard I. "An Application of Correlation Methods to the Results of the 1949 Prohibition Referendum." M.A., University of Oklahoma, 1950.

Plavchan, Robert J. "A History of Anheuser-Busch, 1852-1933." Ph.D., St. Louis University, 1969.

Povenmire, Kenneth W. "The Temperance Movement in Ohio, 1840-1860." M.A., Ohio State University, 1933.

Rorabaugh, W.J. "The Alcoholic Republic, 1790-1840." Ph.D., University of California, Berkeley, 1976.

Rumbarger, John J. "The Social Origins and Function of the Political Temperance Movement in the Reconstruction of American Society, 1825-1917." Ph.D., University of Pennsylvania, 1968.

Sandberg, Maxine S. "The Life and Career of Adolphus Busch." M.A., University of Texas, 1952.

Siegel, Nancy Ray. "A Matter of the Public Welfare: The Temperance Movement in Ante-Bellum Cincinnati," M.A., University of Cincinnati, 1971.

Stegh, Leslie Joseph. "Wet and Dry Battles in the Cradle State of Prohibition: Robert J. Bulkley and the Repeal of Prohibition in Ohio." Ph.D., Kent State University, 1975.

Sterling, Dwayne W. "The Repeal of Prohibition in Oklahoma." M.A., University of Oklahoma, 1965.

Tulk, Roger William. "World War I and Congressional Submission of the Eighteenth Amendment." M.A., University of Western Ontario, 1971.

Turner, James R. "The American Prohibition Movement, 1865-1897." Ph. D., University of Wisconsin, 1972.

Unger, Samuel. "A History of the National Woman's Christian Temperance Union." Ph.D., Ohio State University, 1933.

Vigilante, Emil Christopher. "The Temperance Reform in New York State, 1829-1851." Ph.D., New York University, 1964.

Wahl, Sanford Allan. "The Activities of the Woman's Christian Temperance Union of the State of New York in Relation to Alcoholic Beverage Legislation in New York State, 1934-1960." Ph.D., New York University, 1966.

Watson, Julie P. "The Evolution of the Temperance Movement in Nebraska." M.A., University of Nebraska, 1926.

Webb, Louis Winfield. "A Pedagogical Estimate of Scientific Temperance Instruction." M.A., University of Chicago, 1913.

Weisensel, Peter. "The Wisconsin Temperance Crusade to 1919." M.S., University of Wisconsin, 1965.

West, William Elliott. "Dry Crusade: The Prohibition Movement in Colorado, 1858-1933." Ph.D., University of Colorado, 1971.

Whitaker, Francis Myron. "A History of the Ohio Woman's Christian Temperance Union, 1874-1920." Ph.D., Ohio State University, 1971.

Wilkerson, A.E. Jr. "A History of the Concept of Alcoholism." Ph.D., University of Pennsylvania, 1966.

Wittet, George G. "Concerned Citizens: The Prohibitionists of 1883 Ohio." M.A., University of Western Ontario, 1978.

Zwick, Gwen W. "Prohibition in the Cherokee Nation, 1820-1907." M.A., University of Oklahoma, 1940.

Articles

Albertson, D. "Puritan Liquor in the Planting of New England." *New England Quarterly* 23 (1958): 477-90.

Ashby, LeRoy. "The Disappearing Dry: Raymond Robbins and the Last Days of Prohibition." *North Carolina Historical Review* 51 (1974): 401-19.

Bacon, Selden D. "The Classic Temperance Movement of the U.S.A.; Impact Today on Attitudes, Action and Research." *British Journal of Addiction* 62 (1967): 5-18.

Baird, Edward A. "The Alcohol Problem and the Law: III, The Beginnings of the Alcoholic Beverage Control Laws in America." *Quarterly Journal of Studies on Alcohol* 6 (1945): 335-83; 7 (1946): 110-62, 271-96.

Baldwin, Hanson W. "The End of the Wine Mess." *Proceedings, U.S. Naval Institute* 84 (1958): 82-91.

Barclay, George. "The Keeley League." *Journal of the Illinois State Historical Society* 57 (Winter 1964): 364-79.

Beebe, Lucius. "Moriarty's Wonderful Saloon." *American Heritage* 16 (1965): 65-69, 105-06.

Benson, Lee. "Research Problems in American Political Historiography." In *Common Frontiers of the Social Sciences*, edited by Mirra Komarovsky, pp. 113-83. Glencoe, Ill.: Free Press, 1957.

Beveridge, N.E. "Prohibition Comes Early to the Navy." *American History Illustrated* 3 (1969): 50-51.

Blocker, Jack S. Jr. "The Politics of Reform: Populists, Prohibition and Woman Suffrage, 1891-1892." *The Historian* 34 (1972): 614-32.

Boase, Paul H. "In Cases of Extreme Necessity: The Methodists Take Action against Tobacco Chewing and Spitting in Church Along with the Excessive Use of Alcohol." *Bulletin of the Historical and Philosophical Society of Ohio* 16 (1958): 191-205.

Bohner, Charles H. "Rum and Reform: Temperance in Delaware Politics." *Delaware History* 5 (1953): 237-69.

Bordin, Ruth. "'A Baptism of Power and Liberty': The Women's Crusade of 1873-1874." *Ohio History* 87 (Autumn 1978): 393-404.

Brown, Thomas Elton. "Oklahoma's Bone Dry Law and the Roman Catholic Church." *Chronicles of Oklahoma* 52 (1974): 316-30.

Buenker, John D. "The Illinois Legislature and Prohibition, 1907-1919." *Journal of the Illinois State Historical Society* 62 (Winter 1969): 363-84.

Burnham, J.C. "New Perspectives on the Prohibition 'Experiment' of the 1920s." *Journal of Social History* 2 (1968): 51-68.

Burran, James A. "Prohibition in New Mexico, 1917." *New Mexico History Review* 48 (1973): 133-49.

Byrne, Frank L. "Maine Law Versus Lager Beer: A Dilemma of Wisconsin's Young Republican Party." *Wisconsin Magazine of History* 52 (1958/59):115-20.

Campbell, Ballard C. "Did Democracy Work? Prohibition in Late Nineteenth-Century Iowa: A Test Case." *Journal of Interdisciplinary History* 8 (1977): 87-116.

Canup, Charles. "The Temperance Movement in Indiana." *Indiana Magazine of History* 16 (1920): 3-37, 112-51.

Carson, Gerald. "Bourbon: Amber Waves of Grain—100 Proof." *American Heritage* 25 (1974): 60-63.

——. "The Dark Age of American Drinking." *Virginia Quarterly Review* 39 (1963): 94-103.

Carter, James A. "Florida and Rumrunning during National Prohibition." *Florida Historical Quarterly* 48 (1969): 47-56.

Carter, Paul A. "Prohibition and Democracy: The Noble Experiment Reassessed." *Wisconsin Magazine of History* 56 (1973): 189-201.

Case, George L. "Prohibition Party: Its Origins, Purpose and Growth." *Magazine of Western History* 9 (1888/89): 115-24, 243-49, 373-79, 555-64, 705-14.

Cassedy, James H. "An Early American Hangover: The Medical Profession and Intemperance 1800-1860." *Bulletin of the History of Medicine* 50 (Fall 1976): 405-13.

Caswell, John E. "The Prohibition Movement in Oregon, Part 1, 1836-1904." *Oregon Historical Quarterly* 39 (1938): 235-61.

——. "The Prohibition Movement in Oregon, Part 2, 1904-1915." *Oregon Historical Quarterly* 40 (1939): 64-82.

Chapman, J.K. "The Mid-Nineteenth Century Temperance Movements in New Brunswick and Maine." In *Canadian History before Confederation*, edited by J.M. Bumsted, pp. 444-61. Georgetown, Ont.: Irwin-Dorsey, 1972.

Clark, Dan. "The History of Liquor Legislation in Iowa, 1846-1898." *Iowa Journal of History* 6 (1908): 55-87, 339-74, 503-68.

Clark, Roger W. "Cincinnati Crusaders for Temperance: 1874." *Cincinnati Historical Society Bulletin* 32 (1974): 185-98.

Clayton, John. "The Scourge of Sinners: Arthur Burrage Farwell." *Chicago History* 3 (1974): 68-77.

Coleman, Alan. "The Charleston Bootlegging Controversy, 1915-18." *South Carolina Historical Magazine* 75 (1974): 77-94.

Coulter, E.M. "The Athens Dispensary." *Georgia Historical Quarterly*, 1966, pp. 14-36.

Dana, Charles L., et al. "The Medical Profession and the Volstead Act." *Journal of the American Medical Association* 76 (1921): 1592-93.

Dannenbaum, Jed. "The Crusader: Samuel Cary and Cincinnati Temperance." *Cincinnati Historical Society Bulletin* 33 (1974): 137-51.

——. "Immigrants and Temperance: Ethnocultural Conflict in Cincinnati, 1845-1860." *Ohio History* 87 (Spring 1978): 125-39.

Dodd, Jill Siegel. "The Working Classes and the Temperance Movement in Ante-Bellum Boston." *Labor History* 19 (Fall 1978): 510-31.

Drescher, Nuala McGann. "Organized Labour and the Eighteenth Amendment." *Labor History* 8 (1967): 280-99.

Duis, Perry. "The Saloon in a Changing Chicago." *Chicago History* 4 (1975/76): 214-24.

Engelmann, Larry D. "Dry Renaissance: The Local Option Years, 1889-1917." *Michigan History* 59 (1975): 60-90.

———. "The Iron River Rum Rebellion." *Mid-America* 55 (1973): 37-53.

———. "Old Saloon Days in Michigan." *Michigan History* 61 (1977): 99-134.

Faler, Paul. "Cultural Aspects of the Industrial Revolution: Lynn, Massachusetts, Shoemakers and Industrial Morality, 1826-1860." *Labor History* 15 (1974): 367-94.

Fitzgibbon, John. "King Alcohol: His Rise, Reign and Fall in Michigan." *Michigan Historical Magazine* 2 (1918): 737-80.

Foreman, Grant. "A Century of Prohibition." *Chronicles of Oklahoma* 12 (1934): 133-41.

Fraser, Hugh H.J. "Sidney Peters: The First Commissioner of Prohibition in Virginia Traveled a Rocky Road during Four Years of the Great Experiment." *Virginia Cavalcade* 22 (1973): 28-35.

Garrison, Curtis W. "President Hayes, the Opponent of Prohibition." Historical Society of Northwestern Ohio *Quarterly Bulletin* 16 (1944): 164-77.

Gebhart, John C. "Movement against Prohibition." *Annals of the American Academy of Political and Social Science* 163 (1932): 172-80.

———. "Prohibition: Statistical Studies of Enforcement and Social Effects." In *Statistics in Social Studies*, Stuart A. Rice, ed. Philadelphia: University of Pennsylvania Press, 1930.

Gorrell, Donald K. "Presbyterians in the Ohio Temperance Movement of the 1850's." *Ohio State Archeological and Historical Quarterly* 60 (1951): 292-96.

Gould, Lewis L. "Progressives and Prohibitionists: Texas Democratic Politics, 1911-1921." *Southwestern Historical Quarterly* 75 (1971): 5-18.

Greenberg, Irwin F. "Pinchot, Prohibition and Public Utilities: The Pennsylvania Election of 1930." *Pennsylvania History* 40 (1973): 21-36.

Guese, Lucius E. "St. Louis and the Great Whisky Ring." *Missouri Historical Review* 36 (January 1942): 160-83.

Gusfield, Joseph R. "Prohibition: The Impact of Political Utopianism." In *Change and Continuity in Twentieth Century America*, edited by John Braeman, Robert H. Bremner, and David Brody, pp. 257-308. Columbus: Ohio University Press, 1968.

————. "Social Structure and Moral Reform: A Study of the Women's Christian Temperance Union." *American Journal of Sociology* 6 (1955): 221-32.

Hansen, James E. II. "Moonshine and Murder: Prohibition in Denver." *Colorado Magazine* 50 (1973): 1-23.

Harmon, Wendell E. "The Bootlegger in Southern California." *Southern California Quarterly* 37 (1935): 335ff.

Heffernan, John Paul. "Neal Dow." *New England Galaxy* 16 (1974): 11-19.

Hendricks, E.A. "The South Carolina Dispensary System." *North Carolina Review* 22 (1945): 176-97.

Hines, Tom S. Jr. "Mississippi and the Repeal of Prohibition." *Journal of Mississippi History* 24 (1962): 1-39.

Hohner, Robert A. "Bishop Cannon's Apprenticeship in Temperance Politics, 1901-1918." *Journal of Southern History* 34 (1968): 33-49.

————. "Prohibition and Virginia Politics: William Hodges Mann Versus Henry St. George Tucker, 1909." *Virginia Magazine of History and Biography* 74 (1966): 88-107.

————. "The Prohibitionists: Who Were They?" *South Atlantic Quarterly* 68 (1969): 491-505.

Howington, Arthur F. "John Barleycorn Subdued: The Enforcement of Prohibition in Alabama." *Alabama Review* 23 (1970): 212-25.

Hudson, Peter J. "Temperance Meetings among the Choctaws." *Chronicles of Oklahoma* 12 (1934): 130-32.

Ingraham, Charles A. "The Birth at Moreau of the Temperance Reformation." *New York State Historical Association Proceedings* 6 (1906): 115-33.

Jellinek, E.M. "Recent Trends in Alcoholism and in Alcohol Consumption." *Quarterly Journal of Studies on Alcohol* 8 (1947): 1-42.

Kaplan, H.R. "A Toast to the Rum Fleet." *Proceedings, U.S. Naval Institute* 94 (1968): 84-90.

Kingsdale, Jon M. "The 'Poor Man's Club': Social Functions of the Urban Working Class Saloon." *American Quarterly* 25 (1973): 472-89.

Kirby, Jack Temple. "Alcohol and Irony: The Campaign of Westmoreland Davis for Governor, 1909-1917." *Virginia Magazine of History and Biography* 73 (1965): 259-79.

Kottman, Richard N. "Volstead Violated: Prohibition as a Factor in Canadian-American Relations." *Canadian Historical Review* 43 (1962): 106-26.

Krout, John A. "The Genesis and Development of the Early Temperance Movement in New York State." *The Quarterly Journal of the New York State Historical Association* 4 (1923): 78-98.

Kyvig, David E. "Raskob, Roosevelt, and Repeal." *The Historian* 37 (1975):

469-87.

―――. "Women against Prohibition." *American Quarterly* 28 (1976): 465-82.

Landis, Carney, and Cushman, Jane F. "The Relation of National Prohibition to the Incidence of Mental Disease." *Quarterly Journal of Studies on Alcohol* 5 (1945): 527-34.

Laurie, Bruce. "'Nothing on Compulsion': Life Styles of Philadelphia Artisans, 1820-1850." *Labor History* 15 (1974): 337-66.

Leab, Grace. "Tennessee Temperance Activities, 1870-1899." *East Tennessee Historical Society Publications* 21 (1949): 52-68.

Lee, Alfred McClung. "Techniques of Social Reform: An Analysis of the New Prohibition Drive." *American Sociological Review* 9 (1944): 65-77.

Lender, Mark. "Drunkenness as an Offense in Early New England: A Study of 'Puritan' Attitudes." *Quarterly Journal of Studies on Alcohol* 34 (1973): 353-66.

Levine, Harry Gene. "Colonial and Nineteenth Century American Thought about Liquor as a Cause of Crime and Accidents." Paper presented at the Annual Meeting of the Society for the Study of Social Problems, Chicago, Ill., September 1977.

―――. "The Discovery of Addiction: Changing Conceptions of Habitual Drunkenness in American History." Paper presented at the Annual Meeting of the Society for the Study of Social Problems, New York City, August 1976.

Lonsdale, Adrian L. "Rumrunners on Puget Sound: Olmstead Is About to Commission a 100-foot, 900-horsepower, 40-knot Booze Boat." *American West* 9 (1972): 70-71.

Martin, Asa E. "The Temperance Movement in Pennsylvania Prior to the Civil War." *Pennsylvania Magazine of History and Biography* 49 (1925): 195-230.

Maxwell, Milton A. "The Washingtonian Movement." *Quarterly Journal of Studies on Alcohol* 11 (1950): 410-51.

Mennell, S.J. "Prohibition: A Sociological View." *Journal of American Studies* 3 (1969): 159-76.

Mezvinsky, Norton. "Scientific Temperance Education in the Schools." *History of Education Quarterly* 1 (1961): 48-56.

Moore, John Hammond. "The Negro and Prohibition in Atlanta, 1885-1887." *South Atlantic Quarterly* 69 (1970): 38-57.

Musselman, Thomas H. "A Crusade for Local Option: Shreveport 1951-52." *North Louisiana Historical Association Journal* 6 (1975): 59-73.

Nelson, Larry. "Utah Goes Dry." *Utah History Quarterly* 41 (1973): 340-57.

Nelson, Margaret. "Prohibition: A Case Study of Societal Misguidance."

American Behavioral Scientist 12 (1968): 37-43.

Nethers, John L. "Driest of Drys: Simon D. Fess." *Ohio History* 79 (1970): 178-92.

Pocock, Emil. "Wet or Dry?: The Presidential Election of 1884 in Upstate New York." *New York History* 54 (1973): 174-90.

Quinn, Larry. "The End of Prohibition in Idaho." *Idaho's Yesterdays* 17 (1974): 6-13.

Rattray, Jeannette Edwards. "Rum-running Tales from the East End." *New York Folklore Quarterly* 19 (1963): 3-18.

Renner, G.K. "Prohibition Comes to Missouri, 1910-1919." *Missouri Historical Review* 62 (1968): 363-97.

Roberts, Clarence N. "The Illinois Intercollegiate Prohibition Association, 1893-1920." *Journal of the Illinois State Historical Society* 70 (1977).

Robinson, William M. "Prohibition in the Confederacy." *American Historical Review* 37 (1931-1932): 50-58.

Room, Robin. "Cultural Contingencies of Alcoholism: Variations between and within Nineteenth-Century Urban Ethnic Groups in Alcohol-Related Death Rates." *Journal of Health and Social Behavior* 9 (1968): 99-113.

Rorabaugh, W.J. "Estimated U.S. Alcoholic Beverage Consumption, 1790-1860." *Journal of Studies on Alcohol* 37 (1976): 357-64.

——. "Rising Democratic Spirits: Immigrants, Temperance, and Tammany Hall, 1854-1860." *Civil War History* 22 (June 1976): 138-57.

Ross, Irwin. "Carry Nation—Saloon's Nemesis." *American History Illustrated* 2 (1968): 13-17.

Ryan, Daniel J. "History of Liquor Legislation in Ohio." In *History of Ohio*, edited by Emilius O. Randall and Daniel J. Ryan, pp. 507-41. New York: Century History Co., 1912.

Sansoucy, Debra P. "Prohibition and Its Effect on Western Massachusetts, 1919-1920." *History Journal of Western Massachusetts* 4 (1975): 27-39.

Sheldon, Richard N. "Richmond Pearson Hobson as a Progressive Reformer." *Alabama Review* 25 (1972): 243-61.

Shelp, Willard B., Jr. "Prohibition in the Mojave Desert." *Bulletin of the Missouri Historical Society* 28 (1972): 267-72.

Simkins, Francis Butler. "The South Carolina Dispensary." *South Carolina Historical Magazine* 25 (1926).

Smith, Becky. "Prohibition in Alaska—When Alaskans Voted Dry." *Alaska Journal* 3 (1973): 170-79.

Sponholtz, Lloyd. "The Politics of Temperance in Ohio, 1880-1912." *Ohio History* 85 (1976): 4-27.

Stegh, Leslie J. "A Paradox of Prohibition: Election of Robert J. Bulkley as Senator from Ohio, 1930." *Ohio History* 83 (1974): 170-82.

Streeter, Floyd. "History of Prohibition Legislation in Michigan." *Michigan History Magazine* 2 (1918): 289-308.

Sweeney, Kevin. "Rum, Romanism, Representation, and Reform: Coalition Politics in Massachusetts, 1847-1853." *Civil War History* 22 (June 1976): 116-37.

Vanwoerkom, Gerald. "They Dared to Do Right: Prohibition in Muskegon." *Michigan History* 55 (1971): 41-60.

Von Daache, John. "Grape Growing and Wine Making in Cincinnati: 1800-1870." *Cincinnati Historical Society Bulletin* 25 (1967): 197-213.

Walker, Anna Sloan. "History of the Liquor Laws of the State of Washington." *Washington Historical Quarterly* 5 (1914): 116-20.

Walker, Robert, and Patterson, Samuel C. "The Political Attitudes of Oklahoma Newspapers: The Prohibition Issue." *Southwestern Social Science Quarterly* 42 (1961): 271-79.

Walker, Samuel. "Terence V. Powderly, the Knights of Labor and the Temperance Issue." *Societas: A Review of Social History* 5 (1975): 279-93.

Walton, Hanes Jr., and Taylor, James E. "Blacks and the Southern Prohibition Movement." *Phylon* 32 (1971): 247-59.

Weinbaum, Paul O. "Temperance, Politics and the New York City Riots of 1857." *New York Historical Society Quarterly* 59 (1975): 246-70.

Wenger, Robert. "The Anti-Saloon League in Nebraska Politics 1898-1910." *Nebraska History* 52 (1971): 266-92.

West, Elliot. "Cleansing the Queen City: Prohibition and Urban Reform in Denver." *Arizona and the West* 14 (1972): 331-46.

———. "Of Lager Beer and Sonorous Songs." *Colorado Magazine* 48 (1971): 108-28.

Whitaker, Francis Myron. "The Ohio W.C.T.U. and the Prohibition Amendment Campaign of 1883." *Ohio History* 83 (1974): 84-102.

Whitener, Daniel J. "The Dispensary Movement in North Carolina." *South Carolina Quarterly* 26 (1937): 33-58.

Willcox, Walter F. "An Attempt to Measure Public Opinion about Repealing the Eighteenth Amendment." *Journal of the American Statistical Association* 26 (1931): 243-61.

Williams, Charles Scott. "Dr. Huntington, The Index and the Prohibition Party." *Now and Then* 14 (1963): 79-89.

Williams, G.O. "History of the Seattle Police Department: The Prohibition Era in Seattle." *Sheriff and Police Reporter*, 1951.

Wilson, John, and Manton, Kenneth. "Localism and Temperance." *Sociology and Social Research* 59 (1975): 121-35.

Wiltsee, Herbert. "The Temperance Movement, 1848-1871." *Papers of the Illinois State Historical Society*, 1937, pp. 82-92.

Winkler, A.M. "Drinking on the American Frontier." *Quarterly Journal of Studies on Alcohol* 29 (1968): 413-45.

———. "Lyman Beecher and the Temperance Crusade." *Quarterly Journal of Studies on Alcohol* 33 (1972): 939-57.

Index

Notes on Contributors

B. GAIL FRANKEL received the M.A. in sociology from the University of Western Ontario in 1978. She was formerly Senior Research Assistant, Lake Erie Region, Addiction Research Foundation of Ontario, and is currently Project Director, Study of Italian-Canadians in Ontario for the National Congress of Italian Canadians Foundation (Ontario). She has published articles in the *Canadian Journal of Public Health* and the *British Journal of Addiction*. Her latest publication is *Attitudes and Attitude Change in an Ontario Community: London, 1974-1976* (Toronto: Addiction Research Foundation Substudy no. 860,1977).

PAUL C. WHITEHEAD received the Ph.D. in sociology from the University of Massachusetts in 1969. He is presently Associate Professor and Chairman of the Department of Sociology, University of Western Ontario. He has lectured and published widely on deviant behavior and on drug use and abuse, including articles in the *British Journal of Addiction, International Journal of the Addictions, Public Opinion Quarterly, Canadian Journal of Behavioural Science, Canadian Journal of Criminology and Corrections, Journal of Studies on Alcohol, Toxicomanies, Journal of Health and Social Behavior, Canadian Journal of Public Health, American Journal of Alcohol and Drug Abuse, Addictive Diseases: An International Journal, Journal of Safety Research*, and other journals. His latest monograph is *Alcohol and Young Drivers: Impact and Implications of Lowering the Drinking Age* (Ottawa: Non-Medical Use of Drugs Directorate Monograph Series, 1977).

IAN R. TYRRELL received the Ph.D. in history from Duke University in 1974. He now teaches in the School of History, University of New South

Wales. His study of the antebellum temperance movement in the United States, *Sobering Up: From Temperance to Prohibition in Antebellum America, 1800-1860*, was published by Greenwood Press in 1979.

DAVID R. HUEHNER received the Ph.D. in history from the University of Illinois-Urbana in 1972, and is presently Assistant Professor of History at the University of Wisconsin-Washington County. He is conducting research on student society membership and career patterns of Bowdoin College students in the pre-Civil War era, and is also engaged in a larger study of the relationship between antebellum higher education and the antislavery movement.

CHARLES A. ISETTS received the Ph.D. in history from Miami University (Ohio) in 1974. While working at the Ohio Historical Society he directed the Temperance and Prohibition Papers Microfilming Project, described in Randall C. Jimerson, Francis X. Blouin, and Charles A. Isetts, eds., *Guide to the Temperance and Prohibition Papers* (Ann Arbor: University of Michigan, 1977). He is now Head of the History of Health Sciences Library and Museum of the University of Cincinnati Medical Center.

GEORGE G. WITTET received the M.A. in history from the University of Western Ontario in 1978. His research interest is Ohio temperance politics in the late nineteenth century. He now teaches history at Leaside High School, Toronto, Ontario.

JACK S. BLOCKER JR. received the Ph.D. in history from the University of Wisconsin in 1970, and is currently Associate Professor of History at Huron College, London, Ontario. His latest publication is *Retreat from Reform: The Prohibition Movement in the United States, 1890-1913* (Westport, Conn.: Greenwood Press, 1976). He is currently at work on a study of the Women's Temperance Crusade and the founding of the WCTU.

LARRY ENGELMANN received the Ph.D. in history from the University of Michigan in 1971, and now lives in Evanston, Illinois. He has contributed articles to *Smithsonian, Mid-America, Labor History, Michigan History, Detroit in Perspective, California Today*, and *Young World*. He is currently writing a biography of Helen Wills which will be published by Harper and Row. His book *Intemperance: The Lost War Against Liquor* was published by Macmillan in 1979.

DAVID E. KYVIG received the Ph.D. in history in 1971 from Northwestern University, and is presently Assistant Professor of History and Director of the American History Research Center at the University of Akron. He has contributed articles to *The Historian, American Archivist, Teaching History, American Quarterly, Ohio History*, and the *Indiana Magazine of History*. He edited *FDR's America* (St. Louis: Forum Press, 1976) and co-authored *Your Family History: A Guide to Research and Writing* (Arlington Heights, Ill.: AHM, 1978). He has just completed a book manuscript on the repeal of the Eighteenth Amendment.

JAY L. RUBIN is completing a doctoral dissertation in history at Washington University in St. Louis on American society and alcohol in the post-prohibition era. He has taught at Washington University, St. Louis Community College at Forest Park, and the University of Missouri-St. Louis, and is currently Instructor in History at Southwest Texas State University. He has contributed articles to the *Bulletin of the Broome County Historical Society* and *Phylon*.

JACQUIE JESSUP is a member of the library staff at Huron College, London, Ontario.

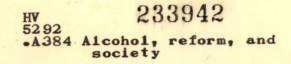

DATE			
MAR 8 198	DEC 17 1985	NOV 20 '90	
MAR 1 1983	FEB 2 '88	FEB 19 31	
MAR 22 1983	OCT 18 '88	APR 09 91	
APR 19 1983	NOV 8 1988	NOV 07 1995	
APR 26 1983	DEC 8 88	NOV 29 198	
NOV 15 1983	FEB 21 '89	DEC 11 1996	
APR 24 1984		OCT 08 1997	
DEC 4 1984	MAR 2 1	DEC 1 3	
OCT 29 1985	APR 11 1989	26 1999	
FEB 25 1986	JUN 29 '89		
APR 15 1986	NOV 14 89		
	AUG 14 1990		